REIMAGINING CHRISTIANITY
AND SEXUAL DIVERSITY IN AFRICA

/ AFRICAN
/ ARGUMENTS

African Arguments is a series of short books about contemporary Africa and the critical issues and debates surrounding the continent. The books are scholarly and engaged, substantive and topical. They focus on questions of justice, rights and citizenship; politics, protests and revolutions; the environment, land, oil and other resources; health and disease; economy: growth, aid, taxation, debt and capital flight; and both Africa's international relations and country case studies.

Managing Editor: Stephanie Kitchen

Series editors

Adam Branch
Alex de Waal
Alcinda Honwana
Ebenezer Obadare
Carlos Oya
Nicholas Westcott

ADRIAAN VAN KLINKEN
EZRA CHITANDO

Reimagining Christianity
and Sexual Diversity in Africa

HURST & COMPANY, LONDON

 International African Institute

Published in collaboration with the International African Institute.
First published in the United Kingdom in 2021 by
C. Hurst & Co. (Publishers) Ltd.,
83 Torbay Road, London, NW6 7DT
Copyright © Adriaan van Klinken and Ezra Chitando, 2021
All rights reserved.
Printed in the United Kingdom by Bell & Bain Ltd, Glasgow

A Cataloguing-in-Publication data record for this book
is available from the British Library.

ISBN: 9781787385719

This book is printed using paper from registered sustainable
and managed sources.

www.hurstpublishers.com

CONTENTS

PART THREE

RESHAPING AFRICAN CHRISTIAN CULTURE

PREFACE

It has been an absolute pleasure for us to work on this project together. We have known each other for over 12 years, since we met at a conference about religion, HIV and AIDS in Durban, South Africa, in 2008. Following that conference, Ezra served as a co-supervisor of Adriaan's PhD research at Utrecht University in the Netherlands. After that, we have frequently collaborated on publishing projects. In 2016, we jointly edited two book volumes on religion and the politics of homosexuality in Africa, to which this book can be seen as a sequel.[1]

We recognise in each other a commitment to engaged academic scholarship that contributes to social transformation. We engage religion critically and empathetically and are keen not only to think about, but also to think with, religion; to identify religious resources for constructive thought and progressive social change. For reasons of transparency, we admit that each of us also has a personal commitment to Christian faith. This should not be taken to mean that we engage Christianity uncritically— on the contrary. Yet it does mean that we recognise from our own experience and understanding the value that religious faith can have, and the contribution it can make to the development of a humanist vision for society. We also have a personal and political commitment to the cause this book centres around. Through his long-term activism and scholarship in the area of

HIV and AIDS, Ezra—who is writing here in his personal capacity—has developed an in-depth understanding of the risks that the marginalisation of sexual minorities in African societies presents to public health and human rights agendas. He has built collaborative relationships with many lgbti activists and communities in his home country of Zimbabwe and across the continent; he has also actively engaged African religious leaders on issues of sexual diversity from faith perspectives. Adriaan has conducted research on religion, homosexuality and lgbti activism for the past ten years, with a focus on Zambia and more recently Kenya. He has built friendships and collaborations with lgbti activists and organisations in these and other countries. Both of us consider ourselves allies of African lgbti communities in their quest for justice, freedom and recognition.

We have realised through our work that an accessible book offering a constructive account on sexual diversity and Christianity in Africa did not exist. Hence the idea emerged for the book you are currently reading, aiming at a range of audiences, from students and academics, to activists and practitioners, to clergy and religious leaders, both based on the African continent and abroad. Whatever your reason for starting to read this book, we hope that it will stimulate and enrich your thinking.

We thank Raga Makawi for her enthusiastic response when the idea for this book came up. We are grateful to Stephanie Kitchen of the International African Institute for her active support, and the reviewers for their helpful comments on the draft manuscript. Thanks also to the editors and publisher of the African Arguments series for making this book project possible.

Adriaan van Klinken and Ezra Chitando
Leeds and Harare, 1 October 2020

INTRODUCTION

SEXUALITY, CHRISTIANITY
AND AFRICAN IMAGINATIONS

There are two dominant imaginations of sexuality and Christianity in Africa. In one, especially popular on the continent, Africa is imagined as a heterosexual continent, where homosexuality is alien and foreign to African cultures: a Western invention imposed on African societies as yet another example of Western imperial hegemony. When presented by African Christians, this imagination often engages the idea of Africa as a Christian continent that must resist the liberal pressure of secularised Western countries. In the other imagination, especially widespread in the West, Africa is envisaged as a homophobic continent in which gay and lesbian people are marginalised and discriminated against, becoming victims of a deeply ingrained homophobia that illustrates the 'backward' nature of African cultures and societies. Christianity, in this imagination, is usually seen as one of the conservative ideologies fuelling this 'African homophobia'. This book interrogates these two narratives by demonstrating the ways in which sexuality, Christianity, and the idea of 'Africa' itself are creatively reimagined within African societies today. It features a selection of African thinkers, organisations, artists and activists who critically engage the intersections of sexuality and Christianity

1

in Africa and stimulate alternative, transformative possibilities of considering these three themes together.

This book is based on three central premises: one, sexuality has become a key site of struggle where African identity is imagined, negotiated, contested and transformed. Secondly, Christianity is a critical discursive field in which this struggle over sexuality in Africa takes place. Following from that is a third premise, that Christianity—as a tradition of faith and thought, a practice of lived religion, a site of institutional power, and a major factor in public culture—can also (and in fact, already does) contribute to the creative re-imagination of sexuality in contemporary Africa. The latter proposition might be the most contested one. After all, given how intricately connected Christian beliefs, leaders and institutions are in the politics of homophobia in African societies, seemingly the most obvious thing to do might be to give up on Christianity altogether. However, as the Cameroonian philosopher Achille Mbembe reminds us, 'Struggle as a *praxis of liberation* has always drawn part of its imaginary resources from Christianity.'[1] Mbembe makes this point with specific reference to the history of transatlantic enslavement, with slavery being legitimised by the church and defended by Christians with the Bible in their hands, but with the enslaved and their descendants themselves appropriating the same corpus of biblical texts and Christian beliefs to develop a spirituality of survival and resistance. In the words of the Kenyan literary writer and theorist Ngũgĩ wa Thiong'o, the negro spirituals that sprouted out of this experience represent an 'aesthetic of resistance, the most consistent and concentrated in world history', as these biblically infused songs have a 'force of beauty and imagery of hope and deliverance' that resonates globally.[2] For Mbembe, Christianity is a contested site for liberatory struggle, and he points out that it was not the church as an institution, nor the formal doctrines about God, that inspired

and supported the enslaved in this struggle. Opposing these formal Christian structures, however, they engaged Christianity as
'a space of truth that ... itself is always opening itself up—it is a
be-coming, a futurity'.[3] In a similar way, the Kenyan scholar,
activist and Nobel Peace Prize laureate Wangari Maathai has suggested that the 'past legacy of Christianity as a partner in the
subjugation of communities' can be redeemed, with this tradition, like other traditions of faith, contributing to 'the struggle
to seek justice and replenish the earth'.[4] The point made here by
these African thinkers is that Christian faith is a site of multiple,
and often conflicting, possibilities, so it can be used for a range
of political visions and social struggles. Its meaning and significance are never fully controlled by its official representatives and
those in positions of authority. On the contrary, its symbols,
texts, languages and rituals can be appropriated, negotiated and
transformed in order to shape counter-narratives and inspire
counter-mobilisations. This book explores this dynamic in the
context of struggles over sexual diversity in contemporary Africa,
demonstrating how Christianity in this context becomes a site of
struggle and allows for alternative imaginations.

In what follows in this introduction, we will briefly outline
and contextualise the above stated premises, by discussing sexuality and the African imagination, Christianity and the African
imagination, and then the intersections between the two.

Sexuality and the African imagination

The Ugandan scholar Sylvia Tamale opens the introduction to
her reader *African Sexualities* with a creative imagination:

> If Sexuality were a human being and she made a grand entrance
> (*l'entrée grande*) into the African Union conference centre, the hon-
> ourable delegates would stand up and bow in honour. But the
> acknowledgement of, and respect for Sexuality would no doubt be

tinged with overtones of parody and irony, even sadness, because although Sexuality might represent notions of pleasure and the continuity of humanity itself, the term conjures up discussions about sources of oppression and violence. In fact, once Sexuality got to the podium and opened her mouth, the multiple complexities associated with her presence would echo around the conference room.[5]

This imaginative vignette draws attention to the ambiguous status of sexuality in African societies and to the various, often conflicting, associations it carries. (To avoid misunderstandings, this ambiguous status of sexuality is not restricted to Africa. However, it takes particular forms on the African continent.)

A major part of the problem is the history of colonial imaginations of 'African sexuality' which continue to shape perceptions and attitudes today.[6] As part of the process of 'othering' that was inherent to colonial discourses, many Western colonial administrators, missionaries and anthropologists constructed African people and their sexuality as exotic, uncivilised and morally unrestrained; as disconnected from (if not incapable of) love and romance; also as wild and 'close to nature'. As a result of the latter, Africans were generally assumed not to be involved in 'unnatural' acts such as homosexuality.[7] Marc Epprecht, a Canadian historian and scholar of African sexualities, documents in his book *Heterosexual Africa?* how these colonial perceptions continue to shape Western ideas about, and interventions in, sexuality in Africa:

> This hypothetical singular African sexuality includes, above all, the nonexistence of homosexuality or bisexuality, along with Africans' purported tendencies toward heterosexual promiscuity, gender violence, and lack of the kind of internalized moral restraints that supposedly inhibit the spread of HIV in other cultures.[8]

As a result of this, the efforts of HIV prevention campaigns focused for a long time on the heterosexual transmission of HIV in African societies, based on the assumption that its spread through homosexual relationships was negligible.

However, the colonial construct of African heterosexuality has continued to thrive not only in the West, but also in Africa itself. In fact it was actively reinforced by several postcolonial African statesmen, which is ironic but perhaps not surprising given their education in colonial mission schools. We deem it ironic in that most African statesmen have positioned themselves as resisting colonialism and its constructs. As the Cameroonian anthropologist Basile Ndjio points out,

> Since the early 1960s, many post-colonial African leaders have taken up the duty of reconstructing an authentic African selfhood perverted by colonialism. In this reformative project, an African 'imagined community' was forged: first, by the political annihilation of any kind of (sexual) difference that could constitute an obstacle to the achievement of nation-building; secondly, by the means of violent exclusion from the post-colonial public sphere of the embarrassing presence of those sexual 'aliens' whose unconventional sexual desires and practices problematize the very ontology of the African subject. In all this process, both African history and culture are selectively reshaped, revised and even reinterpreted by nativist discourses through a deliberate amnesia concerning earlier forms of African sexualities, including male and female same-sex relations.[9]

These efforts have been reinvigorated from the late 1990s. Western societies, which had made significant steps in recognising same-sex relationships, began to include the rights of sexual minorities in a broader narrative of sexual and human rights, and started mainstreaming this in their international diplomacy and development agendas. Recognising gay and lesbian rights was seen as a sign of modernity and progress, and the lack of such recognition in African countries—many of which still had (and have) the colonial anti-sodomy laws in place—was seen as evidence of Africa's backwardness compared to the liberal West. In response to this, African politicians, clergy and other opinion leaders revitalised the already existing discursive repertoires, which allowed them to frame homosexuality and gay rights as un-African and foreign, and as part of a Western neo-colonial imposition. Thus, sexuality again emerged as a key site of narratives of nationhood and as a key marker of citizenship. Needless to say, these politics of sexuality have serious implications, especially for those whose practices of desire, intimacy and love fall outside of the boundaries of a narrowly defined, acceptable 'African sexuality'. The stereotypes involved are obviously misleading and bring serious harm to the people concerned; such stereotypes have broader consequences for public health, social justice and development. Thus, the debates are not merely 'academic' or speculative, but often have life and death implications for flesh and blood human beings.

It is not only scholars of African sexualities who have begun to address these implications and to interrogate the underlying assumptions. Perhaps more importantly, in many African societies, such perceptions are actively and persistently called into question by activists, artists and public intellectuals. Resisting hegemonic discourses, they have courageously generated alternative ways of imagining sexuality in Africa. One example is Binyavanga Wainaina, the late Kenyan writer who, having come out as gay himself, delivered a speech that was tellingly titled 'Conversations with baba', in which he reclaimed Africa as a site of diversity, including with regard to gender and sexuality: 'We, the oldest and the most diverse continent there has been, we, where humanity came from, we, the moral reservoir of human diversity, human age, human dignity.'[10] In a six-part video commentary interrogating the politics of homosexuality in contemporary Africa, Wainaina refers to the homophobia that has been stirred up by many modern African political and religious leaders as illustrating the 'bankruptcy of our imagination'.[11] He underlines the need for Africans to liberate their imaginations and to explore the multiple and complex histories of sexuality on the continent, reclaiming these for the present and the future. A similar call had been made some years earlier by a group of activists from across the continent, who in 2010 released the African LGBTI Manifesto, which states:

> As Africans, we all have infinite potential. We stand for an African revolution which encompasses the demand for a re-imagination of our lives outside neo-colonial categories of identity and power. ... As Africans, we stand for the celebration of our complexities and we are committed to ways of being which allow for self-determination at all levels of our sexual, social, political and economic lives. The possibilities are endless. ... We are specifically committed to the transformation of the politics of sexuality in our contexts. As long as African LGBTI people are oppressed, the whole of Africa is oppressed.[12]

This call for an African queer reimagination is not just about a reimagining of 'African sexuality' but of 'Africa' much more generally, highlighting the interconnectedness of sexual, social, economic and political spheres of life on the continent. The manifesto reflects and inspires an explicitly pan-African spirit, inviting progressive and liberatory imaginaries of African identity and being.[13] Thus, lgbti activists and communities, who are systematically excluded from popular narratives of African authenticity, are 'reclaiming Afrika', as the title of a 2014 essay collection has it. Afrika is spelled here with a 'k' in order to signal that 'we have created our own version of Afrika—a space that cuts across the rigid borders and boundaries that have for so many years made us feel disconnected and fractured'.[14] The question is, can Christianity contribute to this process of imagining new possibilities of sexuality and African identity?

Christianity and the African imagination

The question whether Christianity can be part of the creative reimagination of African sexualities is a contested one, for two reasons: firstly, Christianity is often seen as a colonial religion, thus part of the history that efforts to reimagine Africa seek to interrogate and overcome; secondly, Christianity has become deeply intertwined with the politics of homosexuality in Africa, actively fuelling exclusionary, heteronormative narratives of nationhood and citizenship. Both these points contain critical truths, but also need to be counter-balanced and put in perspective.

In response to the first point, it is obvious that the intricate connection between Christianity and colonialism has enduring legacies, such as the intertwinement of Christianity, politics and the state, the existence of Christian-influenced laws (of which anti-sodomy laws are a notable example), and the prominent role of the Church in sectors such as education and healthcare in many African countries. However, the fact that Christianity was introduced in large parts of Africa during the period of European exploration, colonisation and mission has not stopped Christian beliefs, texts, symbols and languages from becoming part of African imagining practices. Indeed, as demonstrated in a book volume with the apt title *Christianity and the African Imagination*, 'across diverse periods and contexts ... Christianity has captured the African imagination'.[15] In fact, this process far predates the colonial period, as the Christian religion has a history of almost 2,000 years on the African continent.[16] It has had a historical and ongoing presence in countries such as Egypt and Ethiopia since the early centuries of the Common Era. In some parts of West and Central Africa, Christian settlements were established from the fifteenth century. It is correct that much of modern Christianity in sub-Saharan Africa has its origins in the missionary enterprise that came hand in hand with European exploration and colonialism from the nineteenth century. However, these originally Western Christian traditions have gone through complex processes of cultural appropriation, variously referred to using scholarly terms such as 'Africanisation', 'indigenisation', and 'inculturation'. Referring to these long-standing traditions of African Christian thought and practice, the Ghanaian scholar Kwame Bediako, among other theologians, has famously argued that Christianity fundamentally is non-Western and can be seen as an African religion.[17] The appropriation, localisation and 'Africanisation' of Christianity can also be seen in how some African indigenous healers have incorporated aspects of Christianity in their repertoire.

In the twentieth century, Africa witnessed a strong growth of the number of Christian adherents, not least thanks to the emergence of new, revivalist forms of Christianity often classified as 'Pentecostal' or 'Charismatic'.[18] Although Pentecostal Christianity is often associated with North America, and Pentecostal churches in Africa do frequently have direct or indirect links to the United States, African Pentecostalism is certainly not simply an 'American import'. In fact, much of its success and widespread popularity is explained not only through the socio-economic context of neo-liberal restructuring in the 1980s and to the socio-economic aspirations of Africans in a globalised capitalist world, but also through its ability to speak to the spiritual concerns, such as with witchcraft and evil spirits, that emerge from African indigenous religious worldviews.[19] In that sense, contemporary Pentecostal-Charismatic movements can be seen as a new product of Christian imagination in postcolonial African societies. Contemporary Africa is frequently referred to as a marketplace of religions, a term referring to the explosion of the number of religious organisations and movements that compete with one another for followers, social space, public visibility, political influence and financial resources.[20] The idea of a religious market thus emphasises the sense of competition among different religious groups. Pentecostal-Charismatic churches have become highly influential and popular players in this market; it appears that they often engage in politics around issues of gender and sexuality, especially lgbti rights, in order to raise their profile and influence (although this book also suggests that there are other possibilities within Pentecostalism).[21]

With regard to the main Christian sacred text, the Bible, there is a famous anecdote (told in slightly different versions, and variably attributed to Jomo Kenyatta, Desmond Tutu and others) saying that when the European missionaries arrived, they had the Bible and Africans had the land. The missionaries then invited Africans to pray, and when the latter opened their eyes after the prayers, they had the Bible but the missionaries had the land.[22] The anecdote illustrates the ambiguous and contested status of the Bible as a religious text with authority in Africa. However, it is also true that this text—despite the aggressive way in which it was introduced, if not imposed—has been widely appropriated and embraced. As the South African biblical scholar Gerald West poignantly captures in his book about the Bible in Africa, which has the telling subtitle 'From Tool of Imperialism to African Icon':

> Like other classic literature, the Bible has the capacity to generate a surplus of meaning that exceeds its contexts of production, meanings which have formed a reservoir within the public imagination and with which those who have an ear to hear might draw from.[23]

Thus, biblical imagery and narrative have inspired the work of African literary writers such as Chinua Achebe, Ngũgĩ wa Thiong'o, Buchi Emecheta and others, but is also reflected in African popular music and video film, as well as in political speech and in traditional and social media. It is used for a wide range of political ends, reflecting the multiplicity of African cultural and socio-political imaginations. If anything, this demonstrates how the influence of the Bible, and of Christianity more generally, is not limited to the narrowly defined religious sphere; rather it extends much more widely to popular culture and the public sphere in many African societies.[24] Thus, when we think about Christianity and the African imagination, our scope should not be limited to institutional religion in the form of the church, or to formal theological discourse, but should be made much broader to include a wide range of cultural, social and political expressions. We adopt precisely such an approach in this book.

Sexuality, Christianity and alternative African imaginations

Christian institutions, and the Bible as an authoritative Christian text, have certainly been a key part of the African politics of homosexuality outlined above. The critical role of Christian religious leaders and of Christian-inspired political speech in fuelling homophobic campaigns in countries across the African continent has now been widely documented.[25] Thus, Christianity has been a key part of colonial and postcolonial imaginations of Africa as a heterosexual continent, and of African nationhood and citizenship as excluding lgbti people.

As a reaction against this, a number of African queer activists and scholars have seen little point in exploring the potential within Christianity to support African queer imaginations. For instance, in his video commentary 'We Must Free Our Imaginations', Wainaina argues that for Africans to free their imaginations, they have to liberate themselves from colonial and neo-colonial modes of thought. He specifically applies this to Pentecostal Christianity, which in his assessment is a colonising force in the contemporary African public space and a driver behind anti-homosexuality politics. More generally, in the emerging field of African queer studies, little attention is paid to religion; if religious belief and practice are engaged constructively it is usually in relation to African indigenous religious traditions.[26] We acknowledge that there is a considerable queer potential in Africa's indigenous religions, which can be mobilised strategically.[27] However, given the centrality and influence of Christian traditions on the continent, we believe that these should not be side-lined. (The same could be argued in relation to Islam, but that falls beyond the scope of this discussion).[28] Seriously attending to Africa's religious traditions, including Christianity, is a vital part of the process of 'Africanising the discourse on homosexuality in Africa'.[29]

Several of the chapters in this book demonstrate a move to reclaim the indigenous ethics and philosophy of *ubuntu* in the face of the current homophobic climate. For instance, the Cameroonian scholar Elias Bongmba expresses the importance of *ubuntu* to the discourse on homosexuality in Africa as follows:

> *Ubuntu* stresses an ethical responsibility that repudiates scorn and killings, which homosexuals have faced in some African contexts. The vulnerability of lesbians, gay, and transgender people is a cry for an inclusive worldview which respects the dignity of all. It is clear that in contemporary moral discourses in Africa, homosexuals clearly are the absolute contrary others who must not be violated or abused in any way. They must be seen from the African notion of *ubuntu* and within the broad ethics of the other as different.[30]

Thus, the argument can be made that if churches in Africa are serious about inculturation—that is, developing a form of Christianity that integrates the best elements of African cultures—they should not buy into foreign homophobias, instead reclaiming long-standing traditions of recognising difference and promoting respect and harmony.[31]

To some extent, the present book can be seen as a sequel to an earlier book published in 2013 in the African Arguments series, Marc Epprecht's *Sexuality and Social Justice in Africa: Rethinking Homophobia and Forging Resistance*, which strikes a relatively optimistic and hopeful tone in its account of the struggle for sexual rights and justice in Africa. In the chapter about 'Faiths', Epprecht argues that the three main groups—indigenous religions, Christianity and Islam—'have historically been and remain more amenable to accepting sexual difference than is generally understood'.[32] He subsequently underlines the imperative need for scholars and activists not to overemphasise the homophobic tendencies in African religions, and not to position religious faith as unequivocally opposed to the recognition of sexual and gender diversity and lgbti human rights. Such a one-sided account, Epprecht warns, could contribute 'to the impasse between people on the extremes of the debate, and closes down some of the community-building, humanistic potential of those faiths'.[33] In this book, we take up this important suggestion and seek to explore the potential in one of Africa's major faith traditions, Christianity. Or, in fact, we document and reconstruct how this potential has already begun to be explored and mobilised by a number of African thinkers, activists and artists.

This book contributes to a growing body of scholarship that examines how Christian traditions are appropriated and reclaimed to support progressive causes regarding sexual diversity in contemporary Africa. Such scholarship has explored, for instance, the ways in which African lgbti people and communities at a grassroots level identify with and are empowered by religious faith; how they negotiate spaces within Christian communities; and how they develop affirming theologies.[34] It has further documented how formal theological discourses in Africa have addressed questions of sexuality, both in opposing and affirming ways; how the Bible is invoked to support arguments against homosexuality, and how biblical texts can be interpreted in alternative ways; how African Christian leaders have begun to engage with lgbti activists around issues of sexual rights and health; and how lgbti activists creatively appropriate and transform Christian beliefs, symbols, texts and practices in order to advocate their cause.[35] Building on this literature, we aim to offer an accessible overview of the ways in which, across sub-Saharan Africa,

Christianity—as a tradition of faith and thought, a practice of lived religion, a site of institutional power, and a major factor in public and popular culture—has emerged as a site of and resource for the creative re-imagination of sexuality. Doing so, we firmly make religion and specifically Christianity an important site of attention in the field of African queer studies, while foregrounding Africa as a new centre of queer theologies.[36] Indeed, following the call to develop 'theory from the South',[37] we reconstruct emerging queer theologies from the South that decentre Western queer theologies and counter-balance the secular orientation of queer studies. Doing so, we foreground the agency of African scholars and activists who seek to achieve the full liberation of lgbti people on the continent.

About this book

The interest of this book in Christianity automatically implies a focus on that part of the continent where Christianity is more widely spread, thus leaving North Africa, which is overwhelmingly Muslim, out of the picture. Obviously, sub-Saharan Africa is already a vast region and we did not strive to cover it fully. Nevertheless, the voices and material that are featured do cross the continent from the Western part (Cameroon, Ghana, Nigeria) to the Eastern part (Kenya) to the Southern part (Botswana, South Africa). The selection of case studies featured in this book has been informed by our own scholarly expertise and networks, and is therefore somewhat arbitrary by definition. Yet a certain rationale has informed our selection. We have deliberately tried to avoid a firm focus on South Africa with its relatively strong tradition of progressive mobilisations regarding sexuality and Christianity. Although the volume does open with a chapter about the illustrious Archbishop Desmond Tutu, we have sought to feature a wide range of other voices from other parts of the continent. Indeed, we have intended to include those individuals, organisations and contributions that we believe together represent a diverse spectrum of the ways in which Christianity and sexuality can be reimagined in progressive directions. We have done so by including different genres.

Part One explores the writings and other contributions by African Christian thinkers and theologians. Chapter 1, about Tutu, highlights the intersections of thinking about race and sexuality, specifically in the context of post-apartheid South Africa. The second chapter, about Ghanaian theologian Mercy Oduyoye, foregrounds how African feminist thought can provide a basis for constructive engagement with sexual diversity. Chapter 3, about Cameroonian theologian Jean-Blaise Kenmogne, provides a much-needed Francophone perspective in a book that otherwise has a strong Anglophone orientation. The fourth chapter is about Musa Dube, a theologian from Botswana, examining how the theological response to the HIV epidemic has stimulated a progressive approach to sexuality.

Part Two focuses on the activities and programmes of specific Christian organisations. Chapter 5 explores the work of EHAIA, the HIV and AIDS initiative of the World Council of Churches, and the approach they have taken to initiate conversations about human sexuality in Africa (mostly in mainline Protestant churches) using the HIV epidemic as a catalyst. Chapter 6 foregrounds the work of a black Pentecostal organisation from the United States called The Fellowship of Affirming Ministries, which has begun to promote an inclusive form of Christianity on the African continent, framed in a progressive pan-African discourse.

Part Three examines creative expressions of cultural production, featuring a novel and films about same-sex love, as well as lgbti life stories and poetry. The latter section is important, as it foregrounds how Christianity exists outside of institutional boundaries of organised religion and influences broadly defined public and popular culture. Chapter 7 discusses a collection of lgbti life stories from Nigeria called *Blessed Body*, and analyses how through storytelling the narrators reclaim their 'deviant' queer bodies as blessed. Chapter 8 focuses on a collection of African lgbti poetry, highlighting the critique and appropriation of religion in a selection of the poems. Chapter 9 discusses the novel *Under the Udala Trees* by Nigerian author Chinelo Okparanta, considering the ways in which this lesbian love story creatively engages Christian themes. Finally, Chapter 10 highlights two Kenyan films celebrating same-sex love, discussing the critical and constructive representation of Christianity. The fact that two of the four chapters in Part Three relate to material from Nigeria is an illustration of the vibrancy of lgbti communities and queer cultural scenes in this country with its vast population and diaspora.

Our focus on Christianity in sub-Saharan Africa has resulted in a mostly Anglophone orientation. Francophone Africa tends to be Muslim-dominated, with notable exceptions such as Cameroon (see chapter 3) and the Democratic Republic of Congo. Some interesting developments have recently taken place in Lusophone Africa, which is more Christian-dominated, such as the decriminalisation of homosexuality in Mozambique (2015) and Angola (2019). Unfortunately, due to linguistic barriers we have not been able to research progressive Christian voices in this region (however, note that the work of EHAIA discussed in chapter 5 extends to Lusophone Africa, with the Angola-based EHAIA coordinator—at the time of writing, Rev. Luciano Chanhelela Chianeque—referring to ongoing work with sexual minority communities).[38]

African Christianity being incredibly diverse, we have attempted to include a range of Christian traditions in this book. This turned out to be a challenge, and we admit that Protestant Christian perspectives are most prominent, as it was difficult to find examples of Catholic voices explicitly supporting the struggle for sexual minority rights in Africa. Perhaps the most explicit support has been voiced by the Nigerian Jesuit priest, Agbonkhianmeghe Orobator, who (at the time of writing) is the principal of Hekima University College in Nairobi and a well-known African theologian. In a brief response to Pope Francis' 2016 apostolic exhortation *Amoris Laetitia*, Orobator acknowledged that the pope did not make any bold and long-overdue steps on critical issues, such as the recognition of same-sex unions. However, offering a positive interpretation of the document, he states:

> Furthermore, on a continent where at least 38 countries criminalize homosexuality, the pope's trenchant call for respect for human dignity, avoidance of unjust discrimination, aggression, and violence, and respectful pastoral guidance [paragraph 250], should galvanize the church in Africa to embrace wholeheartedly African families and their LGBT members who have been stigmatized, marginalized, and excluded from the life of the church. Church leaders need to dissociate themselves from governments and politicians who persecute gay people, and show example of respect for their dignity. In Africa, we say the church is 'family of God,' implying that it welcomes all without discrimination.[39]

This quotation reflects the more general concern with marginalised communities that Orobator, rooted in the tradition of African liberation theologies, demonstrates in his theological work.[40] Another Nigerian Catholic theologian, Stan Chu Ilo, has also expressed a concern about the conditions of lesbian and gay people in Africa. He calls for an 'inclusive church and society where same-sex persons are treated with respect and dignity as children of God', and further underlines the need for the church to recognise 'the right of two adults to live together in a stable relationship of friendship'.[41] Although these interventions are significant and should be welcomed in the current climate, they are brief and appear to demonstrate more of a pastoral concern than an innovative theological imagination.

In addition to a lack of Catholic perspectives, we also struggled to find examples of Pentecostal voices contributing to the reimagination of sexuality and Christianity. However, the case study of The Fellowship of Affirming Ministries (chapter 6) does bring in a unique Pentecostal perspective and allows for a debunking of the monolithic representation that tends to equate Pentecostal Christianity with homophobia. In fact, the diffuse structures of religious authority, church institutionalisation and religious doctrine mean that individual Pentecostal pastors may (at least potentially) have more flexibility than fellow clergy in the mainline Protestant and Catholic denominations to adopt new ways of thinking about sexual diversity. However, Pentecostal pastors frequently lack higher-level formal theological training, and therefore are less likely to publish their views on these issues in writing. The chapters in Part Three also refer to Pentecostal Christian ideas and practices, such as the concern with demons and the ritual of deliverance. These chapters demonstrate how Pentecostalism and its connection to homophobic cultures are critically represented in contemporary cultural texts.

A note with regard to terminology in this book: it has become a common insight that language not only reflects but also constitutes and shapes reality. This is certainly the case with the language used to conceptualise sexuality. Modern Western terminology is often based on certain assumptions, such as the idea of sexuality as an identity, the binary of hetero- and homosexuality, the seemingly stable signifiers of the lgbti (lesbian, gay, bisexual, transgender and intersex) acronym and of the phenomena to which it refers. These assumptions have been called into question by contemporary scholarship on African sexualities and in African gender and queer studies.[42] However, despite this emerging body of critical and deconstructionist thinking about gender and sexuality in African contexts, an alternative language is yet to emerge. In fact, as a result of complex processes of the globalisation of scholarship, activism, fundraising and networking, originally Western concepts and framings of sexuality and gender are widely adopted by African activists and scholars. In this book, we acknowledge the limitations and shortcomings of terms such as 'homosexuality', 'gay and lesbian', 'sexual minorities', 'LGBTI', 'queer' etcetera, but it is not our aim to critique and theorise these concepts and languages as such. Recognising the problem of terminology, in this book we do not aim to solve that problem. In each of the chapters, we try to stay close to the language and concepts used in that particular case study. However, when employing the acronym lgbti—which nowadays is commonly used by many activists and scholars—we have decided not to capitalise this, as a way of signalling the ambiguous, complex and fluid nature of the categories these letters stand for.[43] Where possible we have also tried to reduce the use of this acronym because this book is mostly about same-sex sexualities and does not deeply engage with issues specifically pertaining to transgender and intersex (or indeed bisexual) people. At the same time, we acknowledge that lgbti categories are fluid; for instance, in our personal experience effeminate same-sex loving men may refer to themselves as gay, but also as transgender. In this book we sometimes use the term 'same-sex loving', as it foregrounds sexuality as a practice rather than as a (stable) identity. We also use the term 'queer', mostly to denote a particular political approach to gender and sexual diversity, as captured by Sokari Ekine and Hakima Abbas when they state: 'We use queer to underscore a perspective that embraces gender and sexual plurality and seeks to transform, overhaul and revolutionise African order rather than seek to assimilate into oppressive hetero-patriarchal-capitalist frameworks'.[44] Although most of the content of this book specifically relates to Christianity and same-sex sexualities in Africa, we hope that the chapters provide stepping stones and suggest directions for further African Christian queer imaginations.

PART ONE

REIMAGINING AFRICAN CHRISTIAN THOUGHT

1

RACE AND SEXUALITY IN A THEOLOGY
OF *UBUNTU*

DESMOND TUTU

Archbishop Desmond Mpilo Tutu is mostly known to the world for his highly prominent role in the campaign against apartheid in South Africa (the institutionalised system of racial segregation in the period 1948–94). Born on 7 October 1931 in Klerksdorp in South Africa, Tutu worked as a teacher in South Africa and later studied theology in both South Africa and England. Between 1972 and 1974, he served as a Vice Director of the Theological Scholar Programme of the World Council of Churches based in London. As general-secretary of the South African Council of Churches (SACC) from 1978–85, Tutu transformed the SACC into a Christian organisation that was highly vocal on the question of race, speaking out against the white Afrikaner nationalist government and its apartheid policies, and calling for non-violent protest and international economic pressure. He continued this very public leadership after he made history by becoming the first black African to serve as Bishop of

Johannesburg (1985–86) and then as Archbishop of Cape Town (1986–96) in the Anglican Church of Southern Africa.[1]

Tutu's role in the struggle against apartheid was internationally recognised by his 1984 Nobel Peace Prize. After the democratic transition in South Africa in 1994, he played a high-profile role as chair of the Truth and Reconciliation Commission, whose public hearings were widely reported in the national and international media. As an indication of Tutu's continent-wide reputation as an African Christian leader, the All Africa Conference of Churches (AACC), with its headquarters in Nairobi, Kenya, named one of its conference halls after him. Tutu served as the president of the AACC for two five-year terms (1987–97).

In more recent years, Tutu, who retired as Archbishop in 1996 and announced his retirement from public life in 2010, has become known for his strong advocacy on issues of sexuality, in particular the rights of lesbian and gay people. Indeed, his biographer John Allen concludes that 'nothing kept Tutu's name in the public eye after his retirement as archbishop more than his attitude toward homosexuality'.[2] For instance, in 2013 he made global headlines with the clear and succinct statement, in typical Tutu fashion, that he would rather go to hell than to a homophobic heaven.[3] Being by far the most high-profile African religious leader to support gay rights has added to his international reputation as a progressive thinker and activist, especially in the Western world, but he was met with suspicion on the continent itself. A fellow Anglican bishop, Emmanuel Chukwuma from Nigeria, even declared him to be 'spiritually dead'.[4] Similarly, Robert Mugabe, former President of Zimbabwe, retorted Tutu's criticism of his leadership by saying that Tutu himself should step down because his pro-gay stance was a 'disgrace'.[5] Yet Tutu's unquestionable moral authority and his firm rootedness in traditions of African theology and spirituality mean that his voice cannot be ignored. Indeed, his thinking on matters of sexuality is an essential stepping stone for the constructive re-imagination of sexuality and Christianity in Africa.

Sexual politics in church and state

As Archbishop of Cape Town, Tutu was also the primate (most senior clergy) of the Anglican Church in Southern Africa. While in that role, he led the 1992 move to offer women ordination into the priesthood, a cause to which he was deeply committed. At the end of his term in office, he also initiated a review of the official church policy on gay and lesbian clergy, which required celibacy of clergy of homosexual orientation. Although Tutu had thus far defended this policy publicly, he had 'privately acknowledged that it was not logically sustainable' and was a form of 'discrimination based on an attribute people could not change'.[6] Already in 1997, Tutu had strongly denounced this policy, describing it as 'illogical, irrational and frankly un-Christlike, totally untenable'.[7] He considered it illogical and irrational for the church to teach that celibacy is a vocation while at the same time making it mandatory for gay and lesbian people. He considered it un-Christlike because the policy denied gay and lesbian people the possibility of expressing their sexuality in ways that allow them to become 'more considerate of each other, more gentle, more compassionate, more ready to engage in self-giving, and so to become more and more like God'.[8] In spite of his strong feelings, Tutu was unsuccessful in changing the church policy on this issue, which remains in place at time of writing. His own daughter, Mpho Tutu, who was an ordained priest, became a victim of it when she married her female partner in 2015 and was subsequently pressured to give up her priestly licence.

It has been described as a tragedy that Tutu's Anglican Church, and many other South African churches which fought successfully against apartheid, have failed to overcome 'another fundamental and equally oppressive division: one that divides straight people from gay and lesbian people' after liberation in the 1990s.[9] In South Africa at large, this division had been addressed more adequately, at least legally speaking. The country's new 1996 constitution was historic for many reasons, including the fact that it explicitly included sexual orientation into the non-discrimination clause. Tutu had actively advocated for this, arguing:

> It would be a sad day for South Africa if any individual or group of law-abiding citizens in South Africa were to find that the Final Constitution did not guarantee their fundamental human right to a sexual life, whether heterosexual or homosexual. I would strongly urge you to include the sexual orientation clause in the Final Constitution.[10]

The inclusion was recognition of the fact that several gay people, such as the first openly gay black anti-apartheid activist Simon Nkoli, had actively participated in the liberation movement, and had successfully 'insisted upon the inseparability of the struggles against apartheid and homophobia'.[11] Tutu had embraced this notion, stressing that apartheid had not only denied blacks, but also gay and lesbian people, of 'their basic human rights and reduced them to social outcasts and criminals in their land of birth.' He urged the writers of the constitution 'to include gay and lesbian people in the "Rainbow People" of South Africa'.[12] Indeed, the new constitution reflected the strong commitment of the country's political and judicial elites to building a legal safety net, remedying past injustices by guaranteeing equal protection and rights to all citizens of the 'new' South Africa. Arguably, these legal provisions did not automatically translate into a change of social attitudes towards lesbian and gay people at a grassroots level, and homophobia remains widespread in South African society at time of writing. Yet on the basis of the progressive constitution, the country's Constitutional Court ruled in 2005 that the common-law definition of marriage should be opened up to same-sex couples, making South Africa in 2006 the first (and so far only) country on the African continent to legalise same-sex marriage. Tutu himself was supportive of the campaign towards this move and also approved of church blessings for same-sex relationships, although he preferred the term 'union' over 'marriage' in order to prevent 'a lot of hassles'.[13]

The 'hassles' Tutu mentioned may be connected to the crisis surrounding issues of homosexuality—in particular, the blessing of same-sex relationships and the ordination of gay and lesbian clergy—that had escalated in the worldwide Anglican Church since the 1998 Lambeth Conference of Anglican bishops.[14] Conservative African bishops, such as Peter Akinola from Nigeria, played a prominent role in protesting against, in their opinion, the too liberal attitudes of American, European and South African Anglican churches, and the conference passed a resolution stating that same-sexual relationships are 'incompatible with Scripture'. Tutu, as a retired bishop, did not attend the 1998 and 2008 Lambeth conferences where the controversy around homosexuality caused deep divisions.

However, in spite of his initial decision not to interfere in these debates publicly, he could not keep quiet for long and 'began to include, in speeches and sermons, careful remarks which made his position clear'.[15] In 2001, he wrote a letter in support of Bishop Christopher Senyonjo, who had been expelled by the Anglican Church of Uganda for his pro-gay stance.[16] A few years later, in 2004, Tutu preached at Southwark Cathedral in London, shortly after the openly gay canon of the cathedral, Jeffrey John, had been forced to withdraw his acceptance of a nomination to become bishop. In his sermon, Tutu saluted John for acting 'with so much dignity and selfless generosity', and stated that 'the Jesus I worship is not likely to collaborate with those who vilify and persecute an already oppressed minority'.[17] Tutu's interventions, to his great frustration, appear to have had little effect in moving the Anglican Communion to a more accepting and affirming position on issues of sexuality. He reportedly wrote to George Carey, then Archbishop of Canterbury, that he felt ashamed to be an Anglican. Nonetheless, his public voicing of these issues has allowed him to become 'perhaps the world's most prominent religious leader advocating gay and lesbian rights'.[18] Consequently, it is important to understand the theological basis of his activism in support of the rights of lesbian and gay people in Africa and other parts of the world.

Homophobia, like apartheid, is a heresy

To distant observers, Tutu's gay rights advocacy might appear to be a recent phenomenon. To his critics, it might serve as an illustration of Tutu becoming a sell-out, striving to be the darling of white liberal audiences in the Western world. However, Tutu's commitment to defending gay rights is far from a new development. As early as the 1970s, he took a relatively 'tolerant' stance on gay issues, a stance that gradually evolved in the following decades towards full acceptance and affirmation.[19] Admittedly, he was operating in a very complex field; this became evident when, as Bishop of Johannesburg, Tutu forced the dean of the cathedral, Mervyn Castle, to resign after the police ensnared him in a trap and charged him for homosexuality, which at that time was legally banned. The decision reportedly 'haunted Tutu for years' and he later tried to make up for it by appointing Castle as his personal chaplain and consecrating him as Bishop of False Bay in 1994.[20]

Tutu has repeatedly made it clear that for him, the struggle for gay rights is very much in continuity with his long-standing resistance against apartheid and his relentless defence of black civil rights in South Africa. At the heart of both struggles is Tutu's strong moral and political commitment to defending the human dignity and rights of all people, and his deep theological conviction that every human being is created in the image of God and therefore is worthy of respect.

Tutu uses the strongest possible theological terminology to reject homophobia and heterosexism when he writes that:

> The church has joined the world in committing what I consider to be the ultimate blasphemy—making the children of God doubt that they are children of God. Lesbians and gays have been made to reject God and, in their rejection of the church, they have been made to question why God created them as they were.[21]

The use of the term 'blasphemy' is particularly significant in the South African context. Ten years before making the above statement, Tutu had used exactly the same word to theologically condemn apartheid: 'Its most blasphemous aspect is ... that it can make a child of God doubt that he is a child of God. For that reason alone, it deserves to be condemned as a heresy'.[22] He made this statement in his contribution to a book called *Apartheid Is a Heresy*, its title inspired by the prophetic declaration with which the World Alliance of Reformed Churches in 1982 categorically rejected the theological justification of apartheid as developed by the South African Dutch Reformed Church.

Although the terms blasphemy and heresy have slightly different meanings, in the South African theological debate about apartheid they were used somewhat interchangeably. As early as 1956, the Johannesburg-based Anglican missionary priest and anti-apartheid activist Trevor Huddleston (who later became a close friend and ally of Tutu) used both words in his anti-apartheid book *Naught for your Comfort*.[23] Apartheid was seen as a heresy because it was considered to go against fundamental Christian beliefs, in particular the belief in the equality of all human beings on the basis of humankind created in the image of

God. Exactly because of this doctrine of the *imago Dei*, the failure to recognise human equality and instead treating people as inferior based on race (or any other trait) was also seen as blasphemy: that is, an insult of God-self.

An echo of the prophetic language that dominated Christian anti-apartheid discourse in the 1980s can be heard in Tutu's above quoted statement about 'ultimate blasphemy'. In the same way in which apartheid, and its false theological justification, wanted black people to believe that they do not fully bear God's image and are less valuable children of God, homophobic and heterosexist theologies make gay and lesbian people believe they are inferior in the eyes of God. Both theologies, Tutu suggests, are fundamentally un-Christian. It is for that reason that shortly after the end of apartheid, Tutu declared:

> If the church, after the victory over apartheid, is looking for a worthy moral crusade, then this is it: the fight against homophobia and heterosexism. I pray that we will engage in it with the same dedication and fervour which we showed against the injustice of racism, so that we may rehabilitate the gospel of Jesus Christ in the eyes of many who have been deeply hurt.[24]

Tutu firmly believes that opposing any form of discrimination and injustice, and defending the full humanity and dignity of all human persons, is at the heart of Christian witness. He criticises the church since, 'instead of being hospitable to all, it has made many of God's children outcasts and pariahs on the basis of something which, like race or gender, they could do nothing about—their sexual orientation'.[25]

Black African theology

Tutu is a theologian deeply grounded in the tradition of South African black theology which emerged in the 1970s as a contextual theology of liberation, prophetically denouncing the injustices of apartheid while constructively affirming black dignity, solidarity and freedom.[26] This theology was inspired by and indebted to the Black Consciousness movement spearheaded by anti-apartheid activist and student leader Steve Biko; by American black theology as developed by James H. Cone whose book *Black Theology and Black Power* was published in 1969; and by African theology as developed by scholars such as John Mbiti from Kenya and Bolaji Idowu from Nigeria. Because of these various sources of inspiration, South African black theology had to negotiate the relationship between blackness as a political category and Africanness as a cultural category, and had to reflect on the problems both these categories posed in the light of the history and contemporary experience of Christianity in a South African context. Tutu, however, saw no such conflict between black and African theology, stating: 'I myself believe I am an exponent of Black Theology coming as I do from South Africa. I believe I am also an exponent of African Theology coming as I do from Africa'.[27] Indeed, his theological thinking, including about the question of sexuality, reflects both traditions.

In the tradition of black and other liberation theologies, God, for Tutu, is the God of the Bible book of Exodus, 'choosing to side with a rabble of slaves, a God who is always concerned with the plight of the widow, the orphan, the alien'.[28] Jesus, for him, reflects the same 'bias' as God, as he was 'firmly on the side of those who had been pushed aside—the hungry, the homeless, the poor'.[29] In the days of apartheid, this belief drove his commitment to denounce racial injustice and to radically affirm the dignity of black people. Yet after political liberation in 1994, the same belief inspired his continued struggle against homophobia and his affirmation of the dignity of gay and lesbian people who, in his perception, simply were the next group of oppressed people in need of liberation. 'The Jesus I worship is a Jesus who was forever on the side of those who were being clobbered, and today it's the gays and lesbians who are being clobbered'.[30]

Emphasising the radically inclusive character of Jesus' ministry, Tutu states that this is what inspired him in the struggle against apartheid, and what inspires him in the struggle against homophobia. Clearly, Tutu is a liberation theologian for whom the question of race and the question of sexuality are part of the same spectrum. Indeed, he has referenced Martin Luther King Jr. as a source of inspiration, not only for his fight against apartheid, but also for his current commitment to the fight for gay and lesbian human rights. 'He [King] encouraged me to see each person as made in the image of God, as someone God loves deeply, and as my own brother or sister in God's colorful family'.[31] According to Tutu, it is time to return to and reinvigorate the dream of Martin Luther King Jr.: 'A world of peace, a world of justice, a world of love without discrimination—this is the dream of Martin Luther King Jr. It should also be the dream of all of God's people. So let us return to the dream!'[32]

Tutu powerfully captured his own dream for South Africa through the metaphor of the rainbow, which he first used in 1989 when addressing the thousands of protesters (from diverse racial backgrounds) participating in an anti-apartheid demonstration as 'the rainbow people of God'.[33] Nelson Mandela later incorporated this notion in the inaugural address after his election as president, referring to South Africa as a rainbow nation. The rainbow metaphor was intended to capture the coming together of people from diverse backgrounds—racially, culturally and linguistically—and it conveyed the belief that the beauty of these groups together, in their differences, exceeded the sum of its parts. It symbolises unity in diversity. Of course, for Tutu the rainbow also has a biblical connotation. In the Old Testament story of Noah and the flood, the rainbow is a sign of God's covenant with humankind, symbolising the divine promise that never again the waters will destroy all life (Genesis 9). Likewise, Tutu's metaphor suggests that under God's covenant with the people of South Africa, all human life is sacred and will not be destroyed by the evils of apartheid, racism and other forms of discrimination. Critics have been sceptical about 'rainbowism', describing it as naïve and sentimental, and as covering up the ever-existing racial and economic inequalities in post-apartheid South Africa. Tutu might agree that it is idealistic indeed, yet for him the ideal is rooted in his understanding of *ubuntu*.

Ubuntu

Tutu's thinking has been aptly described as '*ubuntu* theology'.[34] The engagement with the indigenous southern African concept of *ubuntu* qualifies his theology as a form of African theology, firmly grounded in African cultural concepts and worldviews. *Ubuntu* is an isiXhosa and isiZulu word, and it has been widely adopted in African philosophy as a concept of human existence in community. It is often translated as 'I am because you are' or 'a person is a person through other people'.[35] Tutu, who popularised the word, associates it with values such as generosity, hospitality, care, compassion, openness towards and affirmation of others in recognition of their full humanity, and a celebration of diversity.

For Tutu, *ubuntu* is a theological concept because it is closely connected to his understanding of creation. It provides a correction of the Western theology of salvation, which is traditionally concerned with the individual, instead allowing for an 'emphasis on the integrity of creation and the habitual recalling of our image of God (*imago Dei*) in the midst of human conflict'.[36] To put it simply, from the perspective of *ubuntu*, human beings collectively (rather than individually) present the image of God. The traditional Christian doctrine of the Trinity further enlightens this, because according to this doctrine God exists in three persons—Father, Son and Holy Spirit—and each of these is defined in their relation to the others. Thus, as the Trinity is internally relational and interdependent, so is humankind. It is in our relationality, interdependence and vulnerability—that is, in expressing *ubuntu*—that human beings reflect the image of God.[37]

For Tutu, the implication of *ubuntu* is that 'what dehumanises you, inexorably dehumanises me'.[38] Applying this to the context of apartheid, he argues that those who supported apartheid and perpetrated violence and injustice under this system towards fellow human beings were themselves also victims, as their own humanity was damaged while they inflicted harm on others. This inspired his vision for the Truth and Reconciliation Commission after the end of apartheid, as he believed that the idea of *ubuntu* 'equips you to look at your torturers, to realize that they need your help and to stand ready to enable them to regain their humanity'.[39]

Although Tutu has not systematically reflected on questions of sexuality from the perspective of his theology of *ubuntu*, it is obvious that it considerably shapes his thinking about sexuality. Firstly, *ubuntu* for him is closely connected to the celebration of human diversity, for it is through the complementarity of our differences that we together grow in humanity, affirm one another, and reflect collectively the image of God. This applies to sexual diversity as much as it does to racial diversity. Thanks to his *ubuntu* theology, Tutu could radically imagine society as 'the rainbow people of God'. Secondly, Tutu insists that *ubuntu* calls us to first and foremost recognise the humanity of the other. In particular, this implies an affirmation of those human lives that are marginalised on the basis of societal and cultural norms, and indeed it puts such norms under critique. In the words of Aloo Mojola,

> The *ubuntu* perspective demands a human and compassionate treat-
> ment of and respect for all humans, especially those on the edges and
> the margins. This necessarily includes those whose lifestyles are con-
> sidered deviant, unconventional and non-traditional including those
> espousing alternative sexualities, masculinities and femininities.[40]

Ubuntu makes us attentive to the authentic experiences of people
who live on the margins, thus reminding us that 'sexual politics
is about people—it carries the human face'.[41] Thirdly, in the
same way that the perpetrators of apartheid, according to Tutu,
were dehumanised by their own deeds, one could argue that
those who endorse homophobia and heterosexism are also damaged in their own humanity. This awareness calls for an attitude
of ongoing dialogue with and respect towards those who fail to
recognise the humanity of lesbian and gay people.

Further extrapolating Tutu's thought, one could argue that
ubuntu, as a philosophy of community, might offer a starting
point for an indigenous African philosophy: one that affirms
sexual diversity as an alternative to Western, highly individualised
accounts of lgbti rights. It has been suggested that *ubuntu* can,
in fact, have a negative effect on the debate about homosexuality
in African contexts because of its possible coercive aspects, sup-
pressing individual preferences and freedoms to the interests and
needs of the community.[42] Tutu's conception of *ubuntu*, however,
appears to be more liberationist, as *ubuntu* for him requires the
flourishing of all, and thus the interrogation of any societal
norms that marginalise and oppress certain members of the community. From that perspective, if lesbian, gay, bisexual and transgender people are ostracised because of heteronormative norms
that prevail in a certain community, this not only restricts the
flourishing of these individuals but subsequently also the community to which they belong.[43] Tutu's conception of *ubuntu* also
appears to be more liberal, as he seems to privilege individual
autonomy and freedom, stating that 'to be human is to be free'.[44]

However, for him this freedom is not for self-centred purposes, instead allowing people to contribute to the community in the spirit of *ubuntu*: 'We are created to exist in a delicate network of interdependence with fellow human beings and the rest of God's creation'.[45] While traditional African ways of dealing with sexuality and relationships have often been concerned with the value of biological reproduction, Tutu's understanding of *ubuntu* calls for a broader understanding of human flourishing. In the words of Ghanaian theologian Mercy Oduyoye, further discussed elsewhere in this book (chapter 2), such an understanding acknowledges alternative ways of being fruitful.

Limitations?

It has become clear that Tutu's advocacy for gay and lesbian human rights is shaped by his longstanding commitment to social justice, particularly his struggle against apartheid. His approach to gay rights advocacy reflects a specifically South African narrative in which sexuality is equated to race. This narrative emerged during apartheid, when activists such as Simon Nkoli drew a strong connection between the struggles against racism and homophobia, and it continued to be powerful and effective after liberation. As Ryan Thoreson points out, the considerable legal and political successes achieved by the gay and lesbian movement in post-apartheid South Africa was made possible by the discursive strategy employed by the movement:

> From the outset, GLB activists framed their agenda in terms of identity politics: everyone, they insisted, has a sexual orientation, whether gay, lesbian, bisexual, or heterosexual. Instead of referring to choice ('sexual preference') or practice ('sexuality'), activists insisted upon the terminology of a concrete, immutable identity—'sexual orientation', which was cognate to racial categorisation—and strategically dropped the 'language of fluidity and contingency of

sexuality'. ... Their strategy enabled activists to link their cause to
forms of gender and race-based discrimination that the post-apartheid government had vowed to eradicate, making it more difficult for
religious groups and conservative political parties to argue that public morality and tradition justified discrimination on the basis of
sexual orientation.[46]

Tutu's approach to gay issues reflects this approach; for him
sexual orientation, just like race and gender, is something about
which a person cannot do anything. It is innate and, theologically speaking, part of how God created us. This approach can be
characterised as both biologically and theologically essentialist:

We do not choose our sexuality any more than we choose our race
or ethnicity. As God has made me black, so has God made some of
us gay. And how incredibly wonderful it is that God has created each
of us to be who we are. That's reason for celebration.[47]

This essentialist approach offers a strong basis to oppose discrimination. In Tutu's own words, it is 'always wrong to discrimi-
nate against people because of the way God has made us (black
or white, male or female, gay or straight)'.[48]

There are some possible limitations to this approach, however. Firstly, although it may be a powerful strategy in South
Africa with its history of apartheid, it may not be so effective in
other parts of the continent where the language of culture or
'Africanness' appears to be more prominent than the language
of race or 'blackness'. Secondly, Thoreson suggests that in
South Africa itself, the essentialist emphasis on sexual orientation may be the reason why—in spite of the successes in secur-
ing lesbian and gay rights—'bisexuality has been scarcely visible
and the transgender movement has struggled to secure legal
protections'.[49] Thirdly, one may wonder how long this narrative
will continue to appeal to younger generations in South Africa,
growing up more than 25 years after the end of apartheid. This
question is particularly salient because with the emergence of

queer studies, the language and understanding of sexuality has generally shifted away from biological essentialism to concepts that underscore the fluidity, ambiguity and performativity of gender and sexuality (and perhaps also of race), thus opening up new possibilities for sexual politics.[50]

Conclusion

Nevertheless, Tutu's contribution to the debate about sexuality in contemporary Africa is a major one. He yearns for 'resurrection, new life, new beginning, new hope.'[51] His prophetic commitment to defending human dignity, equality and justice continues to inspire and set an example to many people across the world. Although other parts of Africa have not experienced apartheid, they have experienced colonialism and the systematic racism inherent to it, thus making Tutu's equation of racism and homophobia powerful across the continent. Furthermore, with his theology of *ubuntu* he allows for a conceptualisation of sexual diversity that is meaningful in African contexts and that enhances the human flourishing of gay and lesbian people as part of their communities. *Ubuntu* is clearly based on values such as hospitality and generosity, built on the foundation of solidarity and shared humanity. Therefore, anything that threatens the health and well-being of even one member of the community (for example, through ostracism, stigma and violence) is contrary to the spirit of *ubuntu* extolled by Tutu.

2

GENDER, SEXUALITY AND A THEOLOGY
OF FRUITFULNESS

MERCY ODUYOYE

Can African feminist thought serve as a stepping stone towards reimagining sexuality and Christianity in Africa? It certainly can, as demonstrated in this chapter with reference to the work of leading Ghanaian theologian Mercy Oduyoye.

Mercy Amba Ewudziwa Oduyoye was born in 1934 in Asamankese, Ghana, where she was raised in a Methodist family. She studied at the University of Ghana and at Cambridge University in the UK. In her professional career she held leadership positions in international ecumenical organisations such as the World Council of Churches, and she later founded the Institute of African Women in Religion and Culture at Trinity Theological Seminary in Ghana, where she still serves as director (at the time of writing). A prolific writer, her major books are *Hearing and Knowing: Theological Reflections on Christianity in Africa* (1986), *Daughters of Anowa: African Women and Patriarchy* (1995) and *Introducing African Women's Theology* (2001). Her personal memoir, *Re-membering Me* (2019) is equally informative. The significant contribution she has made to African theology has been recognised with guest lectureships and visiting professorships at universities across the world, as well as honorary doctorates from top universities in South Africa and the United States.

Oduyoye is frequently referred to as 'the mother of African women's theology'.[1] She earned this title thanks to her visionary leadership in including women's voices and perspectives in African theological discourse, where it was hitherto mostly absent. In 1989 she led the establishment of the Circle of Concerned African Women Theologians, which is a continent-wide organisation supporting theological research and writing by African women scholars in the church and the academy.[2] Although Oduyoye has often used the term 'feminist' to describe her work, she and other members of the Circle prefer the term 'women's theology' over 'feminist theology', because of the association of the term feminism with the concerns of white Western middle class women.[3]

Although Oduyoye's work is much more concerned with the category of gender than of sexuality, her thinking is of vital importance to the re-imagination of Christianity and sexuality in Africa. Indeed, as shown below, she herself has made an explicit connection between her concern with the status of women in the church and in society, and the status of sexual minorities. The methods of theological critique and of constructive theological thinking with which she addresses the problem of patriarchy and misogyny in African Christianity can easily be applied to the problem of homophobia and heterosexism in the same context.

Retrieving and transforming African culture

A major theme in Oduyoye's work is the relationship between Christianity and African culture.[4] The question of inculturation (sometimes also called Africanisation or indigenisation) has been a major theme in African theological discourse since the emergence of African contextual theology in the 1960s. Protesting against the negative colonial and missionary interpretations of African indigenous religions and cultures, African theologians in the postcolonial era have sought to bring about a more constructive engagement, and to develop an understanding and expression of Christian faith that is culturally authentic and meaningful.[5] Oduyoye is committed to the project of inculturation, as she is aware of the problematic history of Christianity on the African continent:

> In Africa's history, the arrival of Western Christianity was an assault on the African way of life launched by ethnocentric Europeans in collaboration with colonial administration and colonial violence. This colonization has not ended. In fact new forms of Christianity are arriving in Africa with even more trenchant antipathy for Africa's indigenous religio-culture.[6]

The latter comment criticising new forms of Christianity appears to refer to Pentecostal-Charismatic movements, which have become incredibly popular in Africa since the 1980s and which often use strongly negative rhetoric against African indigenous beliefs and practices. In the dominant theology or ideology of Pentecostalism, African indigenous beliefs and practices belong to the 'old' that must give way to the 'new', namely, born again conversion and the experience of the Holy Spirit.

Vis-à-vis these negative colonial and neo-colonial perceptions of African culture, Oduyoye, like other inculturation theologians, envisions a form of Christianity that affirms and embraces Africanness. She does so, for example, by employing local African idioms, metaphors and symbols to rethink and articulate the meaning of central Christian beliefs, such as about Jesus Christ, salvation, and the church. In her book *Daughters of Anowa*, Oduyoye makes the myths, folktales and proverbs of her own Akan tradition and other West African cultures productive by incorporating them in a constructive theological reflection that can empower women's role in the church and in society. One of her favourite symbols is *Sankofa*, representing the motif of going back and fetching indigenous wisdom. According to Nontando Hadebe, 'It is symbolised by a mythical bird that "flies forward while looking backward with an egg (symbolising the future) in its mouth"'.[7] This symbol in fact captures Oduyoye's own work, especially in *Daughters of Anowa*, as she returns to the African past, specifically of her own Akan tradition, and retrieves its life-giving dimensions to make them fruitful for the present. She does so with a particular view to promoting the position of women, but her work in this regard may present a paradigm for retrieving elements from African cultures and traditions that could help embrace sexual and gender diversity and promote the position of lgbti people. Overall, Oduyoye is a scholar and activist who is decidedly pro-African culture, who contends that the death-dealing aspects of African cultures are aberrations that need to be righted, rather than a norm to be followed uncritically.

Compared to male African theologians working in the paradigm of inculturation, Oduyoye demonstrates a greater awareness that 'African culture' is not just something to be celebrated and embraced. Indeed, she and other women theologians have been rather critical of inculturation theology as developed by many of their male counterparts.[8] As women, they are critically aware of the negative elements of cultural beliefs and practices, especially in relation to gender issues. Although acknowledging that African cultures traditionally have diverse ways of dealing with gender, Oduyoye suggests that both matrilineal and patrilineal societies have patriarchal elements. Missionary Christianity, in her analysis, has reinforced these already existing patriarchal traditions, for instance by introducing an exclusively male image of God. Hence she considers it 'a myth' that Christianity would have brought liberation to African women suffering under patriarchy.[9] She claims instead that the liberation of women is an ongoing task.

Being aware of the way in which African culture and Christianity can serve as canons legitimating the continued oppression and marginalisation of women, Oduyoye advocates a process of inculturation that is critical of both canons while distilling the best elements out of both. This method has been aptly called 'African feminist cultural hermeneutics'.[10] The products of this process would be a transformed African culture and a transformed Christian church. The basic criterion for this transformation is the 'liberation from life-denying circumstances' and the promotion of 'fullness of life' for all.[11] According to Oduyoye, 'For inculturation to mean liberation, it must also be able to stimulate justice, humanity, and equality'.[12]

An interesting illustration of the critical dialogue between African culture and Christianity can be found in Oduyoye's argument about communality. She points out that Western Christianity, as introduced by missionaries in Africa, brought an individualistic outlook which placed emphasis on individual salvation. This was in contrast with the more communal orientation of African societies and of African indigenous religions. Oduyoye argues that with its communal orientation, African culture puts Western individualistic interpretations of Christianity under critique; yet at the same time, the radical message of the Gospel critiques African culture 'for its inability to live up to its principles of harmony and community by extending the meaning of community to include the neighbor', in particular those who belong to minorities or are otherwise marginalised and powerless.[13] Oduyoye indicates that her approach to tradition has been to raise questions:

> My personal mindset towards all that is labelled tradition—what has been handed down from the past, has been questions. I carried this into the Akan traditions and culture I had grown up with. Always

asking, how, why, and who is benefitting and who is being oppressed or silenced. Who is missing from the debates that resulted in the decisions that govern the community's ethos.[14]

Oduyoye's approach to the question of inculturation is directly relevant to questions of sexuality. Her question asking who is being oppressed, silenced or missing from the debates facilitates the inclusion of lgbti people. In the same way that conservative African theologians have used inculturation to argue against the full and equal participation of women in the church and in society—claiming that gender equality would be against African culture—they have also used it to argue against the inclusion of lgbti people. A truly African form of Christianity, the argument goes, does not need to buy in to Western ideas such as homosexuality and lgbti rights.[15] Oduyoye's qualified notion of inculturation as liberating, promoting fullness of life to all, and seeking to include the neighbour, including the sexually 'other', into the community, counterbalances these conservative arguments that rely on static and selective readings of 'African culture'. As discussed below, this understanding allows her to be indeed sympathetic to lesbian and gay people and to begin articulating a theology that affirms them.

Transforming the church

A popular metaphor through which Oduyoye and other African women theologians think about the church is 'church as the household of God'. For Oduyoye, this is an inclusive metaphor:

When in African Religion we speak of the children of God, we mean all human beings. All human beings are the people of God. They belong to God's household housed on this planet and around God in the unseen realms. All of creation is cared for by God, the source of our being.[16]

She applies this inclusivity in two ways. Firstly, God's household is not restricted to Christians, and the church does not hold a monopoly on it. Taking up the notion that in traditional African families, a household could consist of several women who each would have their own 'hearth-hold' (a fireplace shared with everyone whose food security is fully or partially dependent on her), Oduyoye suggests that the Christian church is 'the hearth-hold of Christ within the household of God', but there are many more hearth-holds in the same household, for people with different beliefs.[17] Secondly, women, who are often the centre point of African households, should be fully included in the church as the household of God: 'Women expect the Church to be a household in which all can feel at home because all are accounted worthy'.[18] In the same way, 'Women hope for a transformed Church, because in Africa, the Church remains an institution with a potential for contributing to bringing in the new life that women struggle for'.[19]

Unfortunately, churches in Africa (and across the world) often do not live up to this expectation. In the writings of African women theologians, a recurrent theme is women's struggle with a patriarchal church: the struggle for women's ordination, for women's full inclusion in ministry, for the recognition of women's contribution to the flourishing of Christian communities and society as a whole.[20] The church is often the place where women are 'groaning in faith' because of their experiences of marginalisation, while hoping for and working towards transformation of the same institution.[21] As Oduyoye puts it,

> In Africa, even as participation and justice—including the ordina-tion of women—continue to be disputed, women remain in soli-darity with the Church. They are convinced that the call and the task of the Church are to identify the existing suffering and name it. ... They are in the Church because it is expected to bring joy and abundant life. Their hope is that God will liberate the Church from gender dualism and make all real participants in this house-hold of God.[22]

In the meantime, women 'create for themselves a church within the Church', in the form of women's fellowship groups and women-led churches and ministries.[23]

Thanks to the visionary leadership of Oduyoye and many other African women in theology and church ministry, many churches in Africa have made significant steps in advancing the participation and recognition of women. For instance, many Protestant denominations as well as Pentecostal churches allow for women's ordination and leadership. Churches and Christian organisations have also been actively involved in promoting women's rights and gender equality in society more generally. Obviously, a lot of work remains to be done. The church is far from liberated from gender dualism and hierarchy. However, in addition to the question of the inclusion of women, a next battlefield has emerged: the inclusion of lgbti people in the church. The gender dualism that prevails in forms of African Christianity is not only patriarchal but also heteronormative, thus systematically marginalising and discriminating against people of different sexualities and gender identities. The latter are indeed 'aliens in the household of God'.[24]

Yet just as African women have often stayed within the church, many lgbti people in Africa continue participating in churches that often are so vocal against them. As Marc Epprecht observed with surprise, many African lgbti people 'are proudly, happily and deeply religious'.[25] In some cases, they have created 'a church within the Church', in the form of lgbti Christian fellowships and ministries that offer a safe and affirmative space for those who are ostracised because of their sexuality.[26] In many other cases, they persevere in mainstream congregations, 'groaning in faith' while leading worship, singing in the choir, preaching and participating in ministry.[27] True, when homophobic hate speech becomes too much, some of them withdraw from church and express their faith in God individually. But African lgbti

Christians continue to hope for and strive towards a transformation of the church as a whole. Doing so, they recognise the place that the church as an institution has in African societies, and its potential for contributing to social change and promoting human dignity and rights. In tandem with Oduyoye's vision and call, they push the church to become a more inclusive household, embracing each and every child of God. Like Tutu (see chapter 1), Oduyoye places emphasis on the inherent dignity of every human being. Anecdotally, she narrates that during a trip to Uganda, she filled 'human' in the box for race and got into an argument with the official.[28]

From procreation to fruitfulness

As early as 1993, when there was very little debate in Africa about same-sex relationships, Oduyoye expressed a sensitive and nuanced understanding of the subject. She did so in her contribution to a volume of essays in honour of leading African theologian John Mbiti, from Kenya. In her essay, Oduyoye presents a critique of Mbiti's book *Love and Marriage in Africa*, critically interrogating Mbiti's empathetic account of the societal norms of marriage and procreation, then highlighting the harmful effects of such norms, particularly on women. In the margins of that discussion, she also draws attention to Mbiti's reference to homosexuality. Oduyoye declares herself 'rather horrified by the demonisation of homosexuals' she observes in his book.[29] She further takes issue with the idea that people 'with sexual preferences outside that of the dominant heterosexual orthodoxy' would be 'abhorrent deviants', as suggested by Mbiti and many other Africans.[30] In perhaps the most significant comment, Oduyoye draws a parallel between homophobia and what she calls 'the phobia of childlessness'.[31] She points out that both phobias have their roots in African understandings which link procreation to immortality, as it is through one's offspring that one can become an ancestor. Yet where Mbiti presents such an understanding as a matter of fact, Oduyoye presents a more critical take:

> As Mbiti puts it, it is through marriage and procreation a person becomes immortalised. In contemporary feminism, such an immortality, attached, as it seems, to patriarchal concerns for the perpetuation of the name and the passing on of property, is seen as oppressive. Gay men have opted out of it and lesbians refuse to become victims of the system, though some from both sexual preferences would still adopt children when the rules allow it. For them, as for the rest of human culture, children are important and the care we give them is an expression of our faith in the oneness of humanity and our kinship with God.[32]

She acknowledges that African norms of marriage and procreation are not only patriarchal but also heteronormative, victimising women who are married but do not have children, and people who do not marry nor procreate because of their sexual orientation. In the essay, already we see an allusion to Oduyoye's solution to this problem: by delinking procreation and immortality; and by imagining alternative ways of contributing to humanity in the light of kinship with God, in whose image every human being is created.

This allusion is further elaborated in a later essay, in which Oduyoye gives an intimate autobiographical account of her own experience as a 'childless woman in the West African space'. In her essay, she takes issue with the practice of naming, a practice that in African cultures 'is tied to the experience of childbearing' and has 'religious and spiritual significance' because it is through procreation that the survival of the clan is secured, immortality can be achieved, and the ancestors can 'return to be born into this realm of life'.[33] Women, in particular, bear the brunt of the burden of childbearing. When they succeed in this, they are honoured with the title of motherhood. However, Oduyoye draws attention to 'the experience of women who belong to traditions where naming is according to fruitfulness in childbearing, but who for whatever reason do not join in "increasing and multiplying" the human race'.[34] This is an experience of silence, taboo, stigma and, fundamentally, non-existence in the eyes of the community, because 'one is never really a full and faithful person until one has a child'.[35] The essay is highly personal, narrating her own experience as a married but childless woman, the pressure she faced from her relatives and in-laws, the embarrassment, humiliation and shame. Living through this experience, she has come to understand that there are alternative ways of being fruitful. Fruitfulness is not limited to biological procreation but is about living life to the fullest, in a way that enhances and enriches humanity. Instead of the biblical command of multiplying the human race, Oduyoye came to understand the creative command as:

Increase in humanity.

Multiply the likeness of God for which you have the potential.

Multiply the fullness of humanity that is found in Christ.

Fill the earth with the glory of God.

Increase in creativity.

Bring into being that which God can look upon and pronounce 'good,' even 'very good.'[36]

Obviously, many of the people who know her personally would testify that Oduyoye herself has lived up to this command, as they have been nurtured by her care and inspired by her wisdom.[37]

Oduyoye calls for a church that acknowledges 'the diversity of God's gifts' and that celebrates 'all the ways of bringing forth life'; she calls for a theology that 'embraces forms of fruitfulness, biological and beyond'.[38] This call is as relevant for childless women as it is for people who are unmarried and/or do not have children in a socially-prescribed heterosexual family setting because of their sexuality. Oduyoye's theology of alternative ways of being fruitful is in fact not only feminist but also queer, as it calls into question the heteronormative idea that biological reproduction in the context of a heterosexual marriage and family is the only, or best, way for human beings to achieve their full potential and purpose in life. Instead, her theology calls to recognise the diversity of God-given gifts present in each human being regardless of their reproductive capacities, marital status, gender identity or sexual orientation.

Writing about the traditional Christian belief in 'the resurrection of the body', Oduyoye points out that for African women, this reflects the hope that:

> Christianity will finally come to terms with the fact that we humans are embodied in different forms, but both sexes constitute gifts of God and that women do not have to become men to be human. It is a hope that women themselves will feel fully human in the body God has given them. Thus, women have to come to terms with their particular embodiment.[39]

Again, it does not take much effort to translate this feminist argument into an argument that affirms the humanity of lesbian, gay, bisexual and gender non-confirming people. They do not have to become or present themselves as straight in order to be human; the belief in the resurrection of the body encourages them to come to terms with their sexual embodiment, and to embrace who they are and the unique gifts they have to offer.

Storytelling as a theological method

Oduyoye and other African women theologians have made an important methodological contribution to African theology by utilising storytelling as a theological method. As Sarojini Nadar puts it, 'the work of feminist theologians in Africa bears testimony to this respect for story as a legitimate method and source of theology, and therefore African women theologies have aptly been called "narrative theologies".[40] In Oduyoye's words, accepting 'story as a source of theology' allows women theologians to bring in the experiences and perspectives of people who hitherto have not been part of the theological conversation, particularly women.[41] The methodology is inspired by 'the normative role of stories in Africa's oral corpus, and the role of story in biblical theology'; hence it presents an alternative to 'analytical and deductive forms of theology' because through storytelling feminist theologians 'bring back the personal into academic studies'.[42]

Oduyoye has practised narrative theology in various ways. In her book *Daughters of Anowa*, she retells the story of mythical female figures from the past whose memory can inspire women today. In another essay, she reconstructs the references to Jesus Christ in women's stories and prayers into an oral Christology.[43] As discussed above, Oduyoye has also engaged in autobiographical storytelling, sharing and reflecting upon her own experience as a childless woman, and using that as a starting point for theological reflection. In much of her writing, the stories of women from Africa's past and present, of women in the Bible, and of herself are brought into a creative conversation with each other. It is through such a cross-reading of women's stories that meaning can be given to the narrated experiences, that solidarity can grow, and that healing can occur. As Oduyoye describes the importance of storytelling:

> The stories we tell of our hurts and joys are sacred. Telling them makes us vulnerable, but without this sharing we cannot build community and solidarity. Our stories are precious paths on which we have walked with God, and struggled for a passage to our full humanity. They are events through which we have received the blessings of life from the hands of God. The stories we tell are sacred, for they are indications of how we struggled with God. ... We

share our stories with you as people who believe that true community thrives where there is sharing in solidarity.[44]

Storytelling, as a method to foreground hitherto marginalised
perspectives and experiences, is important not only in relation to
issues of gender but also of sexuality. Thanks to the efforts of
Oduyoye and others, significant progress has been made to
include women in the theological conversation in Africa; yet the
voices of lesbian, gay, bisexual and gender non-conforming
people remain largely silenced, and their experiences excluded.
As far as African women theologians have shared stories about
sexuality, it is in a heterosexual context, problematising women's
sexuality in patriarchal cultures. They 'have hardly begun to tell,
share and reflect upon the stories of women in same-sex relationships, and of lgbti people more generally, and have not yet
developed a systematic critique of heteronormativity'.[45] Yet it is
through storytelling that the joy and pain experienced by lgbti
people can be rendered visible, their voices heard, their struggle
shared, their humanity affirmed, and their lives become a testimony of hope and faith. Such storytelling will reveal the oppressive nature and harmful effects of African hetero-patriarchal
cultural and religious traditions, yet it will also render lgbti lives
as sacred. Thus, building on Oduyoye's work, it can be posed that
narrative methods are the starting point for African queer theology, just as they have served as a starting point for African feminist theology.[46]

Conclusion

Mercy Oduyoye has made a tremendous contribution to African
theology by inserting a critical gender perspective into the theological debate, and constructively engaging women's experiences
as a starting point for theologising. On that basis she has envi-
sioned and contributed to transformations taking place in the

church and society more widely. The discussion in this chapter foregrounds an aspect of her work that has received very little attention so far: that Oduyoye herself was one of the first theologians in Africa to advocate for the human dignity and rights of gay and lesbian people. True, this is not a prominent theme in her writing, yet nevertheless she has explicitly denounced the demonisation of sexual minorities, and she has critically linked patriarchy to heteronormativity by making the connection between homophobia and the phobia of childlessness. It is obvious that her feminist cultural hermeneutics, as well as her feminist narrative theology, present a model for a queer theology in Africa. Such a theology engages critically with African cultures, reclaiming those elements that can be used to affirm fullness of life for all, including people belonging to sexual minorities. Such a theology further attends to the life stories of lgbti people in contemporary Africa, their experiences of struggle as well as the hope and faith that keep them going, and it reads such stories as sacred paths witnessing to people walking with God. Feminist solidarity, for Oduyoye, extends to everyone marginalised on the basis of societal and cultural norms, including people ostracised because of their non-confirming gender and sexual identities. Rather than aliens, they are members of the household of God:

> Women's resistance to anonymity and dehumanization encompasses not only their own humanity but that of all who are marginalized or oppressed or overlooked, as well as a hope for the redemption of the humanity of those who do the oppressing and the marginalizing. The hope for a community of women and men around God's table, is what anchors this theology.[47]

3

REVOLUTIONARY IMAGINATION
AND THE ECOLOGY OF HUMAN RIGHTS

JEAN-BLAISE KENMOGNE

Cameroon, in West Africa, is one of the countries on the African continent that from the 2000s has witnessed an increasing level of social, political and religious homophobia. This chapter focuses on one prominent Christian figure who has intervened in the politics of homosexuality in the country: Rev. Dr Jean-Blaise Kenmogne. It examines the nature of his intervention, and the pastoral and theological lines of thought informing it. Some context of Cameroon is provided as a form of introduction.

A former French colony,[1] Cameroon, when gaining independence in 1960, did not inherit the anti-sodomy laws that the British had introduced in most of their colonies. Yet in September 1972, the first Cameroonian president Ahmadou Ahidjo added an article to the country's Penal Code criminalising 'sexual relations with a person of the same sex' which carried a penalty of maximum five years' imprisonment (Section 347-1). It has been suggested that Ahidjo pushed through this article in order to deflect attention away from the rumours about his own sexuality, but the Cameroonian anthropologist Basile Ndjio has argued that the law was part of a broader socio-political project of post-colonial nation-building, with sexuality being utilised as a key site to promote a sense of national unity and identity.[2] The clause in the penal code, which remains intact to date, was for a long time largely symbolic, with very few cases of arrest and conviction. Yet this changed in May 2005, with a mass arrest taking place at the Victoire bar in Yaoundé.[3] Since then, numerous individuals have been arrested and convicted without any evidence of actual same-sex practice, instead based purely on their real or perceived sexual orientation.[4]

The Catholic Church, which is a powerful institution in the country, has been at the forefront of the current politicisation of homosexuality in Cameroon. A particularly prominent role was played by the Archbishop of Yaoundé, Victor Tonyé Bakot, and the Archbishop of Douala, Cardinal Christian Wiyghan Tumi. On 24 December 2005, Bakot used his sermon on Christmas Eve to denounce the threat of homosexuality and to warn against 'the power of money and the forces of evil [that] want to impose on the people of God that you approve of homosexuality'.[5] On 11 July 2009, Tumi organised a march 'against abortion and homosexuality' and launched a petition against the promulgation of the Maputo Protocol, which is a protocol to the African Charter on Human and Peoples' Rights, protecting the rights of women but which in the Cameroonian debate also became somehow associated with gay rights. Both these events were widely covered by the media and constituted, in the words of the Cameroonian scholar Patrick Awondo, 'decisive elements in the re-politicisation of gender and sexuality in Cameroon'.[6] In January 2006, shortly after Bakot's Christmas sermon, a Cameroonian newspaper and two weekly publications each published lists of names of (presumed) homosexuals in the country, including prominent politicians and business people.

The unfolding media narratives and public discourse, according to Awondo, centred around three 'principal grievances':

> First, a fine line is drawn between homosexual perversion/vice and political power. Second, the relationship between prostitution/*droit du seigneur*/corruption and homosexuality at the heart of the political system. Finally, the link between homosexuality and the 'occult': the idea that homosexuality is symbol of the 'invisible forces'.[7]

Awondo suggests that homophobia provides the general public with an outlet to engage in a socio-political critique of the elites.

Not only Catholic bishops but also other religious bodies and leaders actively fuelled the campaign against homosexuality and gay people in Cameroon. The Council of Protestant Churches in Cameroon officially condemned homosexuality during its annual assembly in Limbe in March 2011. Frida Lyonga draws critical attention to the role of Pentecostal pastors who fuel the idea of homosexuality as the pinnacle of moral corruption that is part of the Devil's agenda.[8] This choir of religious leaders and organisations speaking out against homosexuality illustrates one key factor in the dynamics of the politicisation of homosexuality in African countries: religious competition. When one body speaks out, it is difficult for others not to join the bandwagon, because keeping silent can be interpreted as quietly supporting gay rights. However, in this hostile anti-gay climate, one prominent Christian figure did in fact publicly speak out in support of the rights of sexual minorities.

A pastor speaks out

Rev. Dr Jean-Blaise Kenmogne is an ordained minister in the Evangelical Lutheran Church of Cameroon, which is a relatively small Protestant denomination in the country. He was the founder and serves as general director of a faith-based organisation called International Circle for the Promotion of Creation.[9]

Established in 1990, this organisation is mostly concerned with ecology and sustainable development, but also with human rights advocacy and promotion of democracy. Inspired by an understanding of God's project for creation as concerned with 'life in abundance as revealed through Jesus Christ', it seeks to enhance human flourishing and dignity.[10] Moreover, Kenmogne is rector of the Evangelical University of Cameroon, an institution founded in 2010 by the Evangelical Lutheran Church. Having studied theology and philosophy in France in the 1970s, Kenmogne in 2011 was awarded a doctorate in human rights, from the Catholic University for Central Africa in Yaoundé, with a dissertation in the area of ecology and sustainable development.[11] He has published in areas as diverse as ecological ethics, education, religion, development and peace-building, and HIV. Clearly, Kenmogne is an influential figure not only in his church but in Cameroonian society more generally, as well as ecumenical Christian circles in West Africa and beyond.

Given Kenmogne's high-profile position, his public support of the human rights of sexual minorities in Cameroon is of great significance. In 2011, he published two short articles in Cameroonian newspaper *Le Jour* advocating for the recognition of gay and lesbian human rights. Apart from the praise by local and international gay rights groups who welcomed Kenmogne's intervention, he received a strong backlash; many Christian leaders, including fellow pastors in his own church, spoke out against him. A campaign was launched to have him expelled as an ordained pastor in the Lutheran church, and for him to be dismissed from the post of university rector. Although this attempt was unsuccessful, the smear campaign associated him with heresy, witchcraft and greed. However, this did not stop him. In 2012, Kenmogne participated in a lengthy interview with the director and editor of *Le Jour*, Haman Mana, which was subsequently published in book form under the title *Homosexualité,*

Église et Droits de l'Homme: Ouvrons le débat (Homosexuality, the Church and Human Rights: Let's Open the Debate).[12] In the epilogue to this book, Mana explains that as interviewer he deliberately put himself in the shoes of the average Cameroonian believer, asking Kenmogne the questions that he believed ordinary Cameroonians are asking about the unheard-of phenomenon of a pastor defending gay rights. It makes for a rather aggressive interview style, with Kenmogne trying to explain patiently and empathetically the motivation and rationale behind his position.

The following section offers a detailed analysis of the interview, which is the only text available in which Kenmogne directly engages with the question of homosexuality. Subsequently, his thinking about this topic will be linked to his broader theological thought.

Making a case for homosexuality and human rights

In the course of the interview, Kenmogne develops several arguments regarding homosexuality in Cameroon, which are worth reviewing in detail. Firstly, he makes an analytical distinction between two forms of homosexuality found in contemporary Cameroon: a homosexuality of slavery, and an identity homosexuality. The former is associated with people, especially youth, engaging in same-sex practices on an involuntary basis, as they are forced into it by men who belong to the politically and economically powerful elite. The culture of homosexuality among these elites, Kenmogne suggests, is driven by 'forces of evil', in particular mystical and esoteric forces that infiltrate certain economic, political, intellectual and socio-cultural circles.[13] He associates this culture with secret societies that would promote homosexuality in a pursuit of political and financial power.[14] Without going into detail, Kenmogne appears to allude here to the well-documented popular rumours in Cameroon and more generally in Central and West Africa linking homosexuality to occult practices such as witchcraft, freemasonry and Rosicrucianism, in which anal penetration is key to an economy of power and wealth.[15] Indeed, Kenmogne describes this phenomenon as an unacceptable perversion that should be categorically opposed because it is morally corrupt. Those who fall victim to it need to be liberated.

However, he clearly demarcates this culture of same-sex practice from what he calls identity homosexuality, a term he says he derives from Charles Gueboguo. Here, same-sex activity is motivated by an innate sexual orientation, on the basis of which a person is attracted to someone of the same sex. This orientation needs to be psychologically recognised and accepted as an identity, Kenmogne suggests, in line with modern ideas of sexual identity. There is nothing wrong with this form of homosexuality, he argues, because it is defined by freedom and responsibility, rather than with the domination and exploitation that characterises the other culture of homosexuality.

Secondly, Kenmogne develops a twofold cultural argument about homosexuality in Africa, recognising historical continuity, on the one hand, and calling for evolving cultural understanding, on the other hand. To begin, he refers—seemingly in agreement—to the book by the earlier mentioned Gueboguo, and to a collection edited by Fabien Eboussi Boulaga, which claim that homosexuality has always been practised in the various regions of sub-Saharan Africa, including Cameroon, and present anthropological, historical and linguistic evidence for that claim.[16] He also cites the suggestion of critical theorist Achille Mbembe, also from Cameroon, that contemporary homophobia in Africa is a form of repression and of cultural amnesia.[17] Although Kenmogne recognises that homosexuality may have been a relatively marginal phenomenon in African societies, he also observes that in contemporary Africa it is a 'social fact', the existence of which cannot be denied:

> I start from a very clear contemporary fact: homosexuals exist and they live their homosexuality among us. It is a naturally lived fact. We discover it in our families, in our churches, in our cities, in our countries, in the world. Now we have to know how to deal with this fact.[18]

From there, Kenmogne argues that the new understanding of (homo)sexuality as an orientation, which has emerged in cultures across the world, is part of an evolving anthropological understanding of human identity with which African societies need to come to terms 'in the name of civilisation and humanity'.[19] Refuting the repeated insinuation of his interviewer that he is promoting a Western agenda imposed on Africa (and that he benefits from this financially), Kenmogne emphasises that the question of homosexuality in Africa is 'a problem of Africans confronted with the behaviour of other Africans'.[20] He adds that addressing this problem is therefore an African responsibility, although Africa can learn from developments in other parts of the world.

Thirdly, Kenmogne develops a theological argument, not so much trying to explicitly legitimise same-sex sexuality as such, but to advocate an approach to gay and lesbian people that affirms their human dignity and rights. His interviewer repeatedly pushes a theological discourse of sin, with which Kenmogne reluctantly engages. In response to the question of whether homosexuality is a sin, he proposes a twofold working hypothesis. The first one assumes that homosexuality is a sin, and considers the pastoral and theological consequences of that position. If homosexuality were a sin, Kenmogne argues, there is no theological reason to think that it would be more abominable than other sins that the Bible or the Christian tradition appears to condemn but with which most Christian communities today seem far less concerned. He points to the hypocrisy of many churches not banning people who are involved in adultery, corruption, polygamy, gossip and slander from their midst (and in fact happily receiving their donations), while gay and lesbian people tend to be ostracised. Hence he argues that even if homosexuality is a sin, 'let's leave homosexuals alone', as there is no hierarchy of sin.[21] Kenmogne here cites the words that Jesus spoke to those who brought to him a woman caught in the act of adultery: 'Let any one of you who is without sin be the first to throw a stone at her'.[22] Subsequently Kenmogne calls on those who fiercely condemn homosexuality to take an introspective look at their own lives, and to leave judgement of gay people to God. He reminds his readers of a key Christian principle—namely, the belief in God's mercy—and concludes that even if homosexuality were a sin, we have to 'cover it in the name of Christ in grace, in mercy and in the love of the Lord'.[23] Not doing so, instead sticking to the aggressive spirit of exclusion and stigmatisation towards gay people that currently dominates the Cameroonian churches, would be harmful, according to Kenmogne, for the proclamation of the Gospel of liberation and for the evangelisation of society.

In response to the interviewer pointing out the biblical verses that would condemn homosexuality, Kenmogne underlines the importance of hermeneutics that is, of principles for the interpretation of Scripture.[24] Bringing to mind the fact that the Bible has been used to legitimise slavery, racism and other great injustices in the so-called name of God, he proposes to read the Bible 'with a criterion of humanity', in other words striving to recognise the full humanity in every human being.[25] This is what he calls a 'deep reading' of the Bible which, in contrast to a superficial reading, seeks to interpret and apply the biblical texts in light of what, for Christians, is the essence of the Bible: the revelation of God in Jesus Christ.[26] On the basis of this theological principle of affirming and enhancing the humanity of every human person just as Jesus did, Kenmogne suggests that nothing stops us from affirming the human dignity and rights of gay and lesbian people. Examining what sin fundamentally is—'a radical, fundamental break with God, with his Spirit, with this force, this breath'—he points out that many homosexuals are 'people of great spiritual depth and great ethical height' who are far from sinners at odds with God. Instead 'to everyone's surprise ... [they may well] precede heterosexuals in the Kingdom of God'.[27] The latter claim about gay spirituality can be supported with reference to a rare empirical study, conducted among a group of gay men living with HIV in Douala, Cameroon, which found that for many of these men their faith in God was indeed an important part of their identity and a source of strength.[28] Kenmogne continues his theological argument by stating that God will not judge human beings on the basis of their homo- or heterosexuality, but on the basis of 'our attitude towards the poor, the abandoned, the excluded, the marginalised, the stigmatised'.[29] Here he refers to the biblical scene of the Last Judgement as narrated by Jesus in the Gospel of Matthew, a passage that has also been powerfully invoked by theologian Musa Dube in the context of the HIV epidemic (chapter 4).[30] Both Dube and Kenmogne suggest that in contemporary society, it might well be sexual outcasts such as gay and lesbian people and those living with HIV, who are among the marginalised and stigmatised in whom, according to this parable, Christians can encounter Jesus Christ himself.

Fourthly, what follows from this theological exposition is Kenmogne's pastoral argument about a new attitude of society, particularly Christian communities, towards gay and lesbian people. He distinguishes four pastoral principles that should define that attitude:

1) Love: As discussed above, regardless of whether homosexuality is perceived as a sin, Kenmogne suggests that it must be treated with love. The church should follow the example of

Jesus, who demonstrated love to the marginalised in society, and should subsequently embark on a 'courageous pastoral ministry of love' towards gay and lesbian people, which would be a 'wonderful force for social integration'.[31] Providing a biblical motivation for this, he refers to the parable of the good Samaritan and states that 'it is essential that we become the neighbour of those who suffer from the violence of society instead of clinging to dogmas, rituals and practices of a religiosity cut off from its foundation of love'.[32]

2) Listening: Kenmogne calls for a 'dialogue of life' with gay and lesbian people, in which the church demonstrates an attitude of 'pastoral listening without judgment and without condemnation'. In this dialogue, the church comes to understand the situation of sexual minorities, and through the eyes of Christ it recognises that they are full human beings with rights and duties, holding the 'power to make a positive and profound contribution to the transformation of society, for life in abundance'.[33]

3) Integration: What follows from this process of careful listening to and learning from gay and lesbian people, and the recognition of their talents and gifts, is a step through which the church, and society at large, indeed affirm their 'right to life, to work, to happiness and fulfilment as creatures of God', thus fully integrating them into their midst.[34] This will radically transform the current attitudes of marginalisation and exclusion into one in which gay and lesbian people will be nurtured into human flourishing, benefiting the growth of society.

4) Struggle: The final pastoral principle, for Kenmogne, is a strong commitment to fight for the recognition of the humanity of every human being. The struggle continues, and faith communities should be at the forefront of it. Recognising that gay and lesbian people themselves have already cou-

rageously taken up the struggle to defend their rights, Kenmogne suggests that the church should support them and fight on their side, driven by the Spirit of God who 'knows how to open the ears of the deaf'.[35]

Of course, whether Kenmogne's fourfold argument will convince any of his opponents is yet be seen, and any effect may take a while to become visible. As Joachim Mbetbo has pointed out, popular religious discourse in Cameroon does not see homosexuality just as a sin among other sins, but as fundamentally anti-religious, morally perverse, evil and even demonic.[36] Yet it is exactly against this background that Kenmogne's attempt to humanise gay and lesbian people, and his call for a pastoral attitude towards them, is an important intervention. What gives his intervention intellectual and political weight is that it is motivated by a much more deeply rooted theological line of thought, which opens up an alternative imagination of society and human sexuality as part of it.

Social transformation and a new imagination

In response to the questions of his interviewer, Kenmogne invokes several fundamental theological and ethical notions that appear to guide his thinking, but on which he does not elaborate in the context of the interview. In this section, we offer an interpretation of the views expressed in the interview by linking it to his wider thought and to another key thinker who has influenced him.

Repeatedly, Kenmogne refers to the project of the evangelisation of society. For him, this is not so much about the common definition of evangelism, of the church reaching out to individuals with the Christian message and trying to convert them. Instead, in line with the wider discourse of the theology of reconstruction, which from the 1990s emerged in ecumenical theological circles across the continent, Kenmogne understands this evangelisation as a project of social transformation inspired by the Christian faith. Reflecting on his theological formation, he narrates how he was made aware of 'the project of God for human societies, for my country, for Africa and for the world'.[37] He cites a leading figure in the theology of reconstruction, the Congolese philosopher and theologian Kä Mana (with whom he has worked closely), as a great source of inspiration for his own ethical commitment. Taking up a central concept in Kä Mana's thought, the notion of *imaginaire* (imagination), Kenmogne argues that his commitment to defending the human rights of homosexuals 'aims to revolutionise the African imagination', on the basis of an ethics of solidarity and freedom to build a society of shared happiness.[38] Some deeper understanding of Kä Mana's work, by which Kenmogne is greatly inspired, will provide context to the latter's intervention in the politics of sexuality in Cameroon.

The central problem in Kä Mana's extensive body of writing (mostly published in French, in the 1980s–90s)[39] is the human condition in contemporary Africa, which he argues has been severely damaged by a broken imagination. Africans have been dehumanised as a result of the violent legacy of colonialism and alienating postcolonial conditions. Although Kä Mana is far from ignorant about the way in which Christianity, as a colonial religion, is part and parcel of these damaging forces, with other African theologians he also believes that the core of the Christian message is an 'innovative power capable of injecting a creative dynamism into African traditions in order to initiate an ethical redemption of African social *imaginaire*'.[40] For him, this core message is a form of Christian humanism, according to which God seeks to humanise humankind through Jesus Christ. As Kä Mana puts it, 'the person, message and ideals of Jesus Christ undoubtedly represent a universal solution to our African crisis: the seed of a new passion for living and of a new spirit of resourcefulness for building our future.'[41] In his proposal for the redemption of African imagination, the Christian faith is the basis for a humanist vision of African social life, as 'Jesus Christ offers Africa new possibilities for the struggle against the power-lessness of our being, the inconsistency of our action and the devaluation of our presence in the world today'.[42] Kä Mana believes that through salvation, human beings are made co-creators of the earth as intended by God; along the same lines, according to his African Christian humanism, God makes Africa 'responsible for its own destiny'.[43] This is the essence of his theology of reconstruction, a Christian-inspired vision for the reconstruction and transformation of African society.

In this brief outline, Kä Mana's thinking may appear rather abstract and general, yet throughout his work he applies it to specific situations of social crisis in Africa. Although he has not explicitly addressed the question of homosexuality, he has writ-ten about the HIV epidemic as reflecting a crisis of gender and sexuality in Africa. In Kä Mana's analysis, the epidemic is informed by problematic, patriarchal and heteronormative con-ceptions of masculinity that illustrate a broken imagination. He expresses the hope that the struggle against HIV will herald the advent of 'a new state of mind, a new culture, and a new society' based on a quest for 'shared happiness and mutual enrichment' of men and women.[44] Kenmogne appears to apply this analysis to the current struggle against social and political homophobia, and to translate this hope into a new imagination of human together-ness across genders and sexualities.

The influences of Kä Mana's thought can be observed through-out Kenmogne's exposition about homosexuality, the church and human rights. The latter's statement that addressing the problem of homosexuality is an African responsibility is not just a way for Kenmogne to dissociate himself from international gay rights lobbies, or to avoid the suggestion that he is following a Western agenda; instead, it reflects Kä Mana's central point about Africa being responsible for shaping and achieving its own destiny. Kenmogne's argument that 'the attitude of Cameroonian society towards homosexuals does not assure them of a creative representation of themselves' reflects Kä Mana's concern with the broken imagination in Africa resulting in alienation, dehumanisation and misrepresentation not only of but among Africans, such as in the politics of homophobia.[45] When Kenmogne subsequently underlines the 'need for an ethics of solidarity [and] an ethics of respect for the freedom of all for the construction of a society of shared happiness', we see an echo of Kä Mana's humanist vision. According to Kä Mana, God created the world according to 'a plan of happiness for a free and responsible humanity'; inspired by God's creative spirit, human beings are promoters of life and co-creators of happiness.[46] Indeed, Kenmogne's invocation of a discourse of human rights does not so much reflect his reliance on a Western liberal framework, but is in line with Kä Mana's fundamental concern with the human condition and interrogation of the dehumanising forces at work in African societies.

Yet Kenmogne's expression, 'revolutionising the African imagination', appears to be his own invention. This phrase may well be an indication of what is at stake in the question of homosexuality in contemporary Africa. Too often, in Cameroon and elsewhere, popular arguments against homosexuality have adopted the rhetoric of African authenticity and identity.[47] In other words, this discourse claims to represent an African imagination—defending a reified heterosexual 'African culture' vis-à-vis a perceived Western gay imperialism—and on that basis African gay and lesbian people are being denied both their Africanness and their human dignity and rights. It illustrates one of the dynamics against which Kä Mana warns: attempts to rebuild African identity 'under the guise of restoring traditions'.[48]

Resisting this dynamic as it plays out in relation to sexuality in contemporary Africa, Kenmogne suggests that a revolutionary imagination is required: one that opposes reactionary and conservative tendencies but instead is radically humanistic and, for that matter, Christian, as it recognises and confirms the full humanity of each and every African, regardless of their sexual orientation and practice. Such a revolutionary imagination calls for a new, progressive concept of what it means to be African and to be human, a concept that allows cultures to evolve and societies to grow towards inclusivity, freedom, respect and responsibility for all. As innovative and forward-looking an imagination this is, it can reclaim and expand on the traditions of human community observed by Kenmogne in the history of Cameroon, as well as other African societies that have long since mastered the art of living together. This 'fundamental Africanity' may have been affected by the broken imagination, but is a key resource for the re-imagination of social life:

> It is about faith in oneself as the foundation of living together, in spite of conflicts, tensions, antagonisms, ambitions and passions that are 'human, all too human'. I believe that in Africa there is such a foundation of being together and that it must be reactivated and resuscitated ... on the basis of the faith of Africa in its own values of life.[49]

A humanistic ecology of human rights

As much as Kenmogne is indebted to Kä Mana, he is also a thinker in his own right. Reviewing Kenmogne's publications, it becomes clear that his concern with homosexuality and with gay and lesbian people is not a one-issue agenda. On the contrary, it is part of and informed by his much broader concern with the integrity of God's creation, and the quest for what he calls 'humanistic ecology'.[50] His thinking is deeply ecological, as he pursues the question of how to build a human civilisation that supports the sustainable and holistic development of all of creation. Against this ecological background he considers the question of human rights, which for him refers to a set of ethical and spiritual principles centring around the notion of 'reciprocal responsibility', allowing each human being to participate in, contribute to, and take care of the whole of God's creation.

Kenmogne describes his ethics as an 'ethics of connections', foregrounding the interconnected nature of humankind as connected to the earth, to each other, to the self and to God.[51] He conceives of this constructive ethical vision both by invoking indigenous African concepts, such as the ancient Egyptian concept of *ma'at* and the philosophy of *ubuntu* (see chapters 1 and 4), and Christian concepts such as the Trinity. For Kenmogne, the Trinity (the Christian belief in God the Father, the Son and the Holy Spirit) means that God is essentially a loving relationship between the three divine persons without hierarchy; this God opens itself up to establish a loving relationship with the whole of creation. Humankind—being created in the image of this God, who is defined by love internally and externally—is called to resemble this model. What follows from this ecological theology and ethics is an emphasis on human existence as fundamentally interconnected, and an imperative to affirm life, especially where it is under threat. It appears that for Kenmogne, in the current context of Cameroon, the life and dignity of gay and lesbian people are in danger, and therefore need to be defended and affirmed.

Conclusion

This chapter has foregrounded the intervention by an African Francophone thinker, Jean-Blaise Kenmogne, in the politics of homosexuality in an African Francophone context, Cameroon. Due to the colonial linguistic divide of sub-Saharan Africa in

English, French and Portuguese-speaking regions, there is little interaction and exchange between thinkers who write and publish in different languages. If only for that reason, this chapter is already significant, as it helps to address this divide. Moreover, it is the specific content of Kenmogne's thought that is valuable for broader African conversations about homosexuality and for the reimagination of Christianity and sexuality on the continent. His understanding of the church's mission as participation in social transformation, his call for a reimagining of what it means to be African and human, and his constructive vision of a humanistic ecology, are important contributions towards the development of new ways of engaging issues of sexual diversity and Christianity in Africa from innovative intellectual perspectives.

4

AFFIRMING HUMAN DIVERSITY AND EMBODIMENT IN THE FACE OF HIV

MUSA W. DUBE

Musa W. Dube (born 28 July 1964), from Botswana, is one of Africa's leading biblical scholars and feminist theologians. Her work in the field of postcolonial feminist interpretations of the Bible established her reputation as an internationally acclaimed scholar. Having taught for many years at the University of Botswana, in 2020 she was appointed Professor of New Testament at Emory University in the United States of America (to take up the position in 2021). From the early 2000s, she has attracted attention as an outstanding scholar-activist in the response to the HIV epidemic, undertaking highly innovative and critical work at the intersections of theology, church and HIV and AIDS, writing many publications and organising numerous workshops in this area. She served as a Theology Consultant on HIV and AIDS for the World Council of Churches (WCC) from 2002–04 (see chapter 5), and her status as a scholar-activist has continued beyond her time with the WCC. For example, in 2019, she was elected the General

Coordinator of the Circle of Concerned African Women Theologians (hereafter the Circle).

As an individual, and within institutions such as WCC and the Circle, Dube is among those determined to tread where many others feared to tread, breaking the silence and addressing the stigma around HIV and AIDS, but also on many other issues relating to gender and sexuality.[1] Courageously, she has put the theme of a positive engagement with homosexuality firmly on the agenda of African biblical studies and theology. An earlier study identified Dube as one of the (then) few African theologians who insisted on defending the dignity and rights of gay and lesbian people in Africa.[2] She has remained a vocal and passionate supporter of sexual minorities, challenging African Christians to embrace individuals and communities who experience extreme levels of stigma and discrimination. As we illustrate below, she also appeals to *ubuntu*, the southern African concept of solidarity (see chapter 1), to mobilise African communities to fully accept sexual minorities in their midst.

Admittedly, Dube has not published any in-depth treatise on the subject; instead of singling out the topic, she has sought to mainstream it as part of a much wider agenda of transformative scholarship. Our interpretation of Dube's consistency in upholding the rights of gay and lesbian people in Africa is that it is based on her concept of social justice and human liberation. For Dube, the liberation project by definition is characterised by radical inclusion. This quest for justice, liberation and inclusion is at the heart of the mission of the church in society. Dube's strong personal commitment to this quest is illustrated by the fact that she named her son, Aluta, in recognition of the slogan '*a luta continua!*'—that is, the struggle continues.

In order to locate Dube's commitment to the full acceptance and participation of African gay and lesbian people, this chapter begins by describing Dube's overarching theological convictions.

These are identified as her commitment to full liberation, a focus on the marginalised in society, and a commitment to Jesus' approach of radical inclusion based on justice and love. Also described are the forces undermining these, such as empire, patriarchy and homophobia. In its second section the chapter focuses on Dube's HIV activism, her calls for pragmatism and the theology of compassion to promote the liberation of African lesbian and gay people. In the third section, we review her reflections on *ubuntu* as a resource in the struggle for the rights and dignity of African gay and lesbian people. We then review some of the resources and strategies that have enabled her to be an effective ally of sexual minorities. In conclusion, we maintain that Dube remains one of the leading African theologians to have come out fully in favour of upholding the rights of sexual minorities.

'Created in God's image': Affirming the sacredness of all life

Dube's overarching theological stance is informed by her reading of the Bible, which for her begins with the affirmation that humankind is created in the image of God, and that God affirms the entire creation as good.[3] This provides her with a powerful entry point for the defence of African women's rights, but also of the rights of sexual minorities. If God, who created human beings as reflecting the image of the divine, saw that all of creation was good, who else has the authority to deem certain humans as inferior because of their gender, their sexuality or any other characteristic? As Dube argues,

> All people, regardless of their color, gender, class, race, nationality, religion, ethnicity, health status, age, or sexual orientation, were created in God's image and are loved by God, who is the source of human dignity.[4]

For Dube, since God has already expressed satisfaction in the beauty and dignity of every human being, there is no room for ambiguity: human life, in all its diversity, is sacred. Consequently, for her human rights are not a secular concept, but refer to the sacred quality inherent to each and every human being.[5] This provides Dube with a strong theological basis to defend the dignity and rights of all whose humanity is diminished by the powers of empire (any oppressive system such as patriarchy, racism, colonialism, capitalism and heterosexism).

If anything, Dube is convinced that diversity is part of God's plan for beauty in the world, an idea she explicitly applies to sexuality. In a handbook for inclusive preaching and worship, especially in the context of HIV and AIDS, she includes guidelines for a church service on homosexuality containing the following liturgical text:

Leader: You are the Creator God
        You created us with a range of sexual orientations.

All: We are a beautiful rainbow people
        And you created all of us good.[6]

This is vintage Dube. Many preachers have demonised homosexuality, deploying the so-called 'clobber texts' to suggest that it emerges from the fall of humanity into sin, and reflects the workings of the devil. Yet Dube radically opposes such interpretations, insisting that the range of sexual orientations is part of God's created order (not the 'disorder' with which critics associate homosexuality). Like Desmond Tutu (chapter 1), she appropriates the symbol of the rainbow to express the belief that human diversity, including diversity of sexualities, is part of God's design. Thus, she invites the congregation to affirm that, 'we are a beautiful rainbow people'. The same liturgical text includes the following line: 'In your Garden there are many different flowers. And you created all of them good'.[7] The text illustrates how Dube is pushing the boundaries by recognising sexual diversity as a positive anthropological given. She challenges African Christians to recognise and affirm that gay and lesbian people are beautiful flowers in the colourful garden of God's creation. The instruction for closing the service on homosexuality is as follows: 'Turn to each of your neighbours, hold/fold their hands in your hands, look them in the eye and say, "I love you with the love of God, for I can see in you the glory of God"'.[8] This, again, is highly revolutionary, particularly in its emphasis on seeing the glory of God in every person. Dube seeks to bring about a profound paradigm shift, not only in the way Christians think about homosexuality but, more importantly, in the way they concretely relate to gay and lesbian people. Her liturgical texts serve to move the worshippers from an attitude of condemnation to one of unconditional embrace.

For Dube, the notion that God perceived the entire creation as good provides the basis for an eco-feminist commitment to defending the environment. Thus, her concern with the rights of human beings is part of a broader concern with the flourishing of all creation. Dube's theology seeks to engender what she calls 'justice-loving earth communities' that affirm the sacredness of all creation. This entails adopting a positive approach towards the body: both the body of the earth and the human bodies inhabiting it. Referring to the negative attitudes to embodiment that have long dominated Christian thought, she cautions:

> Denial of the body and its sacredness often means we have no paradigms of thinking that allow us to affirm difference—people of various genders, various races, various sexualities, various ethnicities, various abilities (physical challenge) and the earth body as our parent. We have denied and disempowered the bodies of difference among us by regarding them as inferior, unacceptable, sinful and available for our exploitation. This attitude often allows us to be communities that deny justice to millions of our members including exploiting, oppressing and damaging the earth.[9]

Clearly, Dube's eco-feminist theology affirms the body and the earth, characterised by a commitment to recognise diversity and inclusivity. The same theology allows her to rebut the heteronormative argument that God instructed human beings to 'multiply and fill the earth', suggesting that in the age of overpopulation we may have to privilege other means of being fruitful.[10]

Reading the Bible for life and justice

In addition to the notion of creation that Dube derives from Genesis, her thinking centres around the Gospel stories about Jesus Christ and his divine mission on earth. As a feminist biblical scholar, her hermeneutics (that is, method of biblical interpretation) specifically centres around the theme of *'talitha cum'*. This phrase is derived from the New Testament story of the little girl who was brought back to life by Jesus, with the words *'talitha cum'*, meaning 'little girl, arise'.[11] Dube, like many other African women theologians, takes this story as a paradigm for understanding the overall message of the Gospel and the Bible.[12] In her postcolonial feminist reading, the story 'represents the struggles of African women against colonial powers and patriarchal oppression, with the highly desired results of liberation and life.'[13]

Using this story as a paradigm, Dube produces biblical interpretations that promote fullness of life to all creation, and liberation from the forces of death such as poverty, injustice and discrimination. Although she is particularly concerned with the fate of girls and women in patriarchal African societies, her work demonstrates a much broader concern with structures of marginalisation and exclusion, for instance affecting people living with HIV, and people belonging to sexual minority groups. Clarifying how she reads the Bible, she says, 'I read for justice: justice for women of various backgrounds; justice against historical and contemporary imperialism and justice for all people who are subjected to various forms of oppression. *I read for life'*.[14]

This hermeneutic allows Dube to take a strong stance against any interpretation of the Bible legitimising injustice towards particular groups of people whose lives are deemed inferior or unworthy on whatever grounds, be it gender, sexuality, race or ethnicity. Her work is a repository of identification with all those who were not created 'good' according to biased interpretations of scripture. In a world where whiteness is given priority over blackness, Dube stands with blackness. Where the world privileges the rich, Dube identifies with the poor. Where patriarchy grants citizenship to men and elders, Dube votes to be with women and the young. Where heteronormativity is celebrated, Dube makes a case for diverse sexualities. She consistently argues that patriarchy, homophobia and other systems of oppression must be replaced by life-giving systems of justice and inclusion. In particular, she regards the ministry of Jesus as one of consistent confrontation with forces of death. Dube reads Jesus as one who was keen to break down the barriers of exclusion and to embrace those ostracised by the dominant ideologies of the day. She powerfully applies this to the context of the HIV epidemic, arguing that Jesus would radically embrace those living with HIV and overcome HIV-related stigma.[15] Hence she calls upon the church to follow the example of radical inclusivity and compassion set by Jesus in his ministry.

In promoting these life-giving interpretations of Scripture, Dube regards her mission as one of 'preaching to the converted', that is, to those Christians who may not have fully grasped the radical message of the sacredness of all creation, and of the inclusiveness of God's love.[16] She is fully aware that this mission involves unsettling the church, because the church as an institution has too often maintained structures of discrimination, exclusion and marginalisation. In the context of the struggle for the dignity and rights of sexual minorities, Dube thus calls for a reconversion of Christians and of the church as a whole, in order to overcome cultures of heterosexism and homophobia, to affirm all the rainbow people of God, and defend their human dignity and rights.

Theology of compassion in the face of HIV

Dube's career as a scholar-activist received added impetus when in the early 2000s she took a break from her work as Professor at the University of Botswana in order to serve as the Theology Consultant on HIV and AIDS for the World Council of Churches. Dube's role was essentially on two related fronts: to mobilise the church and theological institutions in Africa and beyond, and to provide effective responses to the HIV pandemic. Dube crisscrossed the continent at a time when AIDS was killing people at a frightening rate, especially in Southern Africa. Essentially, she was challenging faith communities to break the silence on issues of HIV and AIDS, in particular to change their attitudes towards people living with HIV who generally faced stigma and discrimination.

In a context in which the HIV epidemic was widely seen as a punishment from God for 'sexual immorality', Dube insisted that Africans had to embrace a more pragmatic and realistic approach towards people living with HIV. For her, an adequate understanding of and response to HIV starts with acknowledging the systematic social and economic injustices that create the context in which the virus in Africa can thrive, such as neoliberal capitalist globalisation, poverty, gender inequality and indeed homophobia. She argues that the church should be concerned about and fight these injustices, rather than being preoccupied with people's sexual choices. Specifically addressing homophobia, she states that for the overall African response to HIV to be effective, there is need to undertake some strategic reflections and revise current attitudes and practices:

In the HIV/AIDS era the discrimination of homosexuals means they are often deprived of services that pertain to prevention and provision of quality care. This discrimination means that some homosexuals are forced to hide their identity, to marry wives and then to live with a double sexual life, a secret one and a publicly accepted one. In addition, since homosexuality is not openly talked about in most African societies and churches, emerging research indicates that some youngsters are opting for homosexual sex, believing that one would not get HIV/AIDS from it. In short, the discrimination of homosexuals and the silence that surrounds us does not only expose them to HIV/AIDS infection and lack of quality care, it affects all of us—even heterosexuals, for we are a community.[17]

Dube highlights here the complex ways in which cultures of homophobia in Africa are particularly dangerous, indeed life-threatening, in the context of the HIV epidemic. Importantly, she raised these critical points at a time that HIV in Africa was generally thought of as a heterosexual epidemic;[18] in that sense she was ahead of her time. Many of these points have now been incorporated into HIV programming by governmental, non-governmental and faith-based organisations on the continent.

One of the recurrent arguments against same-sex rights in Africa is that homosexuality is alien to the continent. Politicians and church leaders have frequently insisted that homosexuality was brought into Africa by outsiders, and that the call for respecting the rights of sexual minorities is a form of cultural imperialism by the global North. Dube challenges this narrative, arguing that same-sex sexuality has always been a reality in Africa. Thus, 'despite the African churches' rejection of homosexuality, it is certainly a reality amongst African people since some languages have a name for it, indicating that is was always known.'[19]

Dube's argument for engaging sexual minorities in the response to the HIV epidemic is partly based on notions of pragmatism and realism: an adequate and comprehensive public health response to HIV requires acknowledging the different but entangled ways in which the virus is sexually transmitted. However, her thinking on this issue is more than merely pragmatic; it is inspired by her deeply rooted theological and political convictions, which centre around the notion of the interconnectedness of life in the context of HIV. This is reflected in her proposal for what she calls a 'theology of compassion'[20] as a resource for upholding the rights and dignity of sexual minorities.

For Dube, compassion is not a 'soft' term, but it radically enables allies of different oppressed social groups to join hands in their interconnected struggles. At the centre of the theology of compassion is the call for solidarity and justice. As she puts it, *'Compassion is not charity; it is revolution'*.[21] Dube developed this concept primarily in the context of solidarity with people living with HIV and AIDS (PLWHA), yet it is directly applicable to the struggle of gay and lesbian people in Africa. She elaborates as follows:

> Compassion, in other words, does not patronise, silence or replace PLWHA and the affected as active participants in the struggle against HIV and AIDS and its stigma and discrimination. Rather, compassion is empowering companionship. A theology of compassion is a theology of empowerment and liberation that fully recognises the human dignity and supports the initiatives of the oppressed in working out their own salvation.[22]

This quotation captures two key points. Firstly, those who are oppressed and marginalised—in this case, people living with HIV at a time when the disease was widely stigmatised, gave rise to various forms of suffering and too often resulted in death—are active participants in their own struggle as they work towards salvation. Secondly, all people of goodwill who are moved by situations of oppression can stand and act in solidarity with the oppressed, not as a form of patronising charity but as an 'empowering companionship' in support of the initiatives developed by those oppressed. In this way Dube seeks a balance, recognising the agency of the oppressed (and not seeing them as powerless victims), while creating room for concrete expressions of solidarity by allies without the latter taking over the struggle. The same argument can be applied to other oppressive situations, including of women under patriarchy and gay and lesbian people under heterosexism and homophobia. In these various cases, individual Christians and the church as an institution should be at the forefront of the struggle for human liberation, hand in hand with those who are oppressed and marginalised.

Dube's theology of compassion as solidarity is informed by two traditions of thought: Christian theology and African indigenous traditions. Theologically speaking, she sees compassion as rooted in the nature and character of God, whom she sees fundamentally as a God of compassion, as revealed in the divine acts of creation, liberation and redemption, and in the person of Jesus Christ. Dube argues that Christians are called to a radical praxis of compassion as part of serving a compassionate God and a compassionate Christ. Moreover, she argues that the church, which in biblical language represents 'the body of Christ',[23] should embody the compassion that Jesus Christ demonstrated through his ministry. Dube interprets solidarity in the body of Christ in innovative ways, as expressed through her statement that the body of Christ is HIV-positive.[24] This is to say that the mission of the church, in the context of the HIV epidemic, is not to *reach out to* those who are HIV-positive but to radically *identify and side with* them—even if they are sex workers, men who have sex with men, or other groups considered sexual outcasts in society. Dube's argument—that people living with HIV are not 'out there' but are found within the church and are part of the body of Christ—also applies to gay and lesbian people. Thus, the notion that 'when one member [of the body of Christ] suffers, all members suffer with it' applies to the suffering of HIV-related stigma as much as to the stigma resulting from heterosexism and homophobia.[25] Hence, Dube emphasises the importance of storytelling and the church listening to stories of marginalised people, as the beginning of understanding their lived experiences, and working with them for liberation, justice and flourishing.

Botho/ubuntu/buthu *and upholding human dignity*

In addition to these Christian theological ideas, Dube is convinced that the indigenous African concept of community-based solidarity is a resource in upholding the dignity and rights of lesbian and gay people. Politically, we might locate Dube in the radical pan-African, anti-colonial, liberationist paradigm. She constantly protests the marginalisation of Africa in the global system and bemoans the colonial, oppressive character of the form of Christianity now dominant in many communities, particularly in Southern Africa. Dube is a passionate defender of African indigenous religions and cultures. She suggests that one advantage of indigenous religions, compared to Christianity and Islam, is that they are not so concerned with doctrines, and therefore allow more space for ambiguity and flexibility on moral issues. Moreover, she argues that the ethical and spiritual values of indigenous religions bring much to bear on the current controversy over same-sex relationships. However, because she acknowledges the popularity of Christianity on the continent, she does not simply advocate a return to indigenous religions; rather she envisions a contextual transformation of Christianity in line with indigenous ethical values.

Like Desmond Tutu (see chapter 1), Dube utilises the concept of *ubuntu*, for which she also uses the Setswana word *botho* and the TjiKalanga word *buthu*, to defend the rights of all those who are denied their rightful place by oppressive social norms. For her, these concepts are built around communal solidarity that does not suppress one's individuality. Further, they are not given once and for all, but are continually worked and reworked in the wake of emerging challenges. Thus, 'this approach should inform the continual assessment and review of all oppressive relationships and the re-imagination of communities that respect and empower all [their] members regardless of class, gender, age, ethnicity, race, sexuality, nationality and health status.'[26]

For Dube, *botho/ubuntu/buthu* is a philosophy that is built on radical solidarity. It is an ethic of responsibility where the community is responsible for the safety and flourishing of all its members. Vice versa, when some members are subjected to stigmatisation and discrimination, this affects the whole community. Again, Dube has primarily developed this notion in the context of HIV, but it has wider implications:

> In the African world view, such dehumanization of the other is equally the self-dehumanization of all of us, since without respecting its members the community cannot be. As long as the HIV and AIDS stigma and discrimination exists and persists, we need to reflect on the depth of how we have all (the infected and affected) lost our humanity. HIV and AIDS stigma and discrimination, in other words, are symptoms of our compromised humanity. We will do well, therefore, to remember that by dehumanizing PLWHA, we inevitably dehumanize ourselves—we make statements about ourselves.[27]

These powerful insights can be effectively applied to the context of the current homophobic climate in many African societies. They have the potential to defend the humanity of sexual minorities and to overcome the hatred and discrimination found within communities. Dube is convinced that African communities must be united in their search for solutions to unhealthy relationships and brokenness. Collectively, they must seek to heal these faultlines and promote the health and wellbeing of their members, including gay and lesbian people.

Throughout her writings, Dube is consistent in the argument that HIV is not simply a medical issue but a social justice issue.[28] It is characterised by unequal economic structures, unhealthy relationships, unethical uses of power and exclusion of different categories of people. However, she also contends that HIV has provided an opportunity for African communities (and the world at large) to restructure the same oppressive systems. In particular, she contends that the whole approach towards sex and sexuality needs to be transformed in a radical way. These are some of the key themes that run through her theology in solidarity with African sexual minorities. Inspired by her reading of the Bible and the philosophy of *botho/ubuntu/buthu*, Dube is convinced that there can be no justice without the full inclusion and embracing of lesbian and gay people in African families, communities, nations and the entire continent.

Critical interventions

Dube has been courageous in participating in the movement of challenging homophobia and radically advocating for the inclusion of gay and lesbian people in African communities, including in the church. Her ability to do so has been enhanced by her position in a public university, her international exposure and networks, her work with a global ecumenical organisation, and being a lay Christian in Botswana. These positions gave her certain authority, access and independence. She could unsettle church leaders with progressive pronouncements on a range of issues, including sexuality, without fear of repercussions. Dube's thinking provides an important basis for advancing the cause of sexual minorities in Africa, and there are several themes that we seek to underscore in our interpretation of her significant contribution.

Firstly, as with Mercy Oduyoye (chapter 2), Dube's standing as an African woman biblical scholar and theologian has facilitated her advocacy on homosexuality. As one already steeped in the struggle for women's rights in Africa and globally, Dube's reflections on homosexuality have been generated from this crucible. Gender justice is not only about fighting patriarchy, but also heteronormativity and homophobia. She stands in the tradition of liberation theology which posits that oppression anywhere is oppression everywhere. Dube recognises that it is not possible to pick and choose between struggles; neither does she frame these struggles as mutually exclusive. If anything, she adopts a holistic approach to freedom. In her scheme, the struggle for women's full inclusion goes hand in hand with other struggles, including for Africa's dignity and of African gays and lesbians.

Secondly, like Desmond Tutu (chapter 1), Dube has been strategic in building upon the African story of fighting against dehumanisation and discrimination based on race. She invites her African audiences to introspect and seek to re-experience how they felt when they were humiliated for no reason other than that they were black. Such experiences, she argues, must provide impetus for solidarity with gay and lesbian people. Thus, 'as African people, we have witnessed the struggle for black people and for women, who were discriminated for their differences and we have learnt from these to resist identity-based oppression such as the ethnic and sexual based discrimination'.[29] However, Dube is not naïve. She acknowledges that people who themselves have been victims of discrimination 'quite easily forget their experiences and struggles for humanity and become oppressors of other groups on the basis of their differences'.[30] She challenges such tendencies, pricking the consciences of African Christians and others in order to convert them to the intersectional cause of social justice.

Thirdly, Dube's engagement with the question of sexual diversity, and her concern with sexual minorities, are born out of her work in response to the HIV pandemic. At a time when HIV in Africa was widely seen as a heterosexually transmitted disease, she drew critical attention to the possibility of homosexual transmission. She was perceptive in pointing out that many men who have sex with men may also engage in sexual relationships with women—for various reasons, homosexuality in African societies is often not an exclusive practice. Thus she argued that ignoring the possibility of homosexual transmission presents a major public health risk. Indeed, for Dube the culture of homophobia and heteronormativity are part of the structures of injustice that have helped HIV to thrive in Africa. As a result, overcoming this culture is part of her HIV liberation theology. Dube has been critical of her colleagues in the Circle of Concerned African Women Theologians who, in spite of making religion, gender and sexuality their major focus of work in the context of HIV, only very hesitantly (if at all) engaged with issues of same-sex relationships.[31] Where Nyambura Njoroge argued that the HIV epidemic called for a 'U-turn' in theologising, addressing issues that hitherto were taboo, Dube has been a leader in actually making this turn.[32]

Fourthly, Dube's competence in biblical studies is a powerful resource when engaging with African religious leaders. The Bible remains one of the most widely read and authoritative texts in Africa, and features prominently in debates on homosexuality in the continent.[33] Although there has been a tendency to project most African religious leaders as homophobic, it is necessary to recognise that the Bible they received from Western missionaries, and its accompanying interpretation, subsequently made it extremely difficult for them to embrace sexual diversity and accept gay and lesbian people as full members of their congregations. Therefore, it is important to note that the homophobia exhibited by many African church leaders is largely inherited from colonial traditions and missionary Christianity. Dube has utilised her biblical interpretation skills to persuade African church leaders to adopt more progressive interpretations of the Bible in relation to homosexuality.

Fifthly, Dube is a highly creative and effective public speaker and activist. This is a helpful resource, as it is often individuals with such a skill set who are able to move people from deeply entrenched views to new places of tolerance and acceptance. In relation to homosexuality, such views are often held with a sense of conviction and righteousness. Furthermore, some African political leaders have made resistance to homosexuality part of African identity. Dube's ability to use the storytelling method, as well as music, poetry, rituals of healing and other strategies, enables her to connect with religious leaders. She has sought to mobilise them to be more open towards accepting gay and lesbian persons in their families, congregations and communities.

Finally, and critically, Dube deploys powerful and established concepts from within the Christian tradition to defend African gay and lesbian people. While she is conversant with secular human rights discourse, she couches her message in Christian theological terminology. This enables her to reach both African Christians in general and church leaders in particular. Perhaps drawing from her experience in mobilising African churches to respond to HIV, she knows the power of theological concepts when appealing to Christians. She is also aware of Christians' general reticence to embrace secular human rights discourse. Therefore, Dube has been keen to deploy more familiar theological concepts over which there is no dispute, such as God creating everything good, leaving judgement to God and emphasising the power of love. On this latter theme, the power of love, Dube compellingly writes:

> Often, fear gets [i]n the way of love, especially when we meet those who are different, those who are not like us—denominationally, nationally, religiously, racially, culturally, ethnically, sexually, gen-

derly and economically. What is different is unknown, hence sometimes brews fear for it threatens our reality with another reality.
This response to difference is unfortunate and ungodly, for God is
the author of diversity and the author of love. If we know God as
the creator of all, then we will not fear difference, but love, for God
is love.[34]

Conclusion

Dube is representative of a cadre of African biblical studies
scholars and theologians who have come out clearly and unam-
biguously in support of recognising and upholding the full rights
and dignity of African sexual minorities. She has less explicitly
engaged with other experiences and identities under the lgbti
umbrella, but obviously many of her theological arguments about
diversity and embodiment have a wider significance, providing a
basis for an African feminist-queer theology.

Steeped in liberation theology with its holistic approach to the
tenets and process of human liberation, Dube has been unwaver-
ing in calling African Christians to repent in relation to their
general treatment of sexual minorities. Plumbing the depths of
the Bible and Christian theology, and reflecting on both the
potential and demands of *botho/ubuntu/buthu*, Dube comes to an
irrevocable conclusion: true Christianity and true Africanness
demand that one embraces gay and lesbian Africans. She is one
of the leading theologian-activists in Africa who have been on
the frontline of the struggle for the acceptance of sexual minorities in Africa. Cognisant that revolutions are not won overnight,
Dube continues to rally activists and communities with her sig-
nature slogan: *a luta continua*!

PART TWO

TRANSFORMING AFRICAN CHRISTIAN PRACTICE

5

TOWARDS SEXUALLY COMPETENT CHURCHES

THE ECUMENICAL HIV AND AIDS INITIATIVES AND ADVOCACY

This chapter focuses on the contribution of the EHAIA programme of the World Council of Churches (WCC) to discourses on churches and homosexuality in Africa.[1] The Ecumenical HIV/AIDS Initiative in Africa (EHAIA) was formed in 2002 and was renamed Ecumenical HIV and AIDS Initiatives and Advocacy (EHAIA) in 2013. EHAIA has gradually begun to play a major role in transforming the attitudes of churches (and, to some extent, other faith communities) in Africa towards sexual minorities. Building on the WCC's long history of liberation theology, particularly through the WCC's Programme to Combat Racism, EHAIA has sought to challenge homophobia and promote understanding of sexual diversity and positive attitudes towards same-sex loving people.

It is fair to say that the WCC's stance on issues of sexuality is far from unified. Its membership, which includes several Orthodox churches alongside more liberal Protestant denominations, is divided on the matter, and frequently these differences result in internal tensions and conflicts. However, the WCC has opened up a critical space for dialogue about human sexuality, in which churches that would prefer to ignore controversial questions are taken on a journey towards deeper understanding.[2] The WCC leadership, and especially EHAIA, have adopted a relatively progressive approach towards human sexuality, alongside actively supporting women's quest for gender justice.[3] EHAIA has been able to draw on valuable resources from within the ecumenical movement.[4]

This chapter will begin by discussing the historical, cultural and political context in which EHAIA has come to address the issue of same-sex sexuality. The chapter then examines the theologies and methodologies utilised by EHAIA in its engagement with the theme; following this is a preliminary analysis of achievements and challenges. Although EHAIA works ecumenically and even adopts an interfaith approach, this chapter concentrates on its activities with predominantly mainline Protestant churches in Africa. Anglican, Lutheran, Methodist and Presbyterian denominations are the core of WCC membership churches in Africa, and together they represent millions of Christians on the continent.

Churches, human sexuality and HIV in Africa

EHAIA's focus on human sexuality is a direct result of the devastating impact of HIV and AIDS in Africa. Whereas the dominant critique has been that churches (and other faith communities) have not been able to address human sexuality in any meaningful way, the WCC demonstrated remarkable creativity in its response. As early as 1986, the WCC Central Committee called for more effective responses to HIV. The book *Facing AIDS* was ahead of its time in terms of clarity and willingness to address taboo themes.[5] This background facilitated EHAIA's emergence in 2002, bringing together the WCC, its African member churches and ecumenical partners.

From the onset, EHAIA sought to mobilise churches and theological institutions in Africa to be actively involved in the overall response to HIV. With millions dying, many children being orphaned and access to antiretroviral therapy a major challenge, EHAIA called upon churches to be part of the solution. Theology Consultant Musa W. Dube (see chapter 4) worked with regional coordinators in Southern, East, Central, West and Lusophone Africa, as well as the Programme Executive in Geneva, to coax churches to focus on the challenge at hand and not condemn people living with HIV. Where there had been divisive debates on condoms, EHAIA sought to shift the investment towards treatment, care and support, rather than the morality of condoms.

EHAIA engaged the question of homosexuality as part of its programmes from the start, as it sought to develop a holistic approach to human sexuality. Although at the time there was a strong conception that HIV in Africa was a largely heterosexual epidemic, EHAIA drew attention to the concurrent vulnerability and risks of sexual minorities. Dube was forthcoming in breaking the silence and challenging religious leaders to recognise the importance of mainstreaming sexual minorities in HIV prevention and treatment campaigns. EHAIA's goal was to facilitate churches to become 'HIV competent', which includes having knowledge about, and respect for, different sexualities.[6] Although this was and remains a major challenge given the reluctance of local churches to engage with these issues, EHAIA strives to be in solidarity with lesbian and gay communities as part of its Christian duty and commitment to the human dignity of all.

Having recognised HIV as a social justice issue, EHAIA has placed the marginalised at the centre of its theology and approach.[7] Nuancing the popular concept of the church being the voice of the voiceless, EHAIA has sought to provide a platform where different marginalised groups speak for themselves. These include children and adolescents, people with disabilities, people living with HIV, sex workers, gays, lesbians and others. The experiences—joy, vulnerability and challenges—of individuals who belong to these groups are articulated and respected. They are critical to the formulation of an ecumenical HIV theology.[8]

EHAIA seeks to challenge the historical muting through which lesbian and gay people have been rendered invisible in faith communities. It also acknowledges that where faith communities have admitted the presence of sexual minorities, they have mostly demonised and ostracised them. EHAIA calls upon faith leaders and lesbian and gay communities to engage in 'conversations of the mutually vulnerable', facilitating such dialogue in an effort to promote the former's understanding and achieve the latter's security. Where the general tendency has been to talk about 'those homosexuals out there', EHAIA seeks to engender a new language and approach, encouraging religious leaders to refer to 'our daughters and sons who are lesbians and gays.'

EHAIA has also championed the WCC's global efforts against sexual and gender-based violence through the campaign 'Thursdays in Black: Towards a World without Rape and Violence.' In this, it seeks to challenge violence in domestic and intimate relationships.[9] EHAIA protests sexual and gender-based violence, including the rape of lesbian women and violence against sexual minorities in Africa. Thus, EHAIA endeavours to promote life-affirming theologies before church cultures and Christian theologies, which reinforce and legitimate inequality, stigma, violence and injustice.

Transforming the African theological landscape

EHAIA utilises multiple, but complementary, methodologies in its endeavour to precipitate a profound theological transformation in the discourse on human sexualities, in the wake of HIV in Africa and beyond. While the starting point has always been HIV and the vulnerabilities that lead to infection, EHAIA has regarded HIV as a mirror which exposes society's structural weaknesses. Consequently, HIV is seen as an opportunity to heal society in order to promote the wellness of all individuals, communities and the earth. Nyambura Njoroge, the EHAIA Programme Executive (at time of writing) and a leading African woman theologian from Kenya, elaborates that:

> [We] are not just dealing with a virus and a medical condition. The impact of the HIV pandemic goes beyond this, affecting developmental and human rights issues. Essentially we are confronted by deep broken relationships and by many social injustices at different levels and contexts. In effect, we are confronted by massive spiritual, ethical, pastoral and theological challenges, which have deep implications for the church of Christ. As Christians, the pandemic comes to us as a wake-up call and as some have clearly outlined, this is a *kairos* moment.[10]

Whereas some critics fear (with several valid reasons) that linking discourses on homosexuality in Africa to HIV is challenging, particularly because instrumentalist approaches can dominate, EHAIA's approach is instructive, as articulated by Njoroge above. EHAIA views HIV as presenting the church with a *kairos* moment, that is, a decisive moment for revolutionary change.[11] EHAIA maintains that HIV, while a tragedy, is paradoxically also a moment of grace. It offers African communities a highly strategic juncture to rethink 'the Africa that we want'.[12] If this Africa is to be democratic, upholding the rights and dignity of every human being, then it must commit itself to adopting a more progressive stance towards its same-sex loving children.

EHAIA endeavours to contribute towards social transformation by ensuring that the dominant theology becomes liberating. The anticipation is that once communities are steeped in life-giving theologies, they will be well equipped to counter negative forces, wherever these might manifest. Liberating and life-giving theologies are those framed on the mission and approach of Jesus, namely, to confront the forces of death (such as injustice), to interrogate oppressive systems and ideologies, and to bring healing and human flourishing.[13] Such theologies challenge patriarchy, corruption, homophobia, sexism, ableism, exploitation of the environment and other related evils. They are inspired by the key characteristic of liberation theology: its preferential option for the poor and marginalised, based on the belief that God is on their side and supports them in their struggle towards liberation.

Critically, HIV also prefers the marginalised in a very literal way; it is those communities that suffer most from poverty, inequality and discrimination that are most vulnerable to HIV and most impacted by the epidemic. Against that background, EHAIA mobilises faith communities in Africa to engage in a 'mission in the margins' and to work towards justice and fullness of life for all.[14] The incentive for that mission is, fundamentally, the notion of the *imago Dei*: the imperative to see the image of God in the other, including the most marginalised, because according to Genesis all humankind is created in God's image.[15] This includes lgbti people, and the *imago Dei* drives EHAIA's work to help those whom society shuns. EHAIA insists that even when society turns its back, God's face is turned directly and unerringly towards them, even reflected in them. Thus:

> The *imago Dei* reminds us that we all bear the imprint of God. In this way it challenges our tendency to exclude or marginalize others. If God is present in men who have sex with men, sex workers, intravenous drug users, people who are poor, and other key populations, then to ignore or to marginalize them is to ignore or marginalize God.[16]

Publications and transforming African theological education

One of EHAIA's most significant contributions to African theology in the context of HIV has been through publications, many of which were published with WCC Publications. The publication programme allowed EHAIA to publish progressive theological work that may not necessarily reflect the official views of WCC and/or its membership churches, but can help to transform those views or otherwise stimulate debate.

A number of EHAIA publications encourage churches in Africa to engage with questions of sexual diversity, sometimes subtly and sometimes more explicitly. Volumes such as *Listening with Love, Living with Hope, A Window into Hope, Practicing Hope* and *Abundant Life* compel church leaders to adopt pastoral attitudes towards people living with HIV as well as sexual minorities, while also encouraging them to develop more progressive views towards sexuality in general.[17] This has gone some way towards empowering church leaders to adopt less stigmatising attitudes towards lesbian and gay people. A publication, *What's Faith Got to Do with It?*, produced in collaboration with the International Network of Religious Leaders Personally Affected by HIV and AIDS (INERELA), is more forthright in challenging religious leaders to embrace sexual diversity.[18] Contributors to the volume promote a sex-positive theology and encourage religious leaders to realise the role of faith in accepting lesbians and gays as 'fearfully and wonderfully made'.[19] The landmark volume *Africa Praying* has become one of the major resources in equipping African church leaders with methods of mainstreaming discourse about HIV in their sermons and liturgy, and it includes a section about homosexuality (see chapter 4).[20]

The volume *Engaging with the Past: Same-Sex Relationships in Pre-Colonial Zimbabwe* contests a major ideological stance in African discourses on homosexuality, namely, the contention that homosexuality is not indigenous to Africa.[21] Some politicians and religious leaders have absolutised this position, arguing that homosexuality is a product of Africa's encounter with colonialism and foreign cultures; it is on this basis that they reject homosexuality. Contributors to the volume illustrate that homosexuality is not a foreign imposition in Zimbabwe; if anything, it has a long history in the Zimbabwean cultures being reviewed. While acknowledging the importance of marriage, fertility and children as perpetuating lineage, the researchers highlight the flexibility of indigenous spirituality. There were ritual spaces that facilitated the practice of homosexuality, alongside a more tolerant attitude than is found in contemporary missionary religions. Thus the volume seeks to reclaim indigenous cultures of tolerance for the church today.

EHAIA publications contribute towards changing the attitude of many African religious leaders towards homosexuality. Many of them are edited collections with contributions from clergy and scholars from across the continent, thus stimulating local and collaborative theological scholarship. They are distributed free of charge during workshops and from regional offices, and utilised in the training of future religious leaders within many theological training institutions across the continent. Additionally, the collaboration with the All Africa Theological Education by Extension saw the development of modules that address human sexuality in its diversity. This has ensured that candidates who are pursuing Theological Education by Extension (non-residential) are also accessing and benefiting from theological literature that encourages non-stigmatising, progressive approaches towards same-sex loving people in Africa.

With HIV serving as a radical disruption of theological education in Africa, EHAIA has taken steps to ensure that graduates of African residential theological institutions approach homosexuality with higher degrees of competence than has been the case up to the time of writing. The quest to mainstream HIV and AIDS in African theological education has been undertaken alongside studying theology and human sexuality in all its diversity and complexity.[22] Where earlier church leaders could intimidate their congregations by raising their voices on all contentious issues, EHAIA now challenges them to refine their arguments instead (as Desmond Tutu has consistently encouraged his audiences; see chapter 1).

Cultivating safe spaces and intergenerational conversations

EHAIA is one of the faith-based organisations (FBOs) that have prioritised adolescent sexual and reproductive health and rights in Africa. It has developed a methodology it calls 'Safe Spaces for Intergenerational Conversations'. This has been designed to facilitate open and honest dialogue between, on the one hand, adolescents and youth, and religious leaders, parents, teachers, health personnel and other stakeholders on the other. Due to patriarchal practices and the prioritisation of the opinions of elders, adolescents and youth often struggle with issues relating to sexuality, finding no one to talk to. The 'Safe Spaces' platform has been invaluable in opening dialogue on issues of sex and sexuality within faith settings in Africa. Participating adolescents and youth have been liberated to reflect on sexual diversity in contexts where they do not feel judged or condemned. They have also challenged their religious leaders, parents and teachers' homophobia and heteronormativity. It is from such platforms that change can gradually emerge.

Many church leaders have benefited from engaging directly with individuals and groups who are marginalized by mainstream theologies. A dominant 'holier than thou' attitude has often characterised church members who deem themselves as fulfilling the main requirements of righteousness. Particularly in some

mainline churches, men and women who are married appropri-
ately—that is, they have observed the accompanying rites—often
hold high esteem and may even have distinguishing uniforms to
mark their quality of belonging. This tends to generate stigma
and discrimination against those in perceived inappropriate relationships, particularly girls and young women who fall pregnant
out of wedlock, people in same-sex relationships, people involved
in sex work, and so on. Sue Parry, former EHAIA Regional
Coordinator for Southern Africa, writes on the need for churches
to overcome stigma:

> As people of faith, it is our moral duty to examine our own attitudes
> and have the courage to challenge misguided beliefs and attitudes, to
> confess our failings and to be the first to stand with those who are
> marginalized, excluded, denied their rights and who have been made
> to feel lesser human beings on the basis of the judgmental attitudes
> and discriminating hurtful actions of others, especially when it has
> come from within our own ranks.[23]

'Safe Spaces' have enabled many African religious leaders to interface directly with lesbian and gay individuals. This has helped to
clarify misconceptions and distortions, particularly those deployed
by politicians who seek to manipulate the discourse on homosexuality. Such interactions have contributed towards reducing stigma,
as recommended by Parry in the quotation above. More positively,
they have facilitated greater appreciation of the lived realities, joys
and struggles of African lesbian and gay people in families and
faith communities. 'Safe Spaces' have lifted the veil of shame,
silence, secrecy and stigma surrounding discourses on sexuality,
and thus have promoted greater openness.

By generating candid discussions about sexuality, EHAIA has
equipped many religious leaders with a new understanding of
sexual minorities in Africa. In particular, Njoroge has argued
that alongside economic justice, the liberation of gay and lesbian
people is a topic that deserves 'urgent and critical study in the

churches in Africa today'.[24] She has challenged African church leaders by posing one profound question regarding lesbian and gay people, namely, 'From whose wombs have these children come?' EHAIA builds on this approach, insisting that since lesbian and gay people are children of Africa, Africa has no choice but to embrace them. Njoroge's emphasis on 'wombs' serves to connect African lesbian and gay people to the painful process of childbirth and to underline the need for compassion. Interestingly, she also appears to cultivate the virtue of motherhood. Indeed she has argued that women in Africa, and the great care they show for 'life after birth', present a model of embracing care and inclusive love for the church to follow.[25]

Dialogues

One of EHAIA's defining features on the FBOs scene in Africa has been collaboration with like-minded organisations in responding to HIV and related issues. In the specific case of supporting the struggle for the full rights of African lesbian and gay people, EHAIA has partnered with many organisations that focus on this theme. Some of these include INERELA, the Other Foundation, African Men for Sexual Health and Rights (AMSHeR), the Gays and Lesbians Association of Zimbabwe (GALZ), and Southern African AIDS Information Dissemination Service (SAfAIDS).

Dialogues, like the 'Safe Spaces and Intergenerational Conversations', provide ample space for religious leaders to interact directly with lesbian and gay people in environments of respect and trust. However, whereas 'Safe Spaces and Intergenerational Conversations' take place within the context of other trainings (for example, on sexual and gender-based violence, transformative masculinities and femininities, etc.), dialogues are more formal and specifically focused on sexual diversity. One of the major innovations in the dialogue has been the withholding of identities until the very end of the processes. Thus, over a period of four days (for example), religious leaders mix and mingle with lesbian and gay people, allies and facilitators, all outside the more formal presentations on sexual diversity, human rights and other themes. Through this process, transformative conversations are held and friendships are formed. By the time the lesbian and gay participants come out to the religious leaders, there are always gasps of surprise and disbelief. Religious leaders are forced to revise their preconceived ideas and notions about 'those homosexuals' and develop an appreciation of the full humanity of their interlocutors.

Dialogues seek to question theologies that gain popular acceptance but are deeply problematic. For example, many church leaders soothe their consciences by replaying the commonly-used phrase, 'God hates the sin but loves the sinner'. This theology masks homophobia by pretending to equalise all 'sin'; most people who make this declaration proceed to list other sins about which God is said to be equally angry. In this scheme, homosexuals must repent and be integrated into the family of the righteous. Dialogues between church leaders and gay and lesbian people have served to alert church leaders to the need to embrace theologies that acknowledge and respect sexual diversity, or that at least affirm the human dignity of people belonging to sexual minorities.

While the dialogues have sometimes generated serious tension and confrontation, with many lesbian and gay participants expressing their feelings of being wounded by the church, they have also created opportunities for healing and integration. In many of the engagements, church leaders have asked for forgiveness from the lesbian and gay participants in the room, highlighting that their actions have mostly been based on the beliefs and attitudes they received from previous generations. However, often they also share the challenges they face in ministering to those in the majority sexuality. As the late Calle Almedal (former UNAIDS Senior Advisor on Partnerships with Civil Society and Faith-Based Organisations, and a close advisor to the WCC Health and Healing Programme) rightly observed, churches need to acknowledge the multiple challenges they face regarding heterosexuality before they can concentrate on homosexuality.[26] Almedal is credited with coining the term 'AIDS competent churches', requiring churches to address human sexuality in all its complexity and diversity.

Dialogues also serve to bring the Bible into focus. For example, EHAIA facilitators highlight the fact that the Bible has never been a neutral text, instead appropriated and deployed to meet the specific agendas of those who derive benefits from particular interpretations. They emphasise that the Bible has been used to oppress different categories of people, including blacks who were enslaved. For instance, some white masters gave heavily edited versions of the Bible to slaves in order to prevent them from accessing its revolutionary passages. Essentially, EHAIA reminds African church leaders that the Bible remains 'a problem as well as a blessing', to use a phrase of Takatso Mofokeng.[27]

Contextual Bible studies

EHAIA has effectively utilised the methodology of Contextual Bible Study (CBS) that was developed by the Ujamaa Centre in South Africa.[28] CBS serves to democratise the reading and interpretation of the Bible, ensuring that 'the whole people of God' participate in these processes. More critically, 'ordinary' readers—that is, those who have not undergone training in the highly specialised field of biblical studies, especially those from marginalised communities—participate as equals, forming an 'academy of the poor'.[29] In CBS, the facilitator selects a passage that addresses a specific issue. Participants then engage with the text and analyse characters, as well as drawing out implications for themselves, their families and communities of faith.

EHAIA has utilised CBS to open dialogue on critical issues of gender and sexuality. Although this has mainly taken place within the context of addressing HIV and AIDS in Africa, it has contributed significantly to the overall struggle for the rights of African sexual minorities. Where previously such reflections were regarded as taboo, EHAIA's approach has facilitated keen engagement with the Bible. This has been necessitated by the fact that the Bible is a central text in discourses on homosexuality in Africa (and globally). Masiiwa R. Gunda, who has collaborated with EHAIA, offers some helpful insights into the status of the Bible in debates on homosexuality. According to him,

> The Bible is a site of struggle, a place where different groups get their supplies of ammunition to condemn diversity in its multiple manifestations including race, gender, social status and sexual orientation. Some sexual minorities also mine the text of the Bible for ammunition to defend themselves as fully created in the image of and blessed by God and therefore with the same rights as all other human beings, especially the heterosexual majority.[30]

In what follows, this section will highlight two CBSs used by EHAIA. Although in the earlier period the challenge was most church leaders' complete refusal to engage in dialogue around homosexuality, there is at the time of writing a gradual shift, with church leaders in Africa instead trying to keep the issue off the agenda. By this approach, the rights of sexual minorities may be grudgingly acknowledged, but religious leaders are quick to argue that Africa has far more pressing problems than 'the rights of very few people'. These pressing problems are then enumerated to include acute levels of poverty, violence, natural disasters, unemployment, and so on. The argument is then made that Africa needs to prioritise its struggles; hence the issue of the rights of sexual minorities needs to be parked 'for the time being'. Ostensibly, it would then be revived when the 'right time' comes.

The argument about the justification for delaying the rights of African lesbian and gay people is deceptive. It suggests a hierarchical ordering of priorities, acknowledging the rights of sexual minorities but locating these further down the order. One CBS challenging this uses the text from the Gospel of Luke 13: 10–17. In summary, Jesus heals a woman who had been bent over for 18 years. The leader of the synagogue takes issue with the healing because it had taken place on the Sabbath (the day of religious observance for Jews). He suggested that the healing ought to have taken place on any other day. Yet Jesus retorts that it is more important to heal and liberate people whenever the occasion is there, than to adhere strictly to religious conventions. Reading this story in a contemporary context, participants in the CBS almost invariably come to the conclusion that the liberation of all oppressed people, including lesbian and gay people, must be prioritised; what can be done today should not wait until tomorrow. Thus, participants frequently conclude that urgent and concrete steps must be undertaken to nurture the health and wellbeing of sexual minorities in Africa. Jesus does not postpone the liberation of the oppressed; rather, he makes it his core business, engaging in urgent action to restore their dignity. EHAIA builds on this dynamic approach to mobilise churches in Africa to achieve the liberation of all oppressed people, including sexual minorities.

Notions of righteousness and profanity feature prominently in African discourses on homosexuality. Thus, heterosexuality (in the context of marriage) is often associated with holiness, while homosexuality is described as carnal and sinful. The Book of Acts 10: 1–29, where God guides Peter to disembark from his place of assumed righteousness, is used in another CBS to challenge African church leaders in a radical way. In discussions on the passage, church leaders wrestle with the possibility that zeal can face the wrong direction. In particular, the declaration, 'What God has made clean, you must not call profane' emerges for many African church leaders as a powerful and humbling one in relation to African sexual minorities.[31] Passages that exhort Christians to 'love your neighbour as yourself' are also strategic in debating sexual orientation and gender identity in Africa.[32]

Another helpful entry point into discourses on the rights of African lesbian and gay people has been through African struggles against colonialism, racial oppression and injustice. Many church leaders in Africa have adopted an oppositional stance to homosexuality due to the agenda-setting role of African politicians. Moreover, they are also proudly African, cherishing the heroic African quest for self-determination and freedom from oppression. Reflections on why people who were once oppressed themselves (such as Africans) can proceed to oppress others (such as sexual minorities) take place in the context of biblical passages such as Exodus 22: 21: 'You shall not wrong or oppress a resident alien, for you were aliens in the land of Egypt.'

Challenges

EHAIA has contributed to a gradual shift in the attitudes of churches and church leaders in Africa towards African sexual minorities. However, there remain some challenges in this quest. Firstly, the WCC having its headquarters in Geneva leads some African church leaders to retreat into the protective shell of claiming that homosexuality is brewed in the West and exported to Africa. This is partly mitigated by the fact that EHAIA resource persons, including its theological consultants and regional coordinators, are based in Africa, and that the Geneva-based programme director, Nyambura Njoroge, is a leading African theologian and ordained minister in the Presbyterian

Church of Kenya. The programme thus has considerable African ownership, yet the main financial resources do come via Geneva, from the wealthier WCC member churches in the global North.

Secondly, EHAIA resource persons are thinly spread. After igniting the flame of passionate commitment towards the rights of lesbian and gay people, they return to their respective offices in a few capitals across the continent. However, realising meaningful change in theological convictions and pastoral attitudes, and setting up robust local programmes, requires long-term investment. The religious leaders on the ground need constant support, especially as they are likely to face confrontations within their congregations and denominations after participating in EHAIA workshops. Providing such long-term support is difficult for logistical and financial reasons. One critical strategy to address this problem is linking religious leaders to local networks that promote the rights of African sexual minorities.

Thirdly, the role of African lesbian and gay communities in championing their own liberation is rather understated in EHAIA's approach. There is the danger of a well-meaning ally becoming the face of the struggle. Perhaps this is a challenge that is intrinsic to the relationship between those who front a specific struggle and their allies. This challenge is experienced in the response to HIV, which emphasises the greater and meaningful participation of people living with HIV. Therefore, EHAIA will need to do more to ensure that African lesbian and gay people are seen leading their own struggle within the faith sector in Africa.

Fourthly, the bulk of the activities that promote interaction between sexual minorities and religious leaders tends to be concentrated in Southern Africa. Perhaps this is due to the central role of South Africa in providing safe spaces for such dialogues to take place. Other engagements championed by young people have taken place in parts of West Africa, such as Togo.[33] However, in order for the emergence of a critical mass of religious leaders dedicated to supporting the inclusion of African sexual minorities, it is necessary to promote activities in different regions of the continent.

Fifthly, EHAIA has a strong network among mainline Protestant denominations in Africa but struggles to enter other Christian circles, such as the Catholic Church and Pentecostal churches. The extent of its reach is therefore limited, although efforts are made to connect with faith leaders in other traditions within and beyond Christianity. There is also a risk in the diplomacy that is part and parcel of ecumenical organisations such as WCC: in order to maintain good relationships with membership churches and partners, controversial issues need to be addressed sensitively. As a result, theological interventions cannot always be as radical as one might like to see. Nevertheless, providing a space for dialogue and understanding is already a significant step for many church leaders who hitherto have had very little exposure to adequate information about sexual diversity, let alone to people belonging to sexual minority groups.

Conclusion

Building on the WCC's strand of liberation theology and standing with the oppressed, EHAIA was established in the early 2000s to spearhead churches' response to the challenges of HIV and AIDS in Africa. Addressing the general silence in churches on issues of sexuality, EHAIA developed a strategy to make churches 'HIV competent', which included making them competent in matters of sexuality. As part of that work, EHAIA has gradually engaged with questions of homosexuality, seeking to overcome the silence and taboo around same-sex relationships in African Christian circles, and to promote tolerant and inclusive attitudes towards lesbian and gay people in church communities.

One of the side-effects of EHAIA's work being framed in relation to HIV is that much of the concern has been with men who have sex with men. Although efforts have been made to include lesbian women in EHAIA's programmes, the next step would be to engage with the full range of lgbti and queer expressions.

Employing an array of strategies, EHAIA has brought religious leaders and lesbian and gay people to reason together in order to bridge the gap between them. The results of such encounters have been as surprising as they have been inspiring. Many religious leaders have questioned their inherited opposition to homosexuality, while many of the participating lesbian and gay persons have questioned their militancy towards religious leaders. Thus, EHAIA is contributing towards a critical shift in the interface between church and sexual minorities in Africa. Despite facing notable challenges, EHAIA highlights the potential of faith-based initiatives to become catalysts for change. Religious leaders, committed Christians and activists on the ground can all draw on the resources availed by EHAIA to bring about profound transformation in the lives of sexual minorities in Africa.

6

BUILDING A PROGRESSIVE PAN-AFRICAN CHRISTIAN MOVEMENT

THE FELLOWSHIP OF AFFIRMING MINISTRIES

Advocacy for lgbti rights is often perceived in Africa as a form of white Western imperialism, driven by a secular human rights agenda. However, this perception is challenged by several Christian organisations that are actively involved in promoting the human dignity and rights of lgbti people on the continent. The originally South African organisation Inclusive and Affirming Ministries has expanded the regional scope of its work and is active in a range of countries.[1] The same applies to House of Rainbow, founded by the Nigerian-British pastor Rev. Jide Macaulay.[2] This chapter focuses on yet another organisation, which offers a unique pan-African dimension to lgbti advocacy on the continent, with a Pentecostal language and style. The Fellowship of Affirming Ministries is an African American organisation that in recent years has become active in Africa, aiming to build a pan-African progressive Christian, lgbti-affirming movement.

An inclusive black Pentecostal fellowship

The Fellowship of Affirming Ministries (TFAM) was founded in the year 2000 by the black and openly lesbian Rev. Dr. Yvette A. Flunder, who in 2003 was installed as presiding bishop of the organisation. TFAM describes itself as a trans-denominational coalition of Christian churches and ministries committed to the 'mandate from God to proclaim a gospel that is radically inclusive of all persons'.[3]

Flunder (b. 1955) has strong roots in the largest Pentecostal denomination in the United States, the Church of God in Christ, which has a predominantly African-American membership. Her grandfather and father served as bishop and pastor respectively, but she herself could not pursue her calling in the denomination as it did not allow for women's ordination. She worked as pastor, gospel singer and community activist in various churches and organisations until in 1991, after having come out as lesbian, she founded the lgbti-affirming City of Refuge church in San Francisco, of which she is senior pastor at time of writing. She describes herself as 'an unapologetic disciple and proponent of the radically inclusive love of Jesus Christ'.[4] This vision inspired her to found TFAM as a movement of like-minded Christian leaders and laity, mostly of African American descent, who are concerned about cultures of exclusion and oppression that dominate African American Christianity with its morally conservative orientation. TFAM, in Flunder's vision, is 'Metho-Bapti-Costal' in style, an allusion to the various revivalist Christian traditions (Methodist, Baptist, and Pentecostal) from which its members come.

In Flunder's analysis, the African American church suffers from 'oppression sickness', that is, 'internalized oppression that causes the oppressed to be infected by the sickness of the oppressor'.[5] She argues that conservative white American Christian culture, with its moralism, classism, heterosexism and patriarchy, is being mimicked in the black church, in an attempt by African American Christians to overcome their feelings of inferiority resulting from internalised racism. In line with this, TFAM claims that 'many African American churches have achieved substantial power and influence within their respective communities by virtue of marginalising certain segments of society'.[6] The organisation's mission is to overcome this culture of exclusion and oppression, by promoting a theology of 'radical inclusivity'. This theology is inspired by the belief that each and every human being is part of God's diverse creation, by the example of Jesus' ministry of love to those on the margins of society, and by the vision of an all-inclusive Kingdom of God.[7] The notion of inclusivity is applied to a range of demographic groups: people who for various reasons have been stigmatised by and excluded from the church, such as drug users, those living with HIV, homeless people, formerly incarcerated people, and members of sexual and gender minorities (TFAM mostly uses the term 'same-gender loving people').

The theological discourse of TFAM is clearly inspired by progressive black liberation theologies and their commitment to social justice. Importantly, the organisation combines this with its roots in black Pentecostalism, thus making an explicit case for a progressive and inclusive black Pentecostalism. Not only does TFAM claim to stand in the tradition of the biblical Pentecost event, believing that 'God continues to pour out God's spirit upon all persons',[8] but in their style of worship and preaching, the churches and pastors associated with TFAM also generally adopt the charismatic and ecstatic nature of black Pentecostalism. Indeed, according to Ellen Lewin, who wrote a book about the organisation, this is key to their appeal among members and central to TFAM's success as a movement. Inclusivity is not just a message being preached, but an embodied religious experience mediated through the worship practices that have long been the hallmark of the black church. Thus, participatory worship allows TFAM congregants to invoke the memory of 'old-time religion', be emotionally touched and be spiritually empowered.[9] Flunder acknowledges that the roots of black Pentecostal worship are in West African indigenous religious cultures; she has made efforts to explicitly reclaim elements of these cultures, such as ancestor rituals, which, as a symptom of 'oppression sickness' or internalised inferiority, have become perceived as demonic among many African American Christians.[10] For Flunder, this engagement with African traditions is part of her quest for spiritual authenticity, but also reflects her understanding of radical inclusivity, which involves the recognition of spiritual truths from traditions other than Christianity.[11]

The fellowship in Africa

Since the late 1980s, Flunder has taken a leading role in providing a faith- and church-based response to the HIV epidemic, addressing the culture of silence and stigma in the African American community and offering pastoral support to people living with HIV. She gradually expanded this ministry to the African continent, supporting an orphanage in Zimbabwe among other things. This Africa-focused ministry took a new turn when, in 2009, Uganda launched its Anti-Homosexuality Bill. Out of an awareness that conservative evangelical American Christians were driving the anti-gay campaign in Uganda and other African countries, Flunder felt that TFAM had to provide a progressive counter-campaign. She entrusted this responsibility to a TFAM colleague, Bishop Joseph Tolton. Coming from a black Pentecostal tradition and pastoring a church in New York, Tolton, in his own words, became 'a missionary in Uganda' preaching the gospel of radical inclusivity.[12] He was put in charge of a new ministry, The Fellowship Global (now TFAM Global), which soon expanded the scope of its work from Uganda to other countries such as Côte d'Ivoire, Democratic Republic of Congo, Kenya, Rwanda and South Africa.[13] According to its mission statement,

> ·TFAM Global is an international network of faith leaders working to shift Christianity and influence other faith paths for generations to come. We believe this transformation must be powered by a prophetic vision of LGBTI dignity, gender equality, and Pan African justice. Our vision is a world where every human being can pursue a life of authenticity, integrity, and creativity. The heartbeat of TFAM Global is vibrant spirituality grounded in progressive theology that inspires secular advocacy.

To achieve this vision, TFAM Global partners with local faith leaders, grassroots activists and community organisations in order to promote 'the faith-based ideals of freedom and justice' and to 'influence social change'.[14]

One of the words that stands out in the above quotation is 'pan-African'. From the late 1990s, Africa has witnessed 'the rise of a conservative streak of pan-Africanism', that is, a discourse that frames lgbti identities as conflicting with African culture and values, and which legitimises violence against sexual minorities in the name of African authenticity, independence and pride vis-à-vis a perceived Western imperialism.[15] TFAM Global appears to explicitly counter this discourse, by claiming pan-Africanism for a progressive socio-political project. As put on its website,

> The Fellowship Global is positioned to be a catalyst for a pan-African faith movement, connecting the radically inclusive Christian movement led by African Americans and our allies to communities in Africa and throughout the diaspora. We provide pastoral care for LGBTI people and support pioneering efforts to establish an open an affirming African Christian movement. ... As heirs of the civil rights movement, African spirituality, Christian traditions, and pro-

phetic witness we have a vision for a radically inclusive revival to usher in a new era of social justice.[16]

This quotation reflects an emerging narrative of 'queer pan-Africanism' in an explicitly Christian form.[17] Indeed, the vision of TFAM is to connect progressive African American Christians with progressive African Christians to build a pan-African movement that is radically inclusive, lgbti affirming and committed to social justice. In order to legitimate this progressive pan-Africanist discourse, TFAM explicitly invokes the legacy of the American civil rights movement, suggesting that the struggle for lgbti rights in contemporary Africa is a continuation of the earlier struggle for black civil rights in the United States and is inspired by the same vision of freedom about which Martin Luther King Jr. dreamed.

As with the struggle for civil rights, the struggle for lgbti rights in Africa, according to TFAM, has a racial dimension. In Tolton's words: 'As black gay Christians who identify with Pentecostal worship and as people of social justice, we are countering the work of conservative, mostly white American evangelicals who are doubling down on their attempt of spiritual colonization of Africa'.[18] Thus, the widely-documented exportation of American culture wars to Africa is framed here as a struggle between mostly white conservatives (with controversial American pastors such as Scott Lively and Rick Warren as figureheads) and progressive black Christians, both seeking to shape the future of Christianity in Africa.[19] Also noteworthy is Tolton's reference to religiously-driven homophobia in Africa as a form of spiritual colonisation, which is reminiscent of Flunder's concept of oppression sickness discussed earlier. The suggestion is that in the African context, not only are homophobic campaigns directly fuelled by money and ideas from the American Christian Right, but the eagerness with which many African Christians have bought into such campaigns and owned them demonstrates a deep-rooted inferiority complex and a mimicry of colonial and neo-colonial white Christian masters. In TFAM's analysis, a decolonisation of the mind needs to be brought about through a progressive pan-Africanist vision.

This vision is not only pan-African, but also explicitly Christian. According to the above-quoted mission statement, TFAM Global aims to bring about a 'radically inclusive revival', a phrase that combines typically Pentecostal rhetoric of spiritual revival with the progressive theological idea of radical inclusivity. It further refers to the tradition of 'prophetic witness', a term that in this context refers to a progressive Christian commitment to promote social justice as a key value of God's Kingdom, and the belief that the church is called to denounce injustice and speak out against the violation of human dignity and rights.[20] Tolton himself has narrated how being a black Pentecostal pastor engaged in lgbti advocacy in Africa puts him at an advantage compared to, say, a white European secular human rights activist. It allows him to connect to people at an embodied and spiritual level: 'Even when people questioned who I was at the beginning, what they didn't question was the anointing'.[21] Indeed, from watching Tolton preach and observing how people relate to him, it is obvious that his anointing with the Spirit is recognised by his audience; people report that they are touched by his powerful preaching, claiming that the bishop was 'on fire'.[22]

The progressive pan-African faith movement that TFAM Global seeks to nurture is first and foremost concerned with issues of sexuality, promoting a social and spiritual environment that affirms and embraces lgbti African Christians. However, the agenda of social change is not limited to sexuality but pertains to 'pan-African justice' more broadly, which is interconnected and takes into account the multiple structures of oppression and exploitation that impede the dignity and fullness of life of African peoples.[23] As such, the organisation shares the radical vision of queer African activists who work towards 'an African revolution which encompasses the demand for a re-imagination of our lives outside neo-colonial categories of identity and power', and who seek economic, social, political and environmental justice alongside gender and sexual justice.[24]

Building a movement of affirming Africans

In order to build a progressive and inclusive faith movement on the African continent, TFAM Global has established the United Coalition of Affirming Africans (UCAA), which currently has national chapters in five countries, mostly in East Africa. According to a 2013 press statement,

> Each UCAA national group will engage Christian clergy, and LGBTI activists primarily focused on the social, legal, and moral inclusion of LGBTI people in each country with a secondary emphasis on the economic and social concerns of the country.

> ... Ultimately, this grassroots movement with a progressive faith frame can discern a path toward affirming the inherent dignity and equality of the LGBTI community in Africa while positively impacting its economic, social, and health concerns. The intersectional perspective of structural social change is critical as it proactively connects the LGBTI experience in Africa with the totality of the human experience in Africa.[25]

The activities of UCAA centre around two interlinked strategies. First is the creation of progressive, lgbti-affirming congregations. The aim of such ministries is threefold: to offer a spiritual home and 'a beacon of hope' to lgbti people and their allies; to nurture a new generation of Christian leaders in order for them 'to gain stature and social capital as change makers for Africa's inclusive future'; and finally, to have a long-lasting impact on 'the Christian landscape' and on society in the countries concerned.[26] As a result of this strategy, several small lgbti church communities have been planted, one of which, in Kenya, will be discussed in more detail in the next section. The second strategy, linked to the former, is of 'empowering progressive clergy in Africa'.[27] Through awareness workshops, theological training and conferences, UCAA and its local partners identify and engage clergy in established churches and denominations, initiating dialogue about issues of human sexuality and human rights. There is also a plan, still at an early stage, to 'create a certified institute for progressive theology in East Africa', as an alternative to existing (mostly conservative) theological institutions in the region.[28]

TFAM Global claims to have worked with more than 1,000 clergy and faith leaders, engaging them on issues of sexuality and theology.[29] Obviously, the impact of conservative theologies that dominate the African Christian landscape cannot be undone overnight. However, there are some encouraging signs that TFAM's strategy bears fruit. For instance, in 2019 a Methodist congregation in western Kenya, First United Methodist Church Moheto, voted for full equality of lgbti individuals in the life of the church.[30] According to the lead pastor, Rev. Kennedy Mwita, this vote was the result of a years-long process in which he had taken the congregation on a journey to address issues of sexuality and gender, after he himself had become concerned about the levels of religious-inspired hatred and discrimination in Kenya, and had gradually engaged in advocacy for the inclusion of lgbti people in church and society. This journey had started when a mother with an intersex child, who had been cast out by her husband, sought refuge at the church. Interestingly, Mwita comments that because of the legal situation around same-sex sexuality in Kenya, he initially found it easier to advocate the rights of the intersex persons, but gradually this catapulted him into advocacy for lgbti persons more generally. This was stimulated by his encounter with Tolton:

In 2015, I met Bishop Joseph Tolton and this completely changed my approach. After going through a series of trainings on theological lessons with Bishop Tolton, I became more empowered and strengthened to stand and proclaim a prophetic message of inclusion. I learned that all forms of oppression are connected, and Jesus' message to humanity was that of deliverance and inclusion of all. He says he came to his own but his own did not receive him. But to all who have received him—those who believe in his name—he has given the right to become God's children. This is my conviction, that regardless of our sexuality we are children of God. This inspired me to find other sons and daughters of the Lord who have been shut out of the house of God and have been crying out to be heard.[31]

With the support of Tolton and UCAA, Mwita now engages in discussion about issues of sexuality with fellow clergy in his denomination, and has conducted training for the national leadership body of the United Methodist Church in Kenya. This is the kind of snowballing effect through which UCAA hopes to nurture a movement of change, not only in Kenya but also in countries such as Rwanda and Uganda, where the organisation is most active. This grassroots strategy is believed to gradually affect cultural change in the church, laying 'the groundwork for a pan-African progressive Christian movement'.[32]

Affirming church—a case study[33]

One example of a progressive, lgbti-affirming congregation established with the support of TFAM is the Cosmopolitan Affirming Community in Nairobi, Kenya (CAC).[34] This church, which is prominently featured in the documentary film *Kenyan Christian Queer*, is spearheading the struggle for faith, hope and love in the context of a largely conservative society.[35]

Founded in 2013 by local lgbti activists as a space for lgbti people to reconcile their sexuality and faith, CAC leaders received mentorship and theological training from Bishop Tolton. The initiative gradually evolved from an informal prayer and Bible study group into a church, a process that reached a milestone in September 2019 when Bishops Flunder and Tolton officially ordained a team of pastors as ministers in charge. The lead minister at time of writing is David Ochar, who also serves as TFAM Global's Director of Operations and Strategy Kenya.

CAC has weekly fellowship meetings on Sunday afternoon, initially in a rented space, but since 2021 in a purchased property in Nairobi. The number of congregants usually ranges between 30 and 50, most people being in their 20s and early 30s, across the spectrum of lgbti identities and from varying socio-economic backgrounds. Although congregants come from a variety of denominational backgrounds, the worship style—with gospel praise music and dancing, speaking in tongues and prophecy—is generally Pentecostal-Charismatic, reflecting the overall influence of Pentecostalism on Christianity in Kenya. This influence is even more visible in the overnight *keshas* (prayer nights) that CAC frequently holds. The worship addresses the desire of congregants for spiritual empowerment and embodied religious experience. The fact that here they can experience the touching presence of God and the power of the Holy Spirit, in a space that is explicitly affirming of their non-conforming gender and sexual identities, appears to be a crucial factor in the appeal of the fellowship to its followers.

The lgbti-affirming and inclusive Christian message preached in CAC is developed through sermons and Bible studies. Quite some attention is paid to the so-called 'clobber verses', the biblical texts often deployed against homosexuality. CAC leaders neutralise these by locating them in their particular cultural and historical context, and counterbalance the texts by foregrounding the core Gospel message of God's all-encompassing love and Jesus' inclusive ministry towards the marginalised. Moreover, as a congregation at the forefront of the struggle for lgbti rights in Kenya, CAC believes that God is on their side. As put in a sermon, preached on 29 July 2018: 'The truth is that God is a God of love. Not a homophobic god, a transphobic god, a biphobic god, a queer-phobic god. He's a God of Love. That God is our advocate, siding with us in our struggle.' Thus, the common trope in liberation theologies of God being in solidarity with the oppressed, is interpreted here as God being on the side of those who suffer under societal norms of gender and sexuality, supporting them in the quest for liberation and freedom. This message is not just preached but expressed through songs and prayers. One of the most popular gospel songs in CAC is 'I love the way you handle my situations; I love the way you fight for me', the lyrics originally written by a Ugandan pastor known for his anti-gay views, Robert Kayanja. The song may have been introduced in the church by Ugandan lgbti refugees based in Nairobi, who for some time frequented CAC services in considerable numbers. Always sung enthusiastically and wholeheartedly by the CAC choir and congregation, this song sounds like a testimony of lgbti people of faith. It expresses and reinforces their hope and trust in God, amid the struggles of daily life, similar to the gospel spirituals sung by black slaves in the United States a century earlier.

In February 2019, the Kenyan high court was supposed to deliver a ruling on a petition requesting the decriminalisation of homosexuality.[36] On the Sunday before this landmark decision, CAC invited all its partners and allies to an interdenominational prayer service. The choir performed a gospel song, 'We are a rainbow', with the chorus being a prayer to God to shine the rainbow in the sky and to paint the world in the colours of pride, boldness, and freedom.[37] Of course, the rainbow—whose colours always decorate CAC services—stands for diversity and is the international symbol of the lgbti movement, but is also a biblical symbol of God's covenant with humankind.[38] In this song, and in CAC more generally, both meanings come together, the rainbow becoming a sign of God's promise of freedom, justice and peace to lgbti people. During the service, passionate intercessory prayers called upon God to make the promise of the rainbow come true in Kenya. Various speakers called upon the congregation to be hopeful and join God's movement for social change towards freedom for all. Although the court ruling turned out to be unfavourable, CAC claimed that the prayer service had nevertheless been effective:

> The service was both emotional and inspiring as attendees shared about the different experiences they have gone through. Religious leaders present also affirmed and encouraged the queer community, promising support as allies and friends. In the end, the atmosphere was one of hope, as one speaker put it, 'We have already won!' This was in acknowledging the immense work that has already been done to get us to this point.[39]

Obviously, CAC provides a highly important space to lgbti people of faith in Kenya, who often feel marginalised in the religious communities in which they grew up, and who struggle to reconcile their sexuality and faith. Attending CAC, for a shorter or longer period, helps them to come to terms with who they are in relation to their belief in God. A space like CAC, however small, is also important because it shows the wider society—both the Christian community and lgbti activist circles—that Christianity is not necessarily in conflict with lgbti identities, and that lgbti identities are not necessarily secular. In that sense, such a space presents a powerful testimony of the possibility of an lgbti-affirming Christian movement in Kenya and beyond. It is the beginning of a different narrative to be told.

Conclusion

The relationship between Christianity and pan-Africanism has historically been complex, and so is the relationship between

African Americans and the African continent. The case discussed in this chapter presents us with a unique example of the emerging 'partnerships for transformation' between religious communities of the African diaspora and on the continent that, in the words of Roland Nathan, could bring about 'substantial transformation for both Africa and its diaspora'.[40] Arguably, the building of an affirming pan-African Christian movement is a slow process, and there are many challenges to be faced, including overcoming cultural, economic, theological and political hurdles. Yet TFAM Global is inspired by the Book of Acts, which narrates the small beginning of the early Christian church as a Holy Spirit-led movement, one which attracted many because of its enthusiastic faith and radical commitment to the Gospel. A popular saying by Bishops Flunder and Tolton is that TFAM is 'rewriting the Book of Acts', an expression also adopted in CAC to signify its mission.[41] The phrase may sound overly ambitious, and perhaps naively unrealistic, yet it puts great moral and theological weight on the work at hand. Building an lgbti-affirming and inclusive pan-African Christian movement is nothing less than a second Pentecost; it takes the idea of the Holy Spirit being poured out on all flesh to the next level, as it radically includes those groups that through Christian history have been excluded from this movement of God's spirit. In this vision, pressing for lgbti rights is not just a form of secular advocacy, but part of God's plan for the world that Christians are called to help realise. Importantly, it is black African and African American Christians who are believed to be at the forefront of this new movement. They are assigned the historic task of resisting the spiritual colonisation by conservative, mostly white Euro-American Christians and, instead, to rewrite the Book of Acts as a story of freedom and justice for all.

PART THREE

RESHAPING AFRICAN CHRISTIAN CULTURE

7

RECLAIMING THE QUEER BODY

NIGERIAN LGBT LIFE STORIES OF SEXUALITY AND FAITH

The African queer body—that is, the bodies of lesbian, gay, bisexual, transgender and other people perceived to be deviant because of their gender and sexuality—is too often stigmatised and silenced, discriminated against and excluded from the community. The African queer body, so to say, is considered a nobody: not worthy of acknowledgement, recognition and embrace.

In response to this stigmatisation of their bodies and the silencing of their voices, lgbti and queer activists and communities across the continent have resorted to a strategy of storytelling: they reclaim and affirm their embodied existence by sharing the stories of their lives. Collections of African lgbti life stories have been published during the 2010s, from Botswana and Malawi in Southern Africa, Ethiopia, Kenya and Somalia in East Africa, and Nigeria in West Africa.[1] This wave of publications reflects the increased visibility of African lgbti communities, and the vitality of lgbti and queer activism on the continent. Storytelling has long been an important method in feminist, postcolonial and queer activism and scholarship. As the South African scholar Sarojini Nadar puts it, stories are 'data with soul';[2] one might also say that stories are a form of embodied data. The telling of autobiographical stories is particularly meaningful and powerful, as by telling their life stories people who belong to marginalised groups resist the popular narratives told about them. Instead they narrate not just their own struggles but their strategies of survival and, more than that, their joy of living.

In this chapter, we examine one such example of African lgbti life story-telling, the volume *Blessed Body* that was edited by the Nigerian (US-based, at the time of writing) writer and activist Unoma Azuah, in collaboration with Queer Alliance Nigeria.[3] The volume presents 37 stories of members of the Nigerian lesbian, gay, bisexual and transgender community, aged between 20 and 50. The stories were collected in the aftermath of the passing of the Same-Sex Marriage (Prohibition) Bill by the Nigerian government in January 2014. According to Azuah, the presented stories 'reveal the kind of irreparable damage caused by homophobia'. She goes on to highlight the political significance of such storytelling:

> Essentially, it is the hope of the storytellers to literally or metaphorically scream their messages to the world and be heard. Perhaps, through their narratives, they can draw empathy and understanding from their fellow compatriots, and help prevent others from going through the same treatment.[4]

Although Azuah dedicates one section (out of eight) to 'The Church', in reality themes of faith, Christianity and the Church appear throughout the volume.[5] The Church is narrated as an ever-present, controlling and mostly oppressive system.[6] It establishes and endorses heteronormativity. It promotes the idea of sin, only to seek to extinguish it. It controls the interpretation of the Bible and compels parents to police their children on its behalf. It subjects queer bodies to aggressive deliverance.

However, utilising agency and subversion, several narrators also appropriate and deploy the Bible for their own sanity and survival in a highly oppressive environment. They express how, in their own life journeys, they have come to embrace their queer bodies as blessed. As such, these stories also give insight into Nigerian grassroots queer theologies in a narrative form.[7] This chapter offers a reading of *Blessed Body* that specifically focuses on this complex, creative and ambiguous narrative engagement with the themes of institutionalised and personalised Christianity in the context of contemporary Nigeria.

Breaking the silence in Nigeria

The stories in the volume are characterised by openness, wrestling against condemnation, and the quest for identity by individuals whose options are circumscribed by their setting of Nigeria. This setting denotes the closure of possibilities and stifling of identities; as one narrator puts it with some understatement, the country was not 'the best place for me to spread my wings'.[8] Central to this is the pervasive impact of culture, religion and the state. Nigerian space is largely constraining for lgbt persons (and, probably, for most other categories of activists). The stories in *Blessed Body* speak to the toxicity, hyper intolerance and outright violence against sexual minorities in Nigeria.

At an official level and in popular practice, Nigeria has adopted two mutually reinforcing positions regarding the presence of lgbt persons. At one level, they do not exist; they are denied and erased. At another level, they do exist and pose a major threat to the health and wellbeing of the nation. The Same Sex Marriage (Prohibition Act) of 2014 is built on this assumption. There is the conviction that religion and the state must form a tag team to suppress lgbt people, one which appears to unite Nigerian Muslims and Christians, who are otherwise often deeply divided.[9]

Exploring the extent to which homosexuality has been made the straw man and scapegoat for everything that is wrong with Nigeria, Ebenezer Obadare writes:

> The upshot has been a situation in which homosexuality (and the moral degeneracy that it presumably epitomises) is held responsible for problems as varied as the destruction of African families, the HIV/AIDS pandemic, cultism and violence in the universities, female prostitution, increased divorce rates, the erosion of discipline in the military, moral decay in society and natural disasters. Because religious leaders are central to the construction of this discourse, it meshes with an eschatological imaginary which interprets global structural transformations as a sign of the imminence of 'the second coming'. According to this thinking, homosexuality and associated sexual and moral 'perversions' are not just poignant evidence that we are in 'the last days', they vindicate a divine programme whose inexorable climax is the termination of human culture.[10]

It is within such a context that Nigerian lgbt people struggle to exist. Their bodies are marked for violence, at home, school, church, libraries, university halls of residence, public spaces, and so on. In *Blessed Body*, corporal punishment is the default method of inflicting pain and discipline. Fathers use it, teachers utilise it, and security guards apply it liberally. Police officers do not hesitate to use violence on gender non-conforming individuals. Both the postcolonial state and its citizens are subjects of violence. Violence is the grammar of the postcolonial condition;[11] it is direct, structural and symbolic. With the postcolonial state struggling to deliver the dividends of independence, families struggling to thrive and anxiety permeating the fabric of society, lgbt individuals become scapegoats, and the blessed bodies of individuals are subjected to extreme violence. While colonialism thrived on the othering of black bodies, the postcolonial state and its subjects persecute homosexuals, too, on the basis of having bodies that are 'other'.[12] Thus, Sophia narrates how Albert and his partner are victims of mob justice.[13] Finbar informs his readers that he 'did get beaten up when the opportunity came, simply out of hatred'.[14] Ella is almost stripped naked by the traffic warden and his armed colleagues and has been continuously harassed for being a trans woman.[15] Unoma and her friends are whipped viciously.[16] In addition to physical violence, many of the stories narrate emotional, spiritual and verbal abuse of queer bodies. Violence appears to be written into the lgbt experience in Nigeria. As the narratives confirm, many end up performing heterosexuality by getting married, mostly with disastrous consequences. Others continually seek God's face in the quest to be 'cleansed' of homosexuality.

Yet, *Blessed Body* resists these various forms of violence towards lgbt people in Nigeria. By sharing their stories, the narrators refuse to be victimised and silenced. They come out to a world that wishes they would remain subterranean. True, the stories make it clear that Nigerian lgbt persons navigate very difficult contexts, but nevertheless they assert their right to be. They negotiate violence in society, rejection by their families, and strive to remain afloat. This nonfiction anthology is a testament to the resilience of those who must be dead as they defy the odds to continue living. In Nigerian popular culture, especially in Nollywood movies, lgbt individuals are increasingly featured, yet in such a way that usually vilifies them as intrinsically evil and irredeemable.[17] The narrators in *Blessed Body* counter such portrayals. Their stories engender the full range of human emotions. Some are exceedingly funny, others are deeply depressing. Yet others are funnily depressing! It is clear that being a Nigerian queer person is not a stroll in the park, and the narratives, therefore, are stories of courage and tenacity. While breathing the air that is saturated and suffused with homophobia, individuals encounter signposts of tenderness and love. Allies are found in unlikely places and persons, such as Gamal's uncle, an Imam, who asks a fundamental question, 'Who are we to judge?'[18] Kite's grandmother is the epitome of care and solidarity: 'She would urge me to be happy that she loved me just the way I am. She would not exchange me for the best macho grandson in the whole wide world.'[19] Through stories like these, *Blessed Body* alludes to other possibilities, to a different Nigeria. The power of queer storytelling is that it brings these possibilities to life and helps to imagine them more concretely.

Early sexual awakening and adolescent struggle

Against the popular critique of lgbt individuals in Africa, namely, that their sexual and gender identities are learned from the West and are an attempt at being fashionable, many stories in *Blessed Body* show that individuals have their sexual awakening very early on in life. Several narrators tell how they became aware of their sexual orientation from as early as five years old, and most of them had experimented with their sexuality by the age of 12 to 14. Childhood games, frolicking in the early years of secondary school, attractions to someone of the same sex while at church, are some of the opportunities for self-discovery. What is critical is this: none of the narrators chose their sexuality. They were born this way, or to use a phrase from one of the stories, it is part of God's design.[20] For many, matching their feelings with the concept came later, with Seun relying on the dictionary to process and understand his sexual orientation.[21] The key insight here is that modern discourses about lgbt identity do not constitute sexual desire, but do help to name and frame it in particular ways.

Being brought up in families that do not have space for comprehensive sexuality education, the adolescents and youth in *Blessed Body* fumble, experiment and achieve partial knowledge of themselves as sexual beings. Homes, schools, churches and health facilities do not prepare them adequately to come to terms with their sexuality. There is a general mystification of sexuality and the adolescents must undertake the journey of discovery alone. If parents, religious leaders and teachers feature in their narratives, it is mostly to introduce and reinforce a cultural and religious dogma that demonises sexuality in general, and homosexuality especially. Gamal expresses the struggle as follows:

> The change of environment and the intense sexual arousals, the tension and the fear in the household all started to build up in me and there was no one to help me through or talk with me. I felt like a ticking bomb constantly about to explode and I was too young to understand what it was all about.[22]

Adolescents and young people who do not conform to socially imposed gender norms and values experience a lot of trauma. They simply do not fit in. They are jeered at by their peers. They are sharply criticised by their parents. Their teachers seek to force them to conform to the dominant gender script. They experience violence in all its various forms, as well as deep pain, confusion and alienation. They search for meaning in relation to their sexuality and life in general. With no clear answers or support forthcoming, many, like Ekene, cry in search of answers to the mysteries of sexuality.[23] The endless taunting by peers, parents, teachers, siblings and members of the community results in loss of confidence and pushes many lgbt adolescents and youth to the edge. Rowland Jide expresses it painfully:

> As a young boy, I felt isolated, ignored, and sadly, my parents, especially my father, were too busy and too strict to give any attention to opening a space in which such matters [homosexuality] could be discussed.[24]

Conservative attitudes towards sexuality and homosexuality leave most lgbt individuals feeling guilty of the sexual desires they have and the sexual acts in which they engage. Throughout

Blessed Body, individuals narrate such guilt. Ekene discloses his adolescent struggle whereby 'anguish at being bad would frequently overwhelm me soon after my indulgent thoughts'.[25] Frequently this guilt is framed as a spiritual battle, as people seek refuge in religious belief and ritual, pleading with God for forgiveness of and 'healing' from their 'sinful' sexual attraction. As Aze narrates, 'I prayed and cried and fasted and begged God to kill the "spirit of lesbianism" in me'.[26]

The narratives in *Blessed Body* are dominated by adolescents and youth who felt terrible because they have had sexual thoughts and fantasies. They are victims of a puritanical theology that considers sex as essentially evil, but tolerable only in marriage. Older individuals are also not spared from feeling guilty in relation to sex. In this religious culture, the Bible is constantly deployed as the ultimate pleasure-killer, appealed to in order to neutralise sex appeal. The standard theological equation has been as follows: sex = sin. The sin might be mitigated because the people involved would be married, but there is still a lingering belief that sex pollutes. This is more pronounced in the case of lgbt individuals. For example, Bee narrates that, 'After sex, I prayed and asked God for forgiveness from the sin of lesbianism. This shame and self-denial continued into my years as a diploma student'.[27] Sometimes the shame and self-denial could become complex. For example, Kennedy has steamy sex with 'bubblebuttEn'. However, as they are taking a break, the latter takes out a Bible and begins preaching on how being gay is a sin to God. He goes on, quoting from Leviticus and Romans, and preaches against homosexuality for about 30 minutes. After this he asked softly, 'Can we go another round?'[28] This hilarious anecdote could reflect one strategy of neutralising the 'clobber texts': performing them in between performing on each other. It could also be a vivid demonstration of the internalisation of guilt.

Feelings of guilt, the pressure to conform to established gender norms and stigmatisation forced a significant number of narrators in *Blessed Body* to marry someone of the opposite sex. Indeed, the constant refrain from friends and advisors is for queer folk to marry and perform heterosexuality. However, there is a realisation that such an option is not sustainable, as highlighted by Moji.[29] Others, however, have open marriages that they hope will thrive. The struggle is real: Niyi has attempted suicide at least twice, Kite pins his hopes on psychotherapy, while Bee had to battle depression.[30] Chukkie says, 'I wanted to die because I felt destroyed in every layer of my life. There was no comfort'.[31]

Individuals able to overcome the guilt associated with sex work hard to reach a certain level of self-awareness. They contend with the condemnation of homosexuality by the Church and their families. Same-sex loving people who successfully negotiate notions of sin in relation to sex are those who have undergone internal transformation and have undone layers of socialisation and indoctrination. Bee says, 'With time, I started accepting myself. I became kind to myself and cleansed my mind of the nightmares about Sodom and Gomorrah'.[32] Thus, through the painful searches, countless humiliations, gnawing doubts and endless wrestling with God, most narrators have come to a place of self-acceptance. In a context dominated by supreme levels of misunderstanding and dogged refusals to understand, they have achieved inner peace. They have come to realise that no amount of prayer and exorcism will change them from who they are. As Kite simply puts it, 'After all, I was a happy person: gay'.[33] Furthermore, some have turned the labels that are used against them into resources. Finbar declares:

> Today, I'm usually the first person to call myself a sissy because it is a word that has so often been used to ridicule me. So, I got sick of giving that word so much power that I decided to take a

step back, claim it and in doing so, I have disarmed it and I won it completely.[34]

The stories in *Blessed Body* provide an intimate insight into the vulnerabilities of children and youth as they slowly discover that they are different. Yet the stories also convey a deep truth about Nigerian lgbt folk: they are rooted in their families, communities and cultures. They did not simply learn from the West; instead they are sons and daughters of Nigeria, of Africa, who are simply born this way.

Family struggles

In *Blessed Body*, the family plays a major role in policing (homo)sexuality. The parents and siblings of the narrators are at the forefront of prayers against their sexual orientation, just one of the ways in which 'homophobia has vested itself in the family'.[35] Indeed, for many individuals in the volume, true freedom and liberation comes at the price of weaning themselves from their families. JT says, 'I love my parents. I love my family, but I love me more'.[36] Adaeze expresses the tension as follows: 'My family has not accepted me back and still does not want anything to do with me, but I am happy now with my life'.[37] Indeed, some, like Bukola, hope for reconciliation:

> I have faith that the story is not over. I am grounded in my belief that God is abounding in love and mercy, that He seeks reconciliation always. This is the hope I have for my family. My freedom has come at a great price but I can only be who I am, who God fearfully and wonderfully created me to be: an authentic purple square who loves Jesus and her wife very much, with or without the love and support of her family of yellow Circles.[38]

Families are caught up in vicious circles in which there are basically no winners. The society in which they are rooted is driven by heteronormativity. After a certain age, they expect their sons and daughters to get married to members of the opposite sex. There is really no opportunity to step back and question this expectation; society does not leave any room for difference. Since everyone is marinated in this ideology, it comes as a complete shock when a family member indicates that they do not fit into the box that has been set before them, generating serious tension and conflict. Ella describes such a struggle:

> Every day while with my family, I go through the pain of emotional torture, physical torture and even 'spiritual torture.' They used clobber scriptures from the Bible to execute their disdain towards me. They stole my laughter from me and implanted in me sadness that evolved into depression that nearly made me take my life. A lot happened: I was constantly being taken against my will to an unknown destination all in the name of some spiritual cleansing.[39]

Alongside perpetuating cultural norms, Nigerian families also promote the teachings of the Church against homosexuality. Parents are quick to remind their lgbt children of the Bible and what they believe it says about homosexuality. Fathers, in particular, appear to be at pains to bring up their sons to succeed them in a neatly defined patriarchal hierarchy. They use violence to try to force their sons to conform to socially defined gender norms and values. They are cold, impersonal and zealous to ensure that their sons become 'real men'.[40] Fathers appear to have a covenant with patriarchy, and they cannot renege on delivering their part of the bargain, that is, to bring up their sons on the 'straight path'. We read about fathers torturing their sons in a quest to uphold the 'dignity' of patriarchy and masculinity. Their words, actions and non-actions are hurtful, such as Kite's father who denounces his son, saying, 'You disgusting Sissy! You can't even kill a rat!'[41] Mothers equally struggle to accompany their lgbt children. They invest in many prayers of deliverance, and sometimes even take their kids to a centre of exorcism, forcing them to pray and fast for seven days.[42] They read their Bibles with passion and compassion, seeking to have their children delivered from the 'spirit of homosexuality'. Mothers turn their backs on the children they bore, or the children decide to cut off all ties. Ade's mother often cries, asking what she did to deserve the 'fate' of having a son who is gay.[43]

However, there are a few redemptive windows. Lexy's mother is extremely supportive and joins forces with him to confront the thugs who had brutalised him.[44] Jaijay confidently declares that, 'In spite of my struggles as a gay man, I've got a fairly supportive family'.[45] Chukkie's parents reach a certain level of acceptance.[46] Despite their upbringing against homosexuality, a few families still try to stand with members who express a different sexual orientation and gender identity. Thus, as much as the stories present a narrative critique of the family as a queer-phobic space, they also allude to alternative possibilities of families as spaces where children are accepted and nourished. They invite parents to reflect on different models of parenthood and care. They encourage schools, faith communities and other relevant professionals to provide parents and families with adequate support and guidance, able to accompany children as they explore their bodies and desires and figure out who they are.

Critiquing and reimagining the Church

It appears from the stories in *Blessed Body* that the Church in Nigeria—however diverse in terms of denominations—has a standard template when it comes to homosexuality. Firstly, church leaders glean the Bible and use selected verses to bombard lgbt persons. For instance, Kehinde indicates that Sister Odolo referred to passages in Genesis, Leviticus, Timothy, Corinthians and Romans, which are among the so-called clobber verses.[47] Thus, the Bible, together with culture, becomes one of the two canons between which lgbt folks are trapped. Secondly, they resort to prayer and exorcism to try to drive out what they regard as the spirit of homosexuality. For instance, Unoma narrates how her born-again friend Ngozi declares to her, 'The spirit of lesbianism is stubborn and demonic. I can start prayers and deliverance for you now, if you believe'.[48]

This spiritualisation of sexual orientation is typical of Pentecostal-Charismatic movements, which from the 1980s have become the most popular and influential form of Christianity in Nigeria as in other parts of Africa, and has also greatly influenced other denominations. In the Pentecostal worldview, which is reflected in many of the stories, homosexuality is caused by evil spirits and demons that need to be exorcised by pastors and prophets, or other 'strong believers' able to access and mobilise the power of the Holy Spirit. In Kehinde's words, 'certain things are simply spiritual in nature, and only spiritual interventions could get rid of them'.[49] The struggle against sexual desire is not just a battle 'against flesh and blood but [against] principalities and power in heavenly places'.[50]

Interestingly, this Nigerian Pentecostal spiritualised understanding of, and response to, homosexuality is somewhat similar to West African indigenous religious cultures that uphold the belief in 'spirit spouses'. The latter belief is reflected in the story by Moji, who narrates her search for a 'cure' of her homosexuality. As part of the ritual, she was instructed to sleep on a dead man's grave for three nights: 'I was told that my spirit husband resided in the grave. I had to ostracize the spirit. I had to be released so that I can find an earthly husband'.[51] It illustrates what scholars have coined the 'paradox of dis/continuity', in which Pentecostalism preserves indigenous ontologies while at the same time associating them with the devil.[52]

The psychological effects of such beliefs, and of the actual practices of exorcism and deliverance, can be seriously harmful. As Rowland Jide narrates at length:

While I never stopped praying, I also felt cheated by my primary religious community and culture because of their lack of understanding of homosexuality. I believe this led me in my destructive pathway into heterosexuality. I wasn't able to discuss these feelings with anyone. No member of my family or the church, in my mind, would be able to handle my issues; no pastor or youth leader was in my opinion trained beyond the 'casting and binding of the evil spirit of homosexuality.' I was young and mostly naïve about how best to 'deal with' homosexuality. There were no youth programs at church and the only language for homosexuals was the usual message of condemnation, disapproval, denunciation and hell.[53]

Stories such as this present a strong narrative critique of the Church for its spectacular failure to be supportive of adolescents who are struggling with sexual orientation and gender identity, instead only adding to this existential struggle by denying lgbt people the recognition of their fundamental human dignity.

The consistent demonisation of queer sexuality by the Church has contributed to violence against lgbt individuals, as narrated in many of the stories. There probably exists in the minds of many perpetrators of violence the justification that, if Nigerian lgbt people have been condemned by the Church and by the god on whose behalf the Church claims to speak, they do not have any rights at all. No wonder some narrators indicate that they have broken their attachment to organised religion and have given up on the Church. However, throughout *Blessed Body* we also see narrators expressing a strong desire for the Church to be a space of affirmation, liberation and nourishment, a place where lgbt people, like other human beings, are welcomed as 'children of the living God'.[54] In that sense, the stories call for a redemption of the Church—from homophobia, heteronormativity, cultures of exclusion and marginalisation—in a way that is reminiscent of African women theologians reimagining the Church as redeemed from sexism and patriarchy, and changed into a space of inclusion and of abundance of life for all.[55]

The queer appropriation of religion

Arguably, religious institutions and religious beliefs are at the heart of perpetuating public and internalised homophobia in Nigeria, as narrated in *Blessed Body*. However, these stories illustrate what some readers might perceive as a paradox: as much as the storytellers give an insight into their struggle with faith and organised religion, often they do not give up on it altogether. Instead, they appear to appropriate, negotiate and reclaim it. Religion is part of Nigerian queer self-writing, not only as a relic of the past that people have overcome through a process of self-acceptance and coming out, but also as part of the present and the future that remains relevant and meaningful for the story-tellers' understanding of their lives. The narrators build on the ambivalence of religious belief, ritual and sacred texts to develop life-giving theologies. They refuse to internalise their condemnation and turn faith into a resource. The journey of coming to terms with their sexuality involves new ways of understanding faith, the Bible and God. As Bukola narrates:

> Even as I pursued the relationship, I continued to pray, read Bible passages, search for books and articles which address ethics concerning sexual minorities. ... I was able to find reconciliation between my beliefs and my experiences, not because I wanted to justify my actions but because I wanted to do what is right in God's sight. ... I strongly felt God's blessing over my sexuality.[56]

This journey towards reconciliation of faith, sexuality and gender identity is of course deeply personal, and the stories do not provide a template. However, there are several recurring elements. One is the re-interpretation of the Bible: where the Bible has been commonly used to tell lgbt people that they are sinful (if not demonic), some of the narrators come to read it in new ways. Leaving behind literalist and fundamentalist interpretations, they reclaim the Bible as a book of affirmation and liberation, its central message not one of judgement but of love and grace. As Bukola puts it, 'My understanding of the Word pointed me towards Jesus' teaching that the fulfilment of God's word is to love God and neighbor.'[57] Through this understanding of its key message, they are then able to neutralise the so-called 'clobber verses' used against them. Thus, Nigerian lgbt Christians go to the same Bible used by their tormentors, mining it and recovering liberating passages and concepts.

Second is a reimagining of God, from the judgemental and wrathful God who constantly watches people's sexual lifestyles and punishes them for any moral offences, to a God who is the origin of human life in its diversity and who affirms every human being, in particular those considered as outcasts in society. Thus, homosexuality is not from the devil but is believed to be part of 'God's design' and therefore cannot be changed.[58] In this perspective, being gay, lesbian, bisexual or transgender is part of 'who God fearfully and wonderfully created me to be'.[59] Some of the stories turn into testimonies of how the narrators have experienced the love of God in their struggles with family, friends, the Church and society at large. Seun, who not only had to come to terms with his sexuality but also with a diagnosis with HIV, concludes his deeply moving story by saying,

> I know God listens. He doesn't promise us an easy life, but he promised that his hand and heart in our lives will always see us through. I wouldn't deny that he's been on my side. After all, I have faced death and I am still here.[60]

In another moving story, Jaijay contends that, at a deeply spiritual and existential level, there are good things that have come from his personal suffering:

> It has taught me acceptance and love and treating the whole human race as something beautifully diverse and complex. It has taught me not to judge and that life isn't black and white but contains all colours of the rainbow. It has made me draw closer to understanding

who God is and how He is more than our expectations even in the love and grace he provides for us.[61]

These testimonies are worth quoting, not only because of their narrative strengths, but also because the genre of testimonies is part and parcel of contemporary Nigerian Pentecostal-Christian culture. In Pentecostal churches, time and again people testify how God has helped them through certain challenges in life. Some such testimonies may be about how God has 'healed' someone from the 'demon of homosexuality'. *Blessed Body* subverts and enriches this genre of testimonial stories by inserting queer testimonies into the mix. The stories assert that religious faith can become a source of resilience and empowerment. Chukkie dedicates himself to things of the spirit and relies on faith and hope as his guiding light; Rowland Jide would always turn to prayer in his moments of searching for his identity.[62] Stories of struggle become testimonies of affirmation and liberation.

Perhaps this is reflected most explicitly in the title of Bee's story, 'Resurrection'. This title has an explicitly theological connotation, as it invokes the biblical story of the resurrection of Jesus from death, as well as the classic Christian belief, expressed in the Apostles' Creed, in the resurrection of the body. Bee uses these motifs to frame her own experience of finally being able to separate from her husband (though remaining good friends), and to spend her life with the woman she loves: 'She has resurrected me from death. She has changed my world and has brought me to this good place in my life: freedom'.[63] Indeed, similar experiences of resurrection—in the form of freedom to express one's sexuality, to enjoy one's body and sexuality, and to be affirmed in one's identity—are narrated in many of the stories in *Blessed Body*.

Against this background, the title of the volume itself is highly meaningful and evocative. The body occupies a challenging place in conservative versions of Christian theology. Heavily influenced by Hellenistic philosophy where the body is inferior to the soul, the dominant approach in Christian theology has been to condemn the body, having a particular impact on affected bodies considered 'deviant' because of ideologies of race, gender and sexuality. By adopting the title *Blessed Body*, Azuah disrupts this negative theology. The body, and in this case specifically the Nigerian queer body, should not be condemned but affirmed, embraced and celebrated. The body is not the theatre of the devil to tempt God's faithful, but is, in fact, vested with divine presence. It is blessed.

Conclusion

Blessed Body is an intellectually stimulating but emotionally draining anthology. While there are some stories with an overall positive tone, the volume lays bare the life and death struggles of Nigerian lgbt people. The pain that adolescents and youth go through is unbearable; that they have lived to tell the tale is a living testimony of the tenacity of the human spirit. That in several cases they retain their religion is an incredible witness to the power of faith. Haunted by families, hunted by state operatives, humiliated by various actors and hemmed in by religious bigots, lgbt individuals in Nigeria yearn for the day when they can proclaim, 'Free at last! Free at last!'

The power of lgbt storytelling, as reflected in *Blessed Body*, is that it renders visible those lives and voices that hitherto were largely hidden. It is a way of breaking and voicing the silence.[64] In particular, these stories provide narrative insight into struggles with faith, the Bible and with God, and they offer narrative strategies to turn such a struggle into an experience of spiritual empowerment. Life-storytelling becomes a form of queer testimony, with Nigerian lgbt people reclaiming their bodies as divinely blessed.

8

THE ART OF WORDS

LGBTQ POETRY, CHRISTIANITY
AND FLOURISHING IN AFRICA

Where does one go to when stigma suffuses one's life? How does one refuse to go under amid so much negativity? What is there to do when one's whole socialisation goes against who one really is? In addition to social media, which has become an important site of lgbti community and visibility,[1] people often resort to storytelling and poetry. They compose words of encouragement, wisdom and survival. The creative arts of words help to give voice to deeply personal struggles and experiences of trauma, but also to express glimpses of faith, hope and love, and expectations of the future. In addition to the growing number of volumes of African lgbti and queer life stories (see chapter 7), several collections of poetry have also been published. Thus, poetry gives voice to those sexual and gendered 'others' whose voices have hitherto been silenced. The subaltern can speak through poetry, among other forms of 'arts of resistance'.[2] And when now the poets speak, the gods hearken—or, at least, we do.[3]

This chapter focuses on a 2016 collection of African lgbti and queer poetry, the volume *Walking the Tightrope*, which includes texts of poetry and prose by writers from 13 countries across the continent.[4] A good number of the texts included offer a significant entry point into the ambivalence of religion in the lives of lgbtq people in Africa. Vividly, the poets show how religion both oppresses and liberates: in some instances, religion is a major support, as an lgbtq person may utilise it to negotiate and overcome certain challenges; in other instances, religion is a significant roadblock to self-acceptance and embrace by the community. Although in this chapter we shall discuss the two approaches in different sections, these roles of religion can in fact occur together, sometimes within the same text. Through the arts of poetry, religion becomes both the subject of critique and of creative imagination.

In this chapter, we explore how African lgbtq poets present their experiences with religion, specifically Christianity in Africa. We begin by briefly exploring the advantage of using poetry and then proceed to analyse the five poems that we have selected for closer scrutiny. We then make some concluding remarks on the ambivalence of religion in the lives of lgbtq people in Africa, and the capacity for poetry to articulate these mixed experiences with religion and its role in their lives.

Poetry: life in a few words

It is important to reflect on poetry as a genre in order to appreciate why it appeals to certain activists.[5] Why have some lgbtq people in Africa resorted to poetry, and what do they find in poetry that they do not find in other genres? We contend that poetry enables individuals to condense words and to express key points in concise language. Effective poetry (written or oral) is sharp and precise, while at the same time leaving room for the imagination of the audience. It gives the poet the platform to celebrate, agonise, enquire or teach without engaging in a treatise. Poetry can be so penetrating that the genre of lament has unsettled some African politicians. Such politicians have gone ahead to prevent poets from having freedom after speech. For example, although the Malawian poet Jack Mapanje utilised the device of obscuring, the regime he faced was still sufficiently offended to incarcerate him and force him into exile.[6] Likewise, the Ugandan feminist, queer scholar and activist, Stella Nyanzi, was sentenced in 2019 to 18 months in prison for writing poems reportedly criticising the president and first lady.

Poetry can summon deep emotions, not only in the writer but also in the audience. A 2017 psychological study concluded that 'poetry is capable of inducing peak emotional experiences, including subjectively reported chills and objectively measured goosebumps'.[7] Poetry is strategic for emotional expression, as it seeks to grip the audience's feelings. It promotes creative thinking because in some cases the intended meaning is generally obscured, while the audience must engage in critical thinking in order to decipher the message being communicated by the poet. For example, some postcolonial African poets lament the state of the continent: 'In their poetry, we observe that their fears, hopes, aspirations and frustrations in the post-colony are elaborately illuminated'.[8]

Poetry is a strategic vehicle for communicating feelings, aspirations and convictions in a concise way. As we shall illustrate below, it gives those whose voices have been suppressed the platform to articulate their experiences and longings. Throughout history, the oppressed have utilised poetry to speak and be heard. Women, youth, people with disability, prisoners of conscience, environmental activists and others have often resorted to poetry, appropriating it to protest their situation and work towards freedom. It is, therefore, not surprising that lgbtq people in Africa have engaged poetry to evocatively express their trauma, hopes and visions for the future.

Critiquing religious hypocrisy

The poem 'The rapture' by Andi Dube from Zimbabwe is unforgiving in exposing the hypocrisy and intolerance that can be found among religious leaders.[9] Dube opens the poem by going straight into the discourse of a shamed 'man of God' who has been caught in a compromising position. 'Man of God' is the term used by popular charismatic pastors and their followers when referring to them; the phrase suggests that the pastors are closer to God than the rest of us, who are mere mortals. However, the dramatic opening lines of the poem immediately call this claim into question:

> With all this talk about the latest 'man of God' to succumb to his flesh and desires

> With all the talk he gave about the gays and how bad they were and are

The sub-title states that the poem was written on the occasion of the Ted Haggard scandal.[10] Yet by using the word 'latest' it suggests that Haggard is part of a recurrent pattern rather than an isolated incident—in fact, Dube could have chosen similar cases from pastors caught up in sexual scandals from his home country and other parts of the continent. Evangelical and Pentecostal forms of Christianity have generally portrayed themselves as movements dedicated to the disciplining of the flesh in the quest for purity and salvation.[11] In particular, their charismatic leaders have sought to display a 'holier than thou' outlook in interacting with members of the larger society. It is this elevated position that has given them the licence to pass judgement on all other members of society, especially those who are seen as sexual sinners. However, Dube challenges their claim of occupying higher moral grounds by referencing the 'latest' scandal and placing the title 'man of God' between inverted commas. By evoking 'flesh and desires' Dube uses the same language typically used by these pastors in their moralising crusades, but perhaps also inverts it, suggesting that sexuality is integral to human embodiment.

The second line makes it clear that the 'man of God' had condemned 'the gays', saying 'how bad they were and are'. Both in America and in Africa, charismatic pastors are often at the forefront of public campaigns against sexual and gender minority rights, but also against women's reproductive rights; they not only promote the idea that sex can only be enjoyed in the context of a heterosexual marriage, but also tend to stigmatise as a sinner anyone who does not fit in this paradigm. People who identify as lgbtq, in particular, have become the favourite punch bag of African Pentecostal leaders, who generally project them as representing the extreme side of humanity's fall and as justifying God's decisive intervention.[12] However, Dube deflates the Pentecostal rhetoric of the 'bad' gays in this poem by pointing out that the 'men of God' frequently succumb to the 'desires' and promptings of the 'flesh' against which they preach. As such, he draws critical attention to the hypocrisy of these religious leaders.

Having exposed this hypocrisy, the poem shifts to some of the central concepts in popular versions of Pentecostalism: prosperity ('this god of the wealthy'), election ('this god of the evangelicals') and judgement ('this god of war and destruction'). By repeatedly using the phrase, 'this god', without a capital letter, Dube depicts the god of this form of Christianity as a small god, despite the power and might that religious language in those circles typically ascribes to him. Dube clearly considers that the theology driving this form of Christianity alienates it from the rest of the community, specifically impacting the poor and marginalised, those who do not meet evangelical Christian moral standards and who are therefore believed to be subjected to God's wrath and punishment.

The Cameroonian scholar Frida Lyonga has argued that there exists a 'homophobic trinity' in African Pentecostalism, consisting of the prosperity gospel (the belief that God blesses good Christians with material wealth), the healing gospel (the belief that God will heal true believers from illnesses), and the end time gospel (the belief that the world is coming to an end but that God will save the faithful).[13] These three 'gospels', which reflect different strands of Pentecostal thought, in Lyonga's assessment frequently work together in messages against lgbtq people, as they are subjected to rituals of healing and deliverance from their perceived illness; are warned that they will end up in hell if they do not give up their 'sinful' lifestyles; and are believed to put the prosperity of the nation at risk by their 'immorality'. Dube in his poem directly addresses two of these three 'gospels', of prosperity and of the end times. As the title suggests, he is especially concerned with the latter. In the Pentecostal imagination, the presence and acceptance of lgbtq people portend the end of the world.[14] Consequently, there is a strong anticipation of what is called 'the rapture', the moment when God will intervene decisively to make a complete break with history, taking the righteous to heaven while the sinners will be left behind on earth in the hands of the devil.[15] In a powerful move, Dube in his poem invokes this idea of rapture, writing:

> let them have their heaven / the RAPture
> I'm hoping that it is going to happen soon so that those of us who
> are left behind can be left behind
> in peace
> Those of us bad
> Those not 'saved'
> we'll be glad to stay right where we are in peace

Dube queers rapture, expressing it in a new way, 'RAPture.' This rendition makes the concept absurd, and its vocalisation alludes to the violence of 'rape'. Essentially, the poem welcomes the idea of rapture as a liberatory perspective: if the small god of this narrow-minded faith will take his believers to heaven, the earth will be freed from their hypocrisy and from the moral policing that they impose on fellow human beings. For Dube, the 'RAPture' cannot happen soon enough, because it will bring the long-awaited peace on earth to the queer folks and other apparent sinners who will be left behind. The poem ridicules the idea that God wants to promote a select few to glory, while leaving the rest of his creation behind on earth for being 'bad' and 'not "saved"'. Yet it also underscores the importance of peace for lgbtq people, a peace they can only experience away from anti-queer Pentecostals. Using the word 'peace' twice in quick succession illustrates the feeling of being persecuted and the desire for that persecution to come to an end.

Dube's poem is an example *par excellence* of the queer critique of organised religion, in this case evangelical and Pentecostal forms of Christianity and their self-proclaimed men and women of God. The poem does not make an explicit effort to reclaim religion from hypocritical pastors and their followers. Perhaps it does so in a more subtle way, if we read the poem as a prayer of deliverance—not deliverance from the demon of homosexuality, as Pentecostals would have it, but deliverance from Christian hypocrisy and moral narrow-mindedness: 'Let them have their heaven', in order for 'us' to enjoy peace. The poem can also be read as reflecting an earth-embracing spirituality. It reflects a longing not for a disembodied heaven, but for peace on earth when 'succumbing to flesh and desires' is not deemed sinful but is part of our creation as embodied human beings.

Liberation from institutionalised religion

If Dube presents an explicit critique of organised religion, the next text is more ambiguous, capturing both the negative and positive dimensions of religion in relation to queer sexuality. Not strictly a poem but a text of prose, 'Trapped by religion and freed by God' by J. S. Ayebaziwe from Uganda addresses the theme of religious socialisation.

Socialisation is a process through which society seeks to mould individuals to conform to its values and ways of doing and being. While it plays an important role in enabling persons to have a sense of belonging, in many instances it is experienced as a form of tyranny, especially by lgbtq people who at an early stage discover that they are 'different'. At the heart of socialisation is the desire to develop conformity; essentially, society seeks to force individuals to subscribe to its tenets. Thus the home, as one of the most significant theatres of socialisation, is often experienced as oppressive, particularly in terms of religious observances. Ayebaziwe opens the text by saying, 'I grew up in a catholic family; my mother went to church with us as often as possible'.[16] She indicates that she went along with the religious ideology, aspiring to go to heaven as taught by the religious authorities. She attended a girls' school, in Mbarara, Uganda, where 'homosexuality was strongly discouraged / in fact it was punishable by expulsion'. The head cook had taken it upon herself to break up any two girls who walked hand in hand into the dining hall, and she would reprimand them sternly. However, this did not prevent Ayebaziwe from having a teenage crush on her best friend, with whom she literally spent every day for the first three years. Then, she experienced a sudden transformation and knew that something had changed in her. According to her, 'I detached and spent hours alone. I had no one to talk to about the emotional warfare that was plaguing my mind. I was afraid of everlasting fire and becoming a social misfit'.

These two sentences are packed and highly informative. Society has prescribed the parameters of a young woman's sexuality. To 'stray' beyond the narrowly circumscribed definitions of femininity is to court social (and sometimes physical) death. The only mode of existence is to fit in, to be defined by those who have arrogated the right to define what can and cannot exist, and who one can and cannot be/come. Ayebaziwe's description of being 'detached and ... alone' represents an existential and anguished search for identity. She engages in such a search, investing in solitude in an endeavour to discover herself.

The reference to emotional warfare needs to be understood against the background of Pentecostal Christianity, which has popularised the notion of spiritual warfare. By referencing emotional rather than spiritual strife, Ayebaziwe is implicitly critiquing Ugandan Pentecostalism and its fascination with spiritual warfare. For her, the battle is emotional. Furthermore, the power of socialisation is clearly emphasised when she refers to fearing everlasting fire and becoming a social misfit.

The burden placed on Ayebaziwe's psyche by religion is an onerous one. She has to engage in introspection in order to be able to break free. Religion is experienced as a powerful force that weighs down the individual, bequeathing a creator who is a 'harsh monster'. It is religion that creates the fear, shame and self-doubt highlighted by Ayebaziwe in her reflections. Whereas positive religion must be life-giving and liberating, she had imbibed too much of the death-dealing and immobilising religion imposed by society. Using different institutions, persons and strategies, society sought to ensure enslavement and conformity.

However, as indicated in the title of her text, Ayebaziwe felt trapped by religion, but freed by God. This title conveys an important and critical point: that God does not coincide with institutionalised religion, as much as religious leaders may claim to speak on God's behalf. As Ayebaziwe recalls in poetic words:

> I found god in a long bus trip. I felt her energy in the wind / saw her in the tall elegant trees and heard her in the birds. She was ambiguous, unlike the harsh monster I had come to know as the creator.
>
> She was pure energy, neither positive nor negative. She simply flowed.

This epiphany is expressed in a very striking way. Whereas the conventional Christian approach is to refer to God with a capital letter and with male pronouns, Ayebaziwe decides to queer the divine by deploying the lower case and using female pronouns. Clearly, the patriarchal and homophobic male god popularised by society cannot be the same god to whom Ayebaziwe awakens. Using a feminist eco-critical lens to interpret this passage, we can argue that in this text there is a dynamic interface between god, nature, Ayebaziwe and her sexuality.[17] Ayebaziwe awakens to a new female god who is not violent and intolerant but instead reveals herself through nature, is adaptable and flowing. The text does not describe this god in explicitly Christian language, and may instead invoke images of the divine derived from indigenous religions. For instance, among the Lango people in Uganda, the supreme being is traditionally seen as 'intangible, invisible, indivisible and ubiquitous as the wind'; it is believed to 'inhabit trees, hills, and mountains' and it 'may be of either gender'.[18] Although not explicitly Christian, this way of imagining the divine is not alien to biblical and Christian traditions. For instance, the Bible has an account of the prophet Elijah who, after an epic and violent fight to eliminate the prophets of Baal on Mount Carmel, encounters God not in the aggression of a stormy wind, an earthquake or fire, but in the softness of 'a gentle whisper'.[19]

The story can be read as a conversion experience: not a conversion in the conventional sense, where the convert begins to follow religious instructions in their life, but as a liberation from such normative instructions as imposed by religious authorities, and as the beginning of self-acceptance and self-realisation. The experience enables Ayebaziwe to transcend the tyranny of society and its institutionalised religion, and to discover her inner and true self. She shakes off the imposed patriarchal god and moves in rhythm with the goddess. Such an experience is empowering, as she lets go of her shame and self-doubt. The reflection ends with her 'feeling right and free'. While religion weighs her down from very early on, it enables her to find herself and to move ahead with freedom and grace. Religion, emptied of its zealotry and extremism, can provide solace and inner peace—that is, if it overcomes hypocrisy.

Blessed assurance

The reassurance offered by religion can only be appreciated after examining the struggles that lgbtq people endure. As in the case of Ayebaziwe discussed above, a poem titled 'Free' by Ayanda Mkhize from South Africa brings out the impact of socialisation. It is socialisation that weighs heavily on Mkhize, blocking the avenues to freedom; this is expressed in the gripping opening lines: 'I drown / sink'.[20] The first stanza captures the internal ambivalences often experienced by queer people as they negotiate conflicting feelings: dreaming to be 'set free from my desires', while simultaneously 'fighting a longing to keep them'. The struggle with desire is a struggle with the self, and for the self. Gender and sexual socialisation circumscribe which desires are considered acceptable and which not, and how one is supposed to express or suppress them. The second stanza brings out the pressure that comes from such socialisation:

'Morality' offers me a hand
I do not want to retaliate any more
But I want more to be free
Who wants to be strangled by 'norms' and perceptions
In this world 'the truth' lies at the tip
Of many tongues.

Here, the burden caused by socialisation is emphasised through the notion of being 'strangled', laying bare the existential despair that the poet is experiencing. To be strangled is to be killed in a very painful way, and the poem reveals that it is not only acts of physical aggression and violence through which queer people are strangled to death, but also the struggle with internalised 'norms' that restrict the possibilities of human embodied existence.

The poem does not explicitly name which of the established moral concepts in society cause such struggle. But the reader can easily imagine them: a strict male-female binary that presupposes an obvious connection between certain genitalia and some specific ways of being; ideas about the purpose of human sexuality and the acceptable ways in which to enjoy it. Mkhize questions the naturalness of these ideas by placing the words 'morality', 'norms' and 'truth' between inverted commas. This serves to destabilise them and create space to rethink inherited assumptions, norms and ways of being.

The title of the poem is telling in its simplicity: 'Free'. The concept of being free has generated deep theological, philosophical, linguistic and other searches. What does it mean to be free? What does freedom entail? How does one find freedom? In Mkhize's case, as in the case of Ayebaziwe, freedom comes through introspection. It arrives in moments of quiet rest and serious soul searching. Such moments can turn into experiences of existential affirmation and spiritual recovery. The final stanza captures this experience intimately:

> So today, I shall lie down
> Bare, free and empty of it all
> For I know the one that created Me
> And He knows me.

The language here is somewhat reminiscent of biblical language. The phrase 'lying down' echoes the widely known opening words of Psalm 23: 'The Lord is my shepherd, I lack nothing / He makes me lie down in green pastures / he leads me beside quiet waters, / he refreshes my soul'. Indeed, the experiences reflected in this Psalm and in Mkhize's poem appear to be very similar. Likewise, the closing words of the poem echo the equally well known words of Psalm 139: 'You have searched me, Lord / and you know me. ... For you created my inmost being / you knit me together in my mother's womb.' Mkhize uses poetic language with biblical allusions to express the existential experience of finding freedom to be at peace with the self, born out of spiritual knowledge that their being has its origin and purpose in God the creator.

For Mkhize then, there is no more condemnation. Who condemns the one known personally by the creator? This creator is not an abstract principle that initiated motion in the universe. No, the poet has an intimate and personal knowledge of the creator, as demonstrated by the line, 'For I know the one that created Me.' In turn, 'And he knows me.' That the first 'Me' has a capital letter is not a mistake. It expresses the poet's very own personal awareness of the creator, and of being existentially, spiritually and bodily affirmed by that awareness. They might be harassed by the world and strangled by its norms, but they know God and are known and loved by God. The rhetorical effect of the poem is that it raises an unavoidable question for the audience to reflect upon: when God is for queer people, who then can be against them?[21]

Remembering the composer

The just-quoted words of Psalm 139, reflecting a deep personal and affirming knowledge of God as creator, is also somewhat echoed in the poem 'Broken Bodies' by Tsepho Jamillah Moyo from Botswana.[22] True, the poem does not use the word 'God' or 'creator', but it speaks of a 'composer'. Whoever this composer is, it refers to an Other, a sacred reality, not abstract but personalised, through which the poet feels affirmed and nourished. The resulting poem is a moving acknowledgement and celebration of support, such as in the opening lines:

I sometimes forget how well you know my heart.
If ever I get lost in the woods of pain I feel, you'd find me.
If I ever drown in the seas of sadness that often lap over me, you'd
find me.
You know the world's burdens weigh me down, so often you hold
me up.

The extent of the poet's suffering is expressed in evocative terms.
The reference to being 'lost in the woods of pain' and drowning
in the 'seas of sadness' captures this sense of being tormented.
Clearly, the world is not a hospitable place nor a platform for
flourishing. There is a striking contrast between the poet's precarious conditions and how the Sacred will, without fail, intervene to save her and 'hold [her] up'. Moyo uses a clever deploy-
ment of words here. The 'world's burdens' could mean either the
burdens that the poet encounters in the world, or the entire
world's burden being placed on the shoulders of the poet. We
sense the poet's confidence that, whatever the circumstances, the
Sacred will be available to salvage the situation.

In the metaphorical language of the second half of the poem,
the I-person refers to themselves as a 'broken instrument', trying
to play the song of their life. But how can one play a song using
a broken instrument, and who would understand such a song? In
other words, how can one flourish in life when burdened with
pain and sadness, and who could make sense and appreciate such
a life? Contemplating and responding to those questions, the
tone of the poem takes a turn: 'Then I remember you're my
composer / you wrote the notes that make this song'. As much
as the poet may feel like a broken instrument, unfit to perform
the song of her life, she is aware of a sacred reality, an Other,
who is bigger than herself. This Other has not only composed
the song of her life but will also 'fill in the missing notes', and
when she has forgotten exactly how the song goes, the composer
will 'sing my parts'. Thus the poem expresses a close, intimate

relationship between the poet and her 'composer'. It reflects an innate indebtedness of the one who was made, to the radical consistency of the Sacred that made. The poet is secure in the knowledge that the composer will make complete whatever she might be lacking.

The poem is deeply personal, expressing an individual experience, but it can also be read as paradigmatic of African queer life more generally. The portrayal of the lgbtq person as a 'broken instrument' is very apt, capturing the social and internalised burdens that lgbtq persons too often carry. Yet the poem inverts this image in a moving way by suggesting that there is a composer behind the song of precarious queer African lives. Moyo assures us that regardless of the social, cultural, economic and political circumstances restricting those lives to flourish, the sacred song of queer life will be sung to the fullest.

Guiding the people of God

Where the previous two poems provide a deeply intimate insight in religious faith generating an unshaken sense of security, in 'God's People', Ndayisenga from Burundi seeks to remind religious people of the fundamental teachings of their respective religions.[23] Written in a deceptively simple and direct way, the text—a combination of poetry and prose—is a sharp and urgent call to religious people to go back to the basics. To do this means abandoning all judgement and recovering the spirit of love, tolerance and acceptance. Against those who see religion as an instrument that facilitates stigma and exclusion, the poet redirects focus towards religion as a resource for building a better society for all. The poem opens compellingly as follows:

Tolerance toward others,
Respect for others,

Understanding towards others,
Love towards others.

The prose that follows this opening stanza states that these are the values and principles that God teaches in the sacred scriptures of different religions, such as Christianity and Islam. Whereas some activists would like to wage war against religion, the poet regards the challenge at hand to be the misidentification of origin. This evokes the saying, 'the problem is not the faith, but the faithful', by Kofi Annan.[24] In this scheme, if only the faithful would uphold and embody the true tenets of their faith, then the world would be a better place. According to the poet, the values of 'tolerance', 'respect', 'understanding' and 'love' are enshrined in every religion. Although both the Bible and the Qur'an have been implicated in stigma in the context of HIV and the harassment of lgbtq people,[25] the poet suggests that these scriptures can be reclaimed as reservoirs of positive values.

Having crafted a sacred canopy, in the prose section the poet seeks to draw on common sense. However, the two sections are connected in that the advice dispensed in prose is consistent with the ethical values, deriving from religion, which have been outlined in the opening stanza. The prose challenges attitudes of judging others without having full knowledge or understanding of their lives. What is required, the poet maintains, is to gain an appreciation of the person behind aspects that may first appear to deserve judgement. The text is a plea to listen to the full story, to understanding the full person; above all, it emphasises the importance of relationality and for introspection: 'ask yourself if it's worthy to change your views or not'. The recurrence of the word 'think', which is used thrice in one sentence, illustrates the demand for society to step back and engage the brain. Here, the critique is levelled against the emotion that is often unleashed when it comes to lgbtq issues. All rationality is thrown away, including by individuals who are quite gifted intellectually! Taking time to process issues of difference, understanding the stories that shape people and reflecting on why people are who they are would facilitate greater inter-human understanding, the poet suggests.

'God's People' closes with another section of poetry consisting of two stanzas, which includes a call to believers. If they accept the foundational concepts of their religions and live them out, everyone would benefit. The penultimate stanza returns to the fundamental religious concept that human moral attitudes should reflect God's character, and as the first line puts it, 'God is love'. Building on that, the poet suggests that the fundamental belief in God's love provides us with a roadmap to 'a better world for you / a better world for me'. The stanza is laid out in an artistic and impressive format. Whereas 'God is love' is at the centre, it spreads out beautifully to 'love that is ours' and 'our love that defines our steps'. It suggests that once the notion that 'God is love' is affirmed, religious people will be compelled to enact that love in all their interactions. This implies, naturally, love for lgbtq people. Otherwise, to say that God is love and proceed to hate is to nullify the initial premise.[26]

If the penultimate stanza branches out from the love of God to our steps as humans, the final stanza draws inwards from our steps to the better world that we can build—a better world for everyone. This is the lasting vision painted by the poet: clearly, such a world would be characterised by the values outlined earlier in the poem, of tolerance, respect, understanding and love. Thus, based on the concept of God as love, the poem imagines a queer-friendly world, which does not leave room for homophobia and any other forms of hatred and violence, but which allows human beings in all their diversity to live together in peace and harmony.

Conclusion

Poetry gives voice to lgbtq experiences in Africa; it allows lgbtq folk to talk back at society and to write their vision of the world.

It affords them a platform to express their fears and frustration, to lament and protest, and to imagine another world possible. Through poetry, lgbtq persons can critique religion and call out bigotry and hypocrisy. The poems discussed in this chapter draw attention to the dysfunctional role of religion in relation to the dignity and rights of lgbtq people. Religion has been used to deny lgbtq people their right to exist, belong and flourish. As the poets whose voices we have heard in this chapter articulate so eloquently, religion can be a burden and not a blessing to lgbtq people in Africa. Yet these poems also illustrate that religion itself is an ambiguous and contested terrain. They engage with religion critically, but also creatively, as through the arts of language lgbtq writers give sacred meaning to their struggles, signify their lives with religious idiom, reclaim biblical and theological concepts, and give voice to their experiences of faith, hope and love. Through poetry, African lgbtq people tell the stories of their lives and paint tapestries of hope. Poetry enables them to speak themselves into existence, nullify their nullification and instigate the inexorable move towards a peaceful, affirming and loving world in which they, and all people of goodwill, would like to live. Poetic language helps to imagine another world possible, and to bring that world near.

9

INFINITE POSSIBILITIES IN A NIGERIAN LESBIAN LOVE STORY

UNDER THE UDALA TREES

In recent years, a new genre in African literary writing has begun to emerge: queer fiction. Through novels and stories, several up-and-coming writers have boldly, creatively and innovatively addressed and engaged with queer themes. Perhaps surprisingly, given its reputation as a conservative country with a draconian law against homosexuality, much of this queer literary production originates from Nigeria.[1] This chapter focuses on one such text, the acclaimed novel *Under the Udala Trees*, by the Nigerian-born writer Chinelo Okparanta, which was published in 2015.

How can a novel, a piece of fiction, contribute to the re-imagination of Christianity and sexuality in Africa? As Afe Adogame has pointed out with reference to the classics in African literature, such as Chinua Achebe's *Things Fall Apart*:

African novels principally communicate the African milieu's experiences in its historical setting but also critique it. ... The prose, poetry, and drama genres produced by pioneering figures in African literature are overtly suffused with religious and cultural symbolism, meaning, critique, and connotation.[2]

This observation applies to more recent literary writings, by a new generation of authors, as much as it applies to texts by the giants in African literature to which Adogame is referring. Obviously, the context and the concerns have considerably changed from when contemporary African literature emerged in the 1950s–60s, as is obvious from the ways in which issues of sexuality are being addressed. Yet the engagement with religious themes continues to reflect in African literary writing, including in the emerging queer literature. Adogame suggests that such themes emerge in different ways—through symbolism, meaning, critique and connotation, among other modes. But the bottom line is that literary writing allows for a creative representation, but also for a critique and alternative imagination, of religion as part of African social, cultural and political milieus. This is certainly the case with *Under the Udala Trees*, which opens up a conversation about Christianity and same-sex love in a Nigerian context. As the author puts it, written at the time that Nigeria's then president, Goodluck Jonathan, signed the Same-Sex Marriage (Prohibition) Bill into law, the novel 'attempts to give Nigeria's marginalized LGBTQ citizens a more powerful voice, and a place in our nation's history'.[3]

Setting and plot

The setting of the novel is south-east Nigeria, the region known as Igboland, in the years during and after the Biafra war (which was from 1967–70). This historic setting is significant, as Biafra was a watershed period in Nigeria's postcolonial history, representing a battle about Nigerian nationhood. Does Okparanta want to suggest that the current battle about same-sex issues is as divisive, and as fundamental to the understanding of Nigerian identity, as the Biafra war?

Early in the novel, the protagonist, Ijeoma,[4] loses her father during the war because of a bomb raid which destroys their house in the village of Ojoto. Following the tragedy, her mother, deeply shocked by the turn of events, sees no other option but to leave Ijeoma as a house girl with a befriended couple, an elderly grammar school teacher and his wife, who live in a village called Nnewi that is considered to be safer. Although the separation was intended to be short, Ijeoma is only reunited with her mother after more than one and a half years, and it takes the scandal of a forbidden love for it to happen. While at the teacher's house, a friendship between Ijeoma, a Christian Igbo girl, and Amina,[5] a Muslim Hausa girl, blossoms and gradually becomes more intimate. When discovered, Ijeoma returns to her mother, who is determined to cleanse her daughter's soul. This cleansing process is not helped by the fact that the two girls are sent to the same boarding school. Only after the two girls leave school and Amina gets married does Ijeoma hesitantly develop another intimate friendship, with Ndidi. Yet the rising homophobic climate makes her shrink back; pressured by her mother, and out of a desire 'to lead a normal life' and not having 'to constantly worry about being found out', she ends up marrying her childhood friend, Chibundu.[6] Despite the birth of a baby, the unhappy marriage is doomed to fail from the beginning. In the final chapter of the novel, Ijeoma leaves her husband, and with her daughter she returns to her mother. The epilogue narrates that not only did she return to her mother, but, after all those years, also to Ndidi, and that the two of them found a way to make their relationship work as a 'clandestine affair'.[7]

Christianity is a major theme in the novel. In the very first sentence, reference is made to the 'village church', although Ijeoma and her parents attend a different church, Holy Sabbath Church of God.[8] The worship experience there is described as embodied, ecstatic and exhausting.[9] Throughout the novel, *Under the Udala Trees* sketches a religious culture of fervent worship, intense prayer and conservative biblical interpretation. This reflects the wave of Pentecostal revival that at the time was developing in Nigeria, described by Matthews Ojo as the emergence of an 'end-time army'.[10] Such was the culture in which Ijeoma grew up: one which she has to navigate and, increasingly, contest and reinterpret.

The space of church is a prominent one in the lifeworld sketched in *Under the Udala Trees*, and a paradoxical one for that matter. Throughout the novel we find Ijeoma going to church time and again, initially as part of the weekly routine in her family and the village, but later also as a place where she is drawn to herself, seeking refuge and comfort, and where she desperately tries to pray away her sexual desires, which she has been socialised to see as sinful. As much as church is the space where she struggles with her sexuality, ironically it is also the space where she has her first encounter with a community of same-sex loving women.[11] Her girlfriend Ndidi takes her to a club that is hidden in a covert church, called Friend of Jesus Church of God. This name can be read as a subversive suggestion by the author that Jesus was a friend of same-sex loving folk. Yet even the claim to Jesus' love does not offer adequate protection, as the club is discovered and razed by villagers. These varying and conflicting meanings of church can be seen as an allusion to the complex and multifaceted relationship of Christianity to same-sex sexuality, which is indeed a major theme in the novel. Some interpretations of the novel emphasise Okparanta's critique of the church and its credibility as a safe haven for all people.[12] However, in our reading Okparanta renders the space of the church and of Christian faith more ambiguously, as is explored below. The church as an institution—represented by pastors, bishops and other religious authorities—is virtually absent in the novel. Ijeoma's mother is the main religious authority and teaches her daughter an anti-gay understanding of the Bible; yet at the very end of the novel, her mother changes her opinion as she receives a new revelation. As far as she represents the influence of the church in a domestic setting, it suggests that the church is capable of change.

Udala trees and the biblical tree of knowledge

The novel stages the meeting of Ijeoma and Amina under the indigenous udala tree, which is well-known in the Igbo natural environment and symbolic universe. The suggestion is that this tree transcends the different ethnic backgrounds of the girls, as well as the fact that they represent two 'foreign' religions, Christianity and Islam respectively. The fact that the spark between these two girls started under this tree can also be seen as a means to counter popular claims of homosexuality as exogenous. Ijeome and Amina did not learn it from the West, through TV or film, but instead their mutual friendship and desire originated from this very local setting.

The symbolic meaning goes further, as the udala tree is 'a kind of native apple tree, which for the Igbo symbolizes fertility and the spirit of children. ... This is the spirit of sharing, camaraderie and the innocence of children, which the udala symbolizes'.[13] Okparanta's novel implicitly and explicitly refers to these meanings. The theme of fertility is explicitly invoked in the final chapter which opens by explaining the legend surrounding the tree. It describes the indigenous beliefs according to which udala trees are dwelling places of spirits who cause women to be 'exceptionally fertile'.[14] The legend alluded to here reflects and reinforces the broader concern with fertility and reproduction in Igbo culture, as in African indigenous cultures more generally.[15]

Earlier in the novel, the udala tree is associated with the 'spirit of children', not so much with the innocence of children, however, but with the apparent loss of innocence. The setting of a childhood scene in which Ijeoma exchanges her first kiss with her male neighbourhood friend, Chibundu, is not the branch of an udala but of an orange tree.[16] Although seemingly innocent, the scene is loaded with meaning as it occurs shortly before her mother takes Ijeoma away from the village where she grew up, and leaves her as a house girl with the grammar school teacher and his wife. It is there, in that new environment, that Ijeoma meets Amina for the first time, in the shadow of an udala tree—an encounter that turns out to be less simple.

Under that tree, they look each other in the eyes, and from that moment Ijeoma knows that she 'would not be leaving without her'.[17] It is the beginning of a close friendship that gradually becomes more and more intimate. Amina joins Ijeoma at the teacher's house, where they stay in the hovel in the back yard, sleep on the same yellow foam mattress, and bath together. The girls grow closer to each other and begin to explore each other's bodies. In that hovel, on that mattress, the teacher catches them one night when he opens the door and walks in unexpectedly, before the two girls are able to pull their nightgowns back on. Startled by the sight, he cries out, 'Abomination!' This word is used in the King James translation of the Bible (in Leviticus 18: 22) with reference to homosexuality. British missionaries introduced this Bible translation and its archaic terminology into Nigeria and other parts of Africa. Until today it is a popular term among Nigerian Christians to express their disgust of same-sex activity. Following the teacher's shout of this deeply loaded term, the story narrates the feeling of being exposed, explicitly recalling the imagery of Adam and Eve who discover their nakedness after the fall, as narrated in the Genesis creation story. It captures the teacher's moralistic lecture and expresses the humiliation felt by the girls, making them want to hide, just like Adam and Eve sought to hide from God.[18]

Implicitly, the novel here invokes the image of another tree, the biblical tree of knowledge of good and evil. This is the tree from which Eve picked the apple against God's instructions, after having been persuaded by the serpent, the apple which she shared with Adam (Genesis 2–3). After eating this forbidden fruit, Adam and Eve became first aware of their nakedness, and they covered themselves, while hiding from God in the bushes. This biblical story of the first human beings losing their innocence is woven into the storyline of the novel, with the udala tree under which Ijeoma and Amina first met retrospectively becoming the paradisal tree of knowledge of good and evil; with their bodies becoming the forbidden fruit; with the two girls, too, losing their innocence as they realise the apparent shame of their nakedness. However, as with the biblical tree, the question of whether or not the loss of innocence under the udala tree is good or evil remains ambiguous in the novel, with the epilogue suggesting that after all, the novel might well be a narrative of 'paradise lost, growth gained'.[19]

Prayer

One of the major themes running through the novel is prayer. Given the Pentecostal context, this may not be a surprise, since the practice of intense prayer is typical of Pentecostal forms of Christianity. As Nimi Wariboko evocatively captures it, 'the prayer language of Nigerian Pentecostals drips with blood and violence; the voices of the prayer-warriors thunder across the face of the earth as they speed toward heaven, tongues hauling fire bombs to target, and mouths projecting glistering swords at enemies'.[20] In *Under the Udala Trees*, this prayer culture is not only reflected in the narrative, but is narrated in such a way that critical questions are raised about the meaning, purpose and effect of prayer.

These questions emerge from the beginning of the novel. In chapter 2, Ijeoma tells the childhood memory of her first prayer to God regarding the war. It was just before the start of the war, on a Sunday while she attended church, where a boy jokingly told her that bomber planes would soon be coming—a suggestion she vehemently denied because her father had always assured her that war would not happen. However, the suggestion stuck in her mind, and later in the service she prayed for security and protection against all the dangers that the war posed to their health and well-being.[21] However, a year later, Ijeoma found herself hiding with her mother in the bunker that her father had built for them, on the fatal day that her father himself refused to join them and stayed in the house instead. There and then, she prayed again, repeatedly: 'Dear God, please help Papa. Please make it so that the bomber planes don't go crashing into him'.[22] She pleaded with God intensely, while the noise of the planes grew louder and louder. But once the planes had gone, Ijeoma and her mother found her father dead in the ruins of their house. In her recollection Ijeoma cannot but conclude that, 'It didn't appear that God had been bothered to answer my prayer'.[23] Some time later, with another raid, their church building—'that holy construction of a place that was responsible for keeping our faith and hope intact'—was also demolished.[24] The subtext is that along with the building, her faith in God was profoundly shaken, if not lost, as all the prayers for God's intervention appeared to be futile.

Later in the novel, the thought that God is perhaps not even bothered to attend to her prayers appears to affect Ijeoma's ability to pray. The story narrates two incidents where she cannot pray. In both cases, this relates specifically to her sexuality. The first time is after the grammar school teacher catches her and Amina, and Ijeoma's mother has taken her back. Wandering through the new town, the girl enters an empty church, where she is overwhelmed by the sense of holiness of the place and feels an urge to pray for forgiveness for her sexual acts. She has a sense of guilt and wants to ask God to turn her thoughts away from Amina and pursue a different course of action. However, when she opens her mouth to pray, somehow the words of prayer do not come.[25] The novel here illustrates Wariboko's point that in Pentecostalism, 'desire for holiness creates disgust, which in turn haunts it'.[26] Later that same day, when Ijeoma's mother prays with her, asking God to protect her daughter from the Devil and his temptations, Ijeoma cannot concentrate on the prayer, and even struggles to utter the closing word, 'Amen'. The word amen means 'may it be so', and she is clearly not in agreement that it might be so.

The second incident is again with her mother, who has given Ijeoma daily Bible study lessons for months, as part of the process of cleansing her daughter's soul. But on the day they finally reach the end of the Old Testament, Ijeoma tells her that she is still thinking of Amina. It leaves her mother besides herself, and she screams to ask God for forgiveness 'especially for that particular sin in you.'[27] Her mother insists that she must pray, as this is her only hope. However, Ijeoma cannot pray as her mother's screaming orders wreak havoc in her mind. These are orders for her to kneel and pray, and cries that her actions have been sinful, terribly disrespectful, and that only God can save her.

One explanation for the two subsequent failures of prayer, as suggested earlier, is that Ijeoma might be losing her faith, having questioned whether God is bothered to hear her prayers. However, another possible reason is that Ijeoma's faith itself is changing, as she begins to wonder whether or not God has a problem with her sexuality in the first place. As much as the first incident refers to feelings of guilt, two pages later we read that Ijeoma starts to question her mother's interpretation of biblical passages and their relevance for what had grown between her and Amina (as discussed below). Her mother, however, has yet another explanatory framework.

Deliverance

In the style of Nigerian Pentecostalism, in which 'the spell of the invisible' looms everywhere,[28] Ijeoma's mother becomes more and more convinced that whatever is wrong with her daughter is caused by spiritual forces.

Shortly after Ijeoma has rejoined her, away from the temptations at the grammar school teacher's place, and the two of them have started their Bible studies, her mother prays to God to protect her daughter 'from the devil that has come to take her innocent soul away'.[29] Later in the story, after the second incident where Ijeoma is unable to pray, her mother reports back to her: 'I've been thinking. It's not you. ... No, it's not you at all. There's nothing wrong with you. It's the devil causing you to be this way'.[30] This diagnosis is followed by a prayer of deliverance, in which she mobilises her spiritual power in order for the devil to leave her daughter:

> 'In the name of God the Almighty, I order you to come out of her,' she said. Her voice was progressively louder each time she repeated it, but still controlled: 'In the name of the Almighty God, I order you to leave my child alone.'[31]

The belief that demonic forces can infiltrate the body, leading it into sin and making it impure, is widespread in African Pentecostal Christian circles. Homosexuality in particular is often associated with the Devil and seen as a form of spiritual bondage.[32]

As much as her mother loudly prays herself into exhaustion, crying to cast the devil out, it has no effect on Ijeoma; no demon appears to be leaving her body. Like the prayers, the deliverance appears to have failed, too, and is not re-attempted. Yet her mother's suggestion that the love between her and Amina is 'the influence of demonic spirits' does settle in Ijeoma's mind.[33] Later on in the novel, when she is dating Ndidi, she narrates: 'I began to believe myself a witch under the influence of the devil, and if

Mama's exorcism had not worked, then it seemed that I owed it to myself to find something that would. Self-purification was the goal'.[34] The passage illustrates the constant work on the self that Pentecostal forms of Christianity require believers to undertake, battling sinful desires and the spiritual forces that fuel them, and striving to be morally and spiritually pure. However, for Ijeoma as for many same-sex loving people, this struggle is never-ending, because sexual desires and activities affect 'the possibilities for their salvation and the actualization of the saved self'.[35] The sub-text of the novel is that neither exorcism nor self-purification can effectively overcome same-sex attraction. Even Ijeoma's mother, at the end of the book, finally concedes that 'God who created you, must have known what He did. Enough is enough'.[36] Theologically, this is the eureka moment: the profound realisation that, in fact, same-sex sexuality is of God, not of the Devil. The closing sentence of the novel suggests that in this realisation both Ijeoma and her mother find peace and life.

Bible

Woven through the narration of failed prayer and deliverance is the story of the Bible study lessons that Ijeoma receives from her mother. With daily sessions, over a period of six months, they make it through the whole Bible. Where her mother intends these lessons as a space to teach her daughter the 'biblical truth' regarding her forbidden desire, for Ijeoma it becomes a space to increasingly question this truth.

The first lesson, about the Genesis creation story of Adam and Eve, is used by her mother to get the message across that it is supposed to be 'man and wife, Adam *na* Eve', adding that 'if God wanted it to be otherwise, would He not have included it that other way in the Bible?'[37] It conveys the traditional interpretation of the story, reinforcing the norm of heterosexual marriage—a norm that, in the novel, appears to be religious as much as cultural (indeed, as prefigured in the traditional symbolic meaning of the udala tree). The expectation that 'God willing' one day Ijeoma will be married to a husband is instilled in her early on.[38] Later in the story, we learn that she begins to question her mother's interpretation of the biblical story, and thus also to question the norm of heterosexual marriage. Being reminded of a lesson her father once taught her about allegorical and figurative, rather than literal interpretations of stories, she wonders why most readers of the Bible stick to selective literal interpretations of this sacred Scripture. Ijeoma muses that the Bible, and particularly the Genesis creation story, allow for 'infinite possibilities' of interpretation.[39] The message Ijeoma draws out of the story is that Adam and Eve are 'symbols of companionship',[40] but that such companionship can be realised in different forms of relationships, both between people of mixed and of the same sex, as well as 'infinite' other possibilities.

Ijeoma's ability to imagine alternative interpretation of biblical texts often applied to same-sex relationships continues to manifest itself throughout the story. For instance, when her mother reads her the story of Sodom and Gomorrah—which is traditionally used to frame homosexuality as 'sodomy', the sin that led God to destroy these cities—Ijeoma counters that interpretation. She suggests instead that it could 'simply have been a lesson on hospitality', because the people of Sodom were 'selfish and inhospitable and violent'.[41] Later, when they discuss the rather horrible story in the book of Judges, chapter 19, her mother uses it to underline the 'abomination' of homosexuality, but Ijeoma suggests that it is about sexual violence of the worst kind: 'The men offered up the women because they were cowards and the worst kind of men possible. What kind of men offer up their daughters and wives to be raped in place of themselves?'[42] Unsurprisingly, her mother is not impressed by this inquisitive way of reading the Bible and by the possibility of alternative interpretations. For her, 'the Bible is the Bible and not to be questioned'.[43] She represents the fundamentalist approach to the Bible that is dominant in most Nigerian Pentecostal readings of the text.

Struggling with this normative and rigid Bible interpretation, Ijeoma begins to doubt the relevance of the holy book in the first place:

> The Bible was beginning to feel almost negligible, as it was seeming to me more and more impossible to know exactly what God could really have meant.[44]

> I wondered about the Bible as a whole. Maybe the entire thing was just a history of a certain culture, specific to that particular time and place, which made it hard for us now to understand, and which maybe even made it not applicable for us today.[45]

These passages reflect a process that many same-sex loving people, who grow up in a Christian context where the Bible is used against them, may go through: a process in which they begin to question the relevance of Scripture to speak to their experiences and lives, perhaps even question the status of the Bible as the word of God. Yet for Ijeoma, as for many other people in her situation, this process is not straightforward. The socio-cultural status of the Bible as a text with divine authority is strong and deeply ingrained, making it difficult for her to simply liberate herself from it. Instead, as the novel unfolds she does not continue her questioning of the Bible but rather falls back on the way it is commonly interpreted in her environment.

Thus, in a conversation with her first lover, Ijeoma quotes the Gospel of John 3:16, the verse about God's abundant love for humankind as shown in Jesus Christ, in order to convince Amina that 'God loves us all the same' and that 'He didn't put any qualifiers on His love'.[46] Yet later in the novel, looking back at her relationships with women, she believes that 'there was a real possibility of God punishing me for the nature of my love'.[47] Similarly, although Ijeoma at one stage in the novel expresses the belief that she 'had not committed any type of abomination', later she reverts to this again, ready to confess to her then husband the abomination she has committed in the past.[48] Far from presenting a straightforward liberatory trajectory, the novel narrates how Ijeoma continues to struggle with the Bible and the internalised homophobic biblical messages of her youth. This is further reflected in the story about Ijeoma's second love affair, with Ndidi. At the beginning of it, we read that Ijeoma 'had not been convinced by any of Mama's interpretations of the Bible'.[49] Yet still, memories of the Bible studies with her mother rush back to her when she hesitantly enters into the relationship. As a result, she struggles to fully give herself to it. After an intimate evening spent with Ndidi, she finds herself in bed, 'the images of Mama interspersed with a thunderous sound that, in the dream, was the voice of God, scolding also like Mama reprimanding, condemning me for my sins'.[50] Early the next morning she goes to church, but again cannot find the words to pray. She is then reminded of another biblical passage, more affirming this time: John 8, the story about Jesus and the woman caught in adultery. Reminding herself of Jesus' words to the woman's accusers—that those who are without sin can cast the first stone at her—she feels a 'slow rising of relief'.[51] This verse brings her relief, not because it implies that homosexuality is not sinful, but because it suggests that it is one among many other sins, and that for Jesus there is no difference between sinners. It is also an empowering recollection in that it brings forth a Jesus who is understanding, tolerant and forgiving.

In one story, even in a single protagonist, the novel illustrates the multiple possibilities of interpreting the Bible in relation to the issue of same-sex love: from literalist to historical to allegorical interpretations; from messages of punishment and abomination, to forgiveness of sin, to acceptance of the sinner, to inclusive love. The novel further reflects the complex process through which same-sex loving people navigate and negotiate Scripture, as Ijeoma moves back and forth between these conflicting interpretations and messages. Doing so, *Under the Udala Trees* not only recognises that the Bible itself is 'a site of struggle' in which 'the debate about homosexuality is being fought' in contemporary Africa,[52] but also creatively engages with this space, opening up possibilities of alternative ways of reading the Bible.

Conclusion

Under the Udala Trees is a beautiful novel that contributes to the emerging body of queer literary writing in Nigeria and Africa. Where in African queer writing, literary and otherwise, Christianity is sometimes depicted one-sidedly as a source of homophobia, this novel certainly does not ignore that reality but presents a more nuanced and multi-layered picture. In the words of the protagonist, Ijeoma, the novel alludes to 'infinite possibilities',[53] of sexuality but also of Christianity. Indeed, as much as the novel emphasises that normative understandings of the Bible and the Christian faith in Nigeria operate to suppress same-sex desire and oppress same-sex loving people, it also suggests that Christianity is filled with queer possibilities—that there is a potential within Christian traditions to affirm love, sexuality and the erotic in multiple forms. Indeed, this novel is perhaps 'prophetic', because of its 'capacities to anticipate a space for the Christian legitimacy of female same-sex desire'.[54]

Ijeoma struggles for years, with her sexuality, the Bible and her faith in God. Yet at the very end of the novel, in the epilogue, it appears that her struggle has come to an end and has been overcome. She begins to conceptualise God as an artist who utilises the world as his canvas. She now approaches the Old and the New Testaments as testimonies of God's commitment and endorsement of change. In this scheme, the rules of the Bible will not be fixed but will always be in flux. Thus, perhaps God is still speaking and will always continue to do so. She embraces the idea that maybe God is 'still creating new covenants'.[55] This passage presents the reader with an articulation of Christian queer theology. It articulates an understanding in which change—social, cultural, religious change—is part of how God designed the world. Instead of sticking to static and unchangeable interpretations of the Bible and doctrine, this understanding embraces a commitment to transformation, it encourages an ethic and spirituality of flexibility and openness for the future. Thus, critiquing popular forms of Nigerian Christianity with their strongly heteronormative and homophobic inclinations, *Under the Udala Trees* firmly expresses the belief that God is not concerned with conserving an imagined authentically heterosexual Nigerian past, but with making all things new.

10

CHRISTIANITY AND VISUAL ACTIVISM IN KENYAN QUEER FILM

RAFIKI AND *SAME LOVE*

In recent years, several countries on the African continent have witnessed the emergence of a new genre of films: queer-themed audio-visual productions. This reflects an increasingly visible and bold movement of lgbti and queer activism and advocacy who, in addition to traditional forms of social mobilisation, also adopt a range of creative and artistic methods in order to build what Keguro Macharia has called 'queer African archives'.[1] The boundaries of the genre of 'queer film' are diffuse as it includes documentaries, music videos and drama films, which often reflect 'the various material and political constraints faced by African audiences and African filmmakers in a global world'.[2] Writing about documentary films that feature lgbti African lives and experiences, the Nigerian activist and writer Unoma Azuah states that these are forms of 'visual activism'. Her words apply to audio-visual productions more generally:

> The place of documentaries in educating, changing lives, and affecting social changes cannot be overemphasised; visual stories

are easily absorbed compared to textual representation. Documentaries have a reach that is greater than the printed word and is seen by a larger audience.[3]

Conceptualising such films as a 'visual topography where both fiction and the real merge', Azuah suggests that their main purpose is to 'raise people's awareness of the discrimination faced by the LGBT community'.[4] The latter may be true for the specific documentary she discusses (the 2013 documentary *Born This Way*, about lgbti activists in Cameroon). However, with regard to the forms of visual activism under discussion in this chapter, we suggest that in addition to awareness-building, education and sensitisation among the public, there is another important purpose as well: these productions open up spaces for alternative imagination; they manifest new possibilities; they contribute to queer world-making.

In this chapter, we focus on two Kenyan audio-visual productions: the 2016 music video *Same Love (Remix)*, produced by the hip hop group Art Attack led by artist and activist George Barasa, and the 2018 film *Rafiki*, by the director Wanuri Kahiu. Our interest in this chapter is specifically in the way these films engage with Christianity as a key site of struggle about same-sex love in Kenya, but also as a site of alternative imagination. As we will argue, both films critique dominant forms of Christianity in Kenya for their intricate connection to the politics of homophobia, yet they also allude to the possibility of a queer reclaiming of Christianity as a site of affirmation and empowerment of same-sex loving people.

Same Love and Rafiki: *Two Kenyan queer films*

Same Love (Remix) is a remix of the 2012 *Same Love* music video by the American hip hop duo Macklemore & Ryan Lewis. It was produced by the Kenyan hip hop group Art Attack, under the leadership of the openly gay musician and activist, George Barasa (also known as Joji Baro), and was released in February 2016 on YouTube. The Kenyan version has different lyrics and different visual material compared to the American original, although the chorus by Mary Lambert has been left intact. The song tells the story of a young boy growing up, falling in love with another boy, coming out to his parents and being rejected, and finally committing suicide. This dramatic story, which Barasa has claimed is based on his life story, is somewhat in contrast with images that feature both a male and a female same-sex couple having fun and making love.[5] Presented on YouTube as 'A Kenyan song about same-sex rights, gay rights, LGBT struggles, gender equalities, gay struggles and civil liberties for all sexual orientations', the video in its imagery reflects a Kenyan aesthetic. The scenery in which the two same-sex couples enjoy playful, romantic and intimate time together is easy to recognise for the Kenyan viewer, especially from an urban middle class back-ground: the scenes of the young male couple are set in Fourteen Falls Park in Thika, forty miles out of Nairobi, and in Paradise Lost, a recreational resort just out of Nairobi, while the scenes of the young female couple are set in the Arboretum, a park in central Nairobi. In particular the latter setting is politically sig-nificant, as the Arboretum is directly adjacent to State House, the official presidential residence, and has been the setting of several gospel music videos, thus taking part 'in interdenomina-tional religious events that correspond to the vague [Christian] national ideology that cements the country'.[6] The lyrics and part of the imagery of the video appeal to broader (pan-)African aes-thetics and audiences, for instance by mentioning countries such as Uganda and Nigeria, by including visual material from South Africa, Ghana and Uganda, and by referencing the American civil rights movement and the name of Martin Luther King Jr. Indeed, the music genre of the video, hip hop, is typically associated with East African and broader African and black aesthetics. The song, which includes some explicitly religious language, illustrates the fluid boundaries between hip hop and gospel music, while its explicit political message illustrates the way in which popular music serves as a method of social critique.[7] By including visual material of gay culture and socio-political protests across the world, *Same Love* also inscribes itself in a global movement of gay and lesbian pride (the film opens with a rainbow flag) and of human rights and social justice activism.

Rafiki (the Swahili word for 'friend') is a 2018 drama film based on the story 'Jambula Tree' for which Ugandan writer Monica Arac de Nyeko won the 2007 Caine Prize for African Writing. Directed by Kenyan film maker Wahuri Kahiu, *Rafiki* tells the story of an emerging friendship and blossoming love between two young women, Kena and Ziki. The film is set in a vibrant urban middle class neighbourhood in Nairobi complete with *boda boda* (motorbike taxi) drivers, small shops and kiosks, a church and a pastor, and gossiping neighbours. The love story unfolds against the background of political rivalry as the fathers of the two girls compete for the same seat in the county assembly, with Ziki's well-off father having considerably more resources for his campaign than Kena's, who is a small shop owner. Taiwo Adetunji Osinubi argues that Kahiu's film reflects the mission of her company called AFROBUBBLEGUM, to create 'fun, fierce and frivolous African art'; hence the film avoids 'the pessimistic narratives about sexual minorities in African countries', and instead is 'filled with bright colours and set to a vibrant Afro-pop sound track'.[8] Yet the vibrancy of colour and sound cannot hide the reality of day to day homophobia, with the known gay guy (referred to as *shoga*, which is the Swahili equivalent of faggot) in the neighbourhood facing verbal and physical aggression, and with the slowly blossoming love between Kena and Ziki being met with taboo from their parents (apart from Kena's father), the pastor, and the community that, in the end, engages in an act of mob violence against the two girls. The pair are separated, with Ziki being sent to London by her parents. Yet the message of hope that runs through the film prevails as Kena and Ziki are united in the closing scene, the suggestion being that their love has survived and will have a future. As Taiwo Adetunji Osinubi puts the significance of *Rafiki*'s overall plot and representation:

> Kahiu achieves an understated quality through an assiduous aesthetics of loose ends and incompletion that proposes probing questions while gesturing towards horizons of future resolutions. Considering the slow process of LGBTQ rights claims in political domains across Africa, the film's accent on incompletion and its refusal to stitch all narrative strands into exemplary closure captures the spirit of the times.[9]

Same Love and *Rafiki* are very different films, most obviously in their genre (a music video versus a drama film) and in their ending (suicide versus a reunited couple). Yet they both have an interest in making visible the existence of same-sex love in ordinary Kenyan spaces. The films demonstrate, to use Kenyan scholar Eddie Ombagi's words, how Kenya, and urban space in Nairobi specifically, has become 'a site of and frame for the contradictions of queer livability on one hand and queer visibility on the other.'[10] For that reason, both productions became subject to a ban by the Kenya Film Classification Board, which ironically only added to the interest of the public, both locally and internationally, in these films. Among many other podiums, *Same Love* was screened at the Queer Kampala International Film Festival in 2017, and *Rafiki* at the Cannes Film Festival in 2018. Of interest to this chapter is another commonality between the two films: they both engage with Christianity as a critical site of the contestation over same-sex love, but also—subtly, in the case of *Rafiki*, or more explicitly in the case of *Same Love*—as a site that can be reimagined and reclaimed. In *Same Love*, we see images of religious leaders, references to God and to the devil, and a quotation from the Bible. In *Rafiki*, a billboard with a religious message and the symbol of a crucifix appear at the beginning; Kena's mother is depicted as a deeply religious character; the church appears as an important space in the neighbourhood, and the pastor as a prominent and influential figure. Thus, the films demonstrate how Christian language and symbols are part of public and popular culture in Kenya, but more than that, how they are also part of emerging Kenyan queer aesthetics.

Denouncing Christian homophobia

Christianity has become highly invested in the politics of homophobia in many African countries, Kenya included. Both films critically foreground the ways in which Christian institutions and leaders are fuelling the hatred against gay and lesbian people, and in which biblical texts and Christian beliefs are used to legitimise that hatred.

In the *Same Love* video, the rap lyrics state: 'Church rules, street rules / Court rules, school rules / Hate is the new love / kill, maim, talk tough / Homophobia is the new African culture'. These lyrics are accompanied by footage of the 'Protect the Family March', which took place in July 2015 in Nairobi and was organised by several Christian organisations, notably the Catholic Justice and Peace Commission, the Evangelical Alliance of Kenya and the Kenya Christian Professional Forum. The timing of this march was significant; it occurred just ahead of a state visit by US President Barack Obama, the point being, in the words of Bishop Mark Kariuki of the Evangelical Alliance, to make it clear to Obama that he 'should respect the faith, culture and people of Kenya' and 'should not push [homosexuality] as one of his main agendas in the country'.[11] Later on in the song, the lyrics state that the hate gay people face is 'too much, all in the name of piety'. Clearly, the song suggests that the church as a powerful institution in Kenyan society, and religion as a key moral compass of Kenyan people, has made homophobia indeed 'the new African culture', leading to the exclusion of gay people from their families and communities, and to hatred and violence being directed at them.

The latter point is illustrated in *Rafiki*. The two male friends with whom Kena tends to hang out use homophobic slurs against another young man in the neighbourhood, whose effeminate appearance serves to create the impression that he is gay. Referring to him as *shoga* (faggot), one of her friends rhetorically asks, 'Do you think God is just watching men fuck each other?', before aggressively bumping against him. A more elaborate scene is the pastor of the local church in the neighbourhood, who one Sunday begins to praise his wife and the blessing of his heterosexual marriage, and then uses that as a steppingstone towards anti-gay speech:

> What surprises me is that there are Kenyans who are challenging the government because of their stand on same-sex marriage. They say it's a human right. What is a human right? Isn't it God who decides what is right and what isn't? Are we going to ignore God? Don't accept to be lost. Because God's laws don't change like human laws or your country's.

This kind of preaching, directly opposing the recognition of gay and lesbian human rights, is widespread in Kenya as in several other African countries. For instance, in 2019, at a time when the Kenyan high court was dealing with a petition calling for the decriminalisation of homosexuality, many preachers and church leaders explicitly denounced this petition, from the pulpit and in the media. Not only religious leaders but also high-profile politicians, such as Deputy President William Ruto, have frequently referred to the Bible and to Kenyan religious and cultural values to point out that gay rights could never be recognised in the country. Whether or not Ruto and others are driven by personal convictions, or resort to gay bashing in order to gain political mileage, is unclear. But the point is that there is a strong public discourse in Kenya reinforcing the view that homosexuality is a dehumanising act, and that gay and lesbian rights therefore cannot be human rights.

The Bible quotation in the above fragment from the pastor's sermon is taken from Romans 1: 26–27. This is one of the few biblical texts that explicitly refer to female same-sex relationships, and which suggest that same-sex desire, both between men and between women, is 'unnatural'. *Rafiki* appears to counter such a view by giving a human face to its main characters. Kena and Ziki, two young Kenyan women, did not learn homosexuality from the West, nor are they engaging in a same-sex relationship for money or other benefits, as popular Kenyan views would have it. Instead, their love for each other is born out of their hearts; it reflects who they are; there is nothing 'unnatural' about it, and therefore it cannot be beaten out of them.

Later in the film, several people attending the church service appear to be involved in the act of mob violence against Kena and Ziki. In a scene at the beginning, we overhear Kena's deeply religious mother speaking to a friend on the phone, saying: 'We shall not bring upon the afflictions of Egypt.' In the context of the narrative of the film, this can be interpreted as suggesting that homosexuality, for religious Kenyans, is one of the sins that might well bring afflictions upon Kenya. In this view, not only gay people themselves, but the whole of society, will suffer under God's punishment if the country allows such an 'abomination'. This view is far from marginal in Kenya, given that hugely popular Pentecostal figures such as prophet David Owuor, leader of the Ministry of Repentance and Holiness, for many years have pointed at 'sexual sin' as a main reason why God would send his wrath upon the country.[12]

Resisting narratives of demonisation

For Pentecostal figures such as Owuor, homosexuality is not just one among many other sins, but is most directly associated with the Devil. This understanding is widespread in many parts of Africa where Pentecostal Christianity, which often has a strong concern with the reality of demonic forces and of the nearing end times, has become a highly influential discourse shaping people's opinions and public debates.[13] Both *Same Love* and *Rafiki* take on this perception and resist the demonisation of homosexuality and of gay and lesbian people.

In the *Same Love* song, the main character confides in his parents, telling them that he is in love with another boy, only to be harshly rejected by them:

Mummy said I ain't your Mummy, you're the son of the Devil
and Daddy said go fool 'fore I strangle you devil;
and for the last six years my parents have never seen me;
every day I bleed tears hoping that they wish to see me.

The footage accompanying these lyrics show the actor, George Barasa himself, being kicked out of the house. Thus, the song's narrative draws critical attention to the painful effects of beliefs that same-sex love is caused by the Devil: such a discourse of demonisation leads to the rejection of children by their parents and it causes severe alienation between human beings who are united through blood ties.

Rafiki also illustrates the prevalence and effects of such popular Christian views. After Kena has been brutally harassed in an act of mob violence by community members, her father, who is supportive of her, brings her back to her mother, with whom she stayed after the separation of her parents. Her mother, in a highly accusatory tone, says to her father:

Are you forgetting the demons that have possessed this child? You want to accept those demons in this house? I am concentrating on cleansing her. She is full of demons and it is because of you, you and those women out there.

Indeed, this marks the estrangement between Kena and her mother, the latter failing to offer the support and love that her traumatised daughter needs. Instead, Kena is taken to church, where her mother asks the pastor to pray over her daughter and exorcise her from the demons possessing her. The pastor's deliverance prayer is recorded as follows:

> We're humbled and our hearts are broken. We pray to you merciful God to save this soul. We lift up your name. You are able. Show mercy on Kena. Let your blessing cover her life. Let your grace be shown. Show us your power. Oh God be God. Thank you Lord. Thank you, gracious God. We take authority in your name. We say every stronghold is broken.

The term 'stronghold' is typical of the Pentecostal terminology of deliverance and spiritual warfare. The underlying belief is that specific spaces and places are the playing ground of malicious forces that can only be conquered by calling upon the power of God. In this case, it is Kena's body that is believed to be spiritually contaminated and therefore in need of deliverance, demonstrating the Pentecostal concern with the spiritual purity of the body, particularly the female body.[14] In the worldview of spiritual warfare practitioners, making a positive confession—stating that 'every stronghold is broken' in the name of God or Christ—is a way to claim back spiritual territory from demonic agents and to subject it to the authority of God. However, in the narrative of the film, it appears that the deliverance fails. Kena is as tomboyish, masculine-performing and same-sex loving after the ritual prayer as she was before. In this way, the film suggests that non-conforming gender identity and sexual orientation cannot be 'healed' or 'corrected' through spiritual interventions, the main reason being that there is nothing wrong or unnatural with it in the first place. Kena's mum may believe in Jehovah-Rapha, that is, God who heals, but perhaps it is she herself, rather than her daughter, who needs healing.

God of the impossible, God of love

As much as both films are critical about the way in which Christianity is driving the attitudes against gay and lesbian people, they also allude to the potential of Christian faith to serve as a site of affirmation and empowerment of same-sex loving people. *Rafiki* does so in a more subtle way, while *Same Love* does so more explicitly.

At the beginning of *Rafiki*, we see a billboard with the text: 'I have no other God but you. You have done what no man has done. You will do what no man can do.' This line is taken from a gospel song, 'No Other God', by the Nigerian gospel artist Nathaniel Bassey. At first sight, the image of the billboard illustrates the way in which Christian language, through music and in other forms, infuses public culture and has become part of the street aesthetics of urban life in a country like Kenya. However, this specific text on the billboard entails a promise and can be read as prophetic. Watching the film, one may reach the conclusion that gay rights are impossible in Kenya, indeed that same-sex love cannot be recognised or even exist in the country. However, God has done what no man has done, and God will do what no man can do. In other words, with God all things are possible.[15] With God, even the recognition of love between people of the same gender is not something that might eventually happen, sometime in the distant future; instead it is actually within reach. The film does not elaborate on this, but its positive ending with Kena and Ziki being reunited does allow for such an optimistic interpretation. Earlier in the film, we hear the pastor asking rhetorically, 'Isn't it God who decides what is right and what isn't?' It appears as if the closing scene of *Rafiki* is an answer to this question, underlining the title of the film: friendship will prevail, love will prevail, because these are the things that are right in God's eyes.

The *Same Love* video allows more directly for such a theological interpretation, because the lyrics explicitly adopt religious language. At the end of the song, the rapper recites a passage from the Bible (1 Corinthians 13):

Love is patient
Love is kind
Love is selfless
Love is faithful
Love is full of hope
Love is full of trust
Love is not proud.

This quotation is concluded with the statement 'Love is God and God is love', which is not part of the passage of 1 Corinthians but reflects a more general biblical theme identifying God with love.

The insertion of a biblical passage in the *Same Love* song is significant, as it illustrates how the Bible, and Christian language, is incorporated into a text of popular culture such as a music video. It further demonstrates how the Bible is engaged and appropriated not only by those who oppose same-sex relationships and gay and lesbian rights, but also by those who defend them. This speaks to the malleability of the Bible, and its openness to multiple interpretations. In this case, the specific choice of biblical text is highly significant because 1 Corinthians 13 is commonly used in church wedding services, making it a symbolic text for Christian marriage. The song reclaims this text and applies it to the love between same-sex couples. This is not so much in order to advocate same-sex marriage, but to make a more fundamental claim for the recognition of the validity of same-sex loving relationships, as equally grounded in God as the source of love that exists between human beings. Thus the song conveys the key message that loving relationships, both between people of the same and of different genders, are inspired by and embedded in God's all-encompassing love. The emphasis on love is, simultaneously, a critique of the violence, rejection and demonisation of same-sex loving people.

The *Same Love* song's centring of a language of love—Christian love, for that matter—is important, because popular discourses about homosexuality in Kenya and other parts of Africa often reduce same-sex relationships to sex. Even in public health discourses, gay people are reduced to 'men who have sex with men' or 'women who have sex with women', as if sex between people of the same gender is merely a physical act and is unrelated to intimacy, romance and love. Thus, the language of love in the song helps to humanise same-sex relationships and the people involved in them. Just like any other human beings, they experience, express and enjoy love in its manifold forms. The importance of recognising this truth is made evident in the contrast between the lyrics and the footage in the video. While the rapper recites the above-quoted biblical text about love, and concludes by stating that God is the source of love, in the video we see the main character collapse on the floor after swallowing some pills, followed by a suicide note appearing on the screen. The note reads:

> I'm tired of the pressure, tired of the pain, tired of the stigmatisation.
> Tired of the insults and the attacks and the hate!
> Goodbye world!
> Mummy, I love you.
> Wish I wasn't born this way.

The implicit message of the video is that this is what happens when we continue to denounce fellow human beings for whom and how they love. When people are denied the possibility of love, they find death. On the other hand, when people are affirmed in their ability to love, they find life in abundance.

The *Same Love* video includes yet another reference to God. The lyrics mention two countries, Nigeria and Uganda, which in 2013 both gained international headlines for the passing of new anti-homosexuality legislation that harshened the penalties for same-sex practices and the 'propaganda' of homosexuality. Addressing this tendency to further criminalise homosexuality, the song continues by stating:

> It's time for new laws
> Not time for new wars
> We come from the same God,
> Cut from the same cord,
> Share the same pain
> And share the same skin.

These few lines are loaded and deep. They speak of a shared humanity and a shared identity. The shared cord is a powerful cultural symbol. The idea of coming from the same God negates the popular idea raised earlier that gay and lesbian people are 'of the devil'. There is the contrast between the time for new (more same-sex friendly) laws versus new wars, that is, more hatred and violence. There is also the repetition of the word 'same' (God, cord, pain, skin), which is a refusal to endorse the 'othering' of gay and lesbian people.

The lyrics here reflect the belief in the unity of African people as being created by God. This is rooted in a religious version of pan-Africanist thought, represented by illustrious figures such as W. E. B. Du Bois, whose poem 'Credo' opens with an affirmation of faith in God who created all humankind, but which then continues by highlighting the particular beauty and strength of 'the Negro race', and expresses the belief in the fundamental liberty and freedom of all people.[16] There is no evidence that the makers of *Same Love* were directly inspired by Du Bois, but they do appear to be inspired by the African American civil rights struggle. The lyrics refer to the spirit of Martin Luther King Jr., which is claimed to 'live on' in those Africans who fight for gay and lesbian human rights today. The opening statement of the song draws a direct connection between the civil rights movement and the African gay rights movement:

> This song is dedicated to the New Slaves, the New Blacks, the New Jews, the New Minorities for whom we need a civil rights movement, maybe a sex rights movement. Especially in Africa.

In this way, the *Same Love* video inscribes itself, and its cause of same-sex rights, into a broader narrative of African and Black liberation. This allows for a creative and progressive reimagining of African identity—an imagination that, importantly, is rooted in the belief in God as supportive of this long-term struggle for human dignity and freedom.

Conclusion

The film *Rafiki* and the music video *Same Love* are important forms of visual activism as they make visible what hitherto has largely remained invisible to Kenyan audiences: the reality of same-sex love in Kenyan spaces, and the existence of same-sex loving people as part of Kenyan communities. Both audio-visual texts criticise the narratives of homophobia that dominate Kenyan society, and the religious ideologies fuelling them. Yet they also allow for an alternative imagination of what it means to be Kenyan and what it means to be African. In a context such as Kenya, public space and popular culture has become 'Pentecostalised', that is, deeply influenced by Pentecostal forms of Christianity. Both *Rafiki* and *Same Love* reflect the central role of this popular religious culture, incorporating its manifestations in their audio-visual texts. Yet they also speak back to it, challenging the conservative Christian monopoly on defining what is morally acceptable and salvific in postcolonial Africa. Doing so, they allude to ways in which Christian beliefs, texts and symbols can also inspire and buttress an alternative imagination. Thus, in fact both films open up alternative ways of imagining Christianity, as a source of progressive politics that affirms the human dignity and rights of people, regardless of their gender and sexuality.

CONCLUSION

We intended this book to reconstruct, explore and stimulate emerging imaginative narratives of sexuality and Christianity in Africa. Hopefully, reading this book has sparked the imagination of the reader, and we eagerly look forward to seeing the results in any form possible. However, as the Nigerian literary scholar Chielozona Eze reminds us, 'imagination is not an altogether innocent affair'. 'The act of remembering', he points out, 'is in itself not always complete; it is largely selective. Imagination constructs, or rather reconstructs what is in some way (selectively) contained in the memory to produce new ideas'.[1] On that note we would like to conclude this book, fully aware of the incomplete, selective and open-ended account offered in the preceding pages. We do so in the hope, and with the expectation, that the material presented here has demonstrated how sexuality and Christianity can be, and are being, creatively thought together in innovative and progressive ways, enabling new imaginations of African futures.

Although we were tempted to leave this book open-ended, without a conclusion, Eze's comment about imagination not being innocent inspires us to address a concern that some readers may have had while reading this book: a concern about the very idea of Christianity as a possible constructive source for imagining Africa's future in a queer direction. Some readers might feel that this book, and the arguments and perspectives it has foregrounded, are naïve if not downright ignorant of the problematic historical and contemporary manifestation of Christianity on the continent. Especially in the light of the current debates about decolonisation, one might be rather hesitant to suggest that Christianity, as a religion associated with colonialism, neo-colonialism and ongoing forms of coloniality, can play any constructive role in a decolonial African queer political project. It is telling that in a 2018 book about decolonising Africa, *Epistemic Freedom in Africa* by Sabelo Ndlovu-Gatsheni, Christianity is only mentioned a few times, each time in relation to the practice of forced conversion.[2] Has Christianity not lost its innocence? Does a decolonisation of the mind, to use Ngũgĩ wa Thiong'o's phrase, not require a de-Christianisation of the African psyche? Have we as authors not been too selective and perhaps subjective in foregrounding Christianity as a possible, even critical, resource for imagining an African future free from the oppression that is apparently inscribed in the history of this religion on the continent?

Arguably, the question of the relationship between Christianity, decolonisation and queer politics in Africa is too big and complex to deal with here in any satisfactory way. Partly, our response to the above concern is pragmatic: Christianity is too popular in contemporary African societies, embraced by millions of people—including many lgbti people—at a grassroots level as a tradition that helps them to imagine and engage the world. A project of de-Christianisation is unlikely to have any widespread appeal and impact any time soon. If anything, Christianity appears set to continue holding a significant share of the African religious market, inserting itself into the public domain, and influencing society, politics and popular culture. Given that situation, it might be strategic to engage Christianity critically, creatively and constructively and explore its potential for opening up alternative possibilities and futures. But this is not merely pragmatic; it is rooted in the conviction that Christianity, as any other religion, is not homogenous and monolithic but is, in fact, a site of multiple, often competing and conflicting, expressions and interpretations. Neither we as authors, nor the thinkers, organisations, activists and artists whose work we have discussed in this book, are ignorant of the problematic manifestations and impacts of Christianity in African societies, historically and to date. In fact, the awareness of this problem is reflected throughout this book, as each of the presented case studies indicates critiques of dominant forms of Christianity and their social and political effects. However, they also allude to the possibility of alternative theologies and politics that are emerging from Christian ideas, practices and symbols. Thus, by means of a conclusion, let us briefly capture the contours of these alternative, decolonial and queer African Christian theologies and politics that we see slowly emerging from the case studies presented.

Intersectionality

Any constructive reimagination of sexuality and Christianity in Africa will need to foreground the importance of intersectionality. This is the idea that different social categories such as of gender, sexuality, race, class, and ethnicity, create interdependent and overlapping inequalities and structures of oppression and marginalisation. The quest for social justice therefore is comprehensive. As the popular saying goes, 'Justice denied to one is justice denied to all'. As a result of this insight, the struggle for sexual and gender diversity in contemporary Africa cannot be a single-issue campaign, or such a campaign will reinforce the already existing idea that lgbti rights are a middle class issue driven by Western-inspired agendas. In various ways, the chapters in this book have foregrounded how different categories of oppression and marginalisation are interconnected and can reinforce each other. Tutu powerfully connected the struggle for racial equality to the struggle for gay and lesbian rights. Oduyoye effectively used her feminist commitment to gender equality to demonstrate how hetero-patriarchal cultures marginalise not only women but also sexual minorities. Dube and EHAIA foreground how HIV in Africa puts those who are socially and economically marginalised at the greatest risk: the poor, women, sex workers and sexual minorities. Kenmogne and Dube both build on their concern with the environment to articulate thoughts that emphasise the holistic nature of creation, affirming the earth as a Body and therewith all the human and other bodies inhabiting it.

Thus, African traditions of black theology, feminist theology, liberation theology and eco-theology all contribute critical insights to a newly emerging theological discourse that affirms the human dignity and rights, and the fullness of life, of all people, including those with sexual and gender variance. An emerging African Christian queer imagination may be specifically concerned with issues of gender and sexuality, but not exclusively or narrowly so. It mobilises Christian, biblical and theological resources for a social ethics that reflects the intersectional agenda of African queer politics as quoted from Sokari Ekine and Hakima Abbas in the introduction to this book—an agenda of transforming, even revolutionising, African order,[3] or in the words of the African LGBTI Manifesto, 'self-determination at all levels of our sexual, social, political and economic lives'.[4]

Communality

In several chapters in this book, we have outlined how the thinkers and activists under discussion emphasise the communal nature of African social life, for which they refer to indigenous ethical and philosophical values such as *ubuntu* (or *botho/buthu*). These indigenous values are reclaimed and mobilised in the quest to recognise and affirm abundance of life for all, for the community as a whole. The argument is that if certain members of the community are excluded or marginalised, for instance because of their sexuality or gender identity, this affects the cohesion and well-being of the entire community. Although the authors under discussion are not ignorant of the way in which communal ethics can serve, and have served, as a straitjacket forcing those members who are 'different' to adjust and fit in, they believe that these ethics can also be applied in a way that recognises difference within the community, but in a spirit of respect and harmony.

Two points are relevant here in our quest to reimagine sexuality and Christianity in Africa. Firstly, methodologically speaking, we observe openness within these traditions of African Christian thought to engage creatively and constructively with indigenous religions, philosophies and ethics for the development of new social thought and practice. The way in which Dube, for instance, links the indigenous concept of *botho/ubuntu/buthu* with the biblical idea of the body of Christ as a metaphor for community is an excellent example of a creative, inculturated ethics of embodiment, diversity and solidarity that is contextually meaningful. Secondly, politically speaking, the emphasis on these communal concepts is a critical correction of one-sided individualistic accounts of lgbti rights that often dominate Western discourses and programmes. In line with the Banjul Charter that speaks of human and peoples' rights,[5] meaningful thinking about the rights of sexual and gender minorities in Africa will need to balance individual and communal perspectives. From our case studies it appears that religious language might provide ways of doing so. In addition to the language of *ubuntu*, there is also the language of the *imago Dei* in several of the case studies, which serves to reinforce the idea that human-kind as a whole, in all its diversity, reflects the image of God, and that each human individual does so at the same time. These various religious ideas can feed into what has been called 'the inculturation of human rights' in contemporary Africa, which in turn can inspire new ways of imagining sexuality and Christianity.[6]

Bodies and spirits

Thirdly, we suggest that an emerging African Christian queer imagination must centre around the notions of embodiment and enspiritment, that is, influenced by the spirit world, thinking these two notions together in creative and constructive ways. Several of the chapters in this book have touched on the practice of deliverance of the African queer body. In contemporary African popular religious cosmologies, the queer body is frequently stigmatised and violated because it is believed to be possessed by an evil spirit that needs to be exorcised for the body to be freed and un-queered. The contemporary demonisation of the queer body, as narrated in cultural texts such as the novel *Under the Udala Trees*, and the film *Rafiki*, is clearly inspired by Christian, particularly Pentecostal-Charismatic concerns with the devil and demonic realities. One might be tempted to counter such demonisation, and the resulting violent practices of deliverance, by promoting a disenchanted view of the body, emphasising the biological and socio-psychological factors that shape sexual and gender identity. However, such a Western secular account would ignore the fact that the idea of sexual desire and gendered embodiment being enspirited is deeply rooted in African indigenous religious cultures. Instead of explaining away such beliefs, it may be more pertinent to engage them creatively and constructively.

Stella Nyanzi has pointed out that 'cultural and indigenous understandings of gendered spirits of ancestors who may possess individuals offer socially appropriate notions of handling fluid, transient gender identities. Queer Africa must reclaim such African modes of blending, bending and breaking gender boundaries'.[7] Nyanzi makes the important suggestion that local enspirited understandings of gender and sexuality provide an alternative to the 'loaded westernized frame of the LGBTI acronym', and therefore need to be adopted and embraced by local queer activists and communities as a more meaningful lexicon. Nathanael Homewood has applied this to contemporary African Pentecostal circles, where such enspirited understandings de facto largely create sexual hierarchies and practices of exclusion and violence, but in his opinion also potentially 'open up additional interpretative possibilities and opportunities for resistance'.[8] In chapter 6, we quoted Bishop Tolton alluding to one of these alternative interpretative possibilities, pointing out that people recognise his spiritual anointing as a gay preacher. Indeed, given the popularity of Pentecostal Christianity in Africa, the work of Tolton's organisation, TFAM Global, and of similar ministries, is of great importance. It presents the promise of an enspirited progressive and queer African Christian imagination. Here, the dynamic interplay of body and spirit no longer serves to demonise sexual and gender 'deviants', but rather to embrace sexual and gender diversity as a gift of the Spirit, and to reclaim the African queer body, in Azuah's words (chapter 7), as blessed.

To return to Achille Mbembe's words with which we opened this book: 'Struggle as a *praxis of liberation* has always drawn part of its imaginary resources from Christianity.'[9] The ten case studies of this book have demonstrated the many different ways in which various thinkers, activists, organisations and communities in contemporary Africa engage Christianity as a site from which they take constructive resources for imagining and working towards a liberatory African future. Only the future will tell what will become of this.

NOTES

PREFACE

1. Chitando and Van Klinken 2016.

INTRODUCTION: SEXUALITY, CHRISTIANITY AND AFRICAN IMAGINATIONS

1. Mbembe 2017, p. 174.
2. Ngũgĩ wa Thiong'o 2009, p. 45.
3. Mbembe 2017, pp. 174–75.
4. Maathai 2010, p. 170.
5. Tamale 2011, p. 1.
6. See Arnfred 2005.
7. See Epprecht 2008, pp. 38–44.
8. Epprecht 2008, p. 2.
9. Ndjio 2013, pp. 126–27.
10. Wainaina 2015.
11. Wainaina 2014.
12. African LGBTI Manifesto 2010.
13. See Van Klinken 2020b.
14. Matebeni and Pereira 2014, p. 7.
15. Maxwell 2002, p. 3.
16. See Isichei 1995.
17. Bediako 1992, 1995.
18. See Kalu 2008.
19. See Lindhardt 2014.
20. Grillo, Van Klinken and Ndzovu 2019.

21. Van Klinken and Obadare 2018; Kaunda 2020.
22. See West 2016, p. 318.
23. West 2016, p. 477.
24. E.g. see Englund 2011.
25. E.g. see Chitando and Van Klinken 2016; Kaoma 2017; Van Klinken and Chitando 2016; Van Klinken and Obadare 2018.
26. E.g. see Nyanzi 2014.
27. E.g. see Van Klinken and Otu 2017.
28. E.g. see Gaudio 2009.
29. Chitando and Mateveke 2017.
30. Bongmba 2016, p. 31.
31. On inculturation, see Martey 1993; Oduyoye 2003.
32. Epprecht 2013, p. 67.
33. Epprecht 2013, p. 67.
34. See Mbetbo 2013; Muparamoto 2016; Phiri 2016; Van Klinken 2015.
35. Bongmba 2015; Chitando and Mapuranga 2016; Gunda 2010, 2017; Van Klinken and Gunda 2012; van Klinken 2019.
36. On African queer studies, see Nyeck 2020; on queer theologies, see Greenough 2020.
37. Comaroff and Comaroff 2015.
38. See Chianeque 2015.
39. Orobator, quoted in Joshua J. McElwee, 11 April 2016. 'African theologian responds to Amoris Laetitia'. Available at: https://www.ncronline.org/news/african-theologian-responds-amoris-laetitia (accessed 27 March 2020).
40. E.g. see Orobator 2005.
41. Ilo 2019, pp. 227–28.
42. E.g. Tamale 2011; Moreau and Tallie 2020.
43. Following Epprecht 2013, p. 23.
44. Ekine and Abbas 2013, p. 3.

1. RACE AND SEXUALITY IN A THEOLOGY OF *UBUNTU*: DESMOND TUTU

1. At that time, the church was called Church of the Province of Southern Africa. It adopted its current name in 2006.

2. Allen 2006, p. 372.
3. BBC News, 26 July 2013. 'Archbishop Tutu "would not worship a homophobic God"'. Available at: https://www.bbc.co.uk/news/world-africa-23464694 (accessed 22 January 2020).
4. Quoted in Brittain and McKinnon 2018, p. 2.
5. News24, 28 July 2013. 'Mugabe attacks "gay-supporting Archbishop" Desmond Tutu'. Available at: https://www.news24.com/Archives/City-Press/Mugabe-attacks-gay-supporting-Archbishop-Desmond-Tutu-20150429 (accessed 24 March 2020).
6. Allen 2006, p. 281.
7. Tutu 1997, p. x.
8. *Ibid.*
9. De Gruchy and Germond, 1997, p. 2.
10. Quoted in Massoud 2003, p. 303.
11. Thoreson 2008, p. 680.
12. Thoreson 2008, p. 687.
13. Allen 2006, p. 373.
14. Hassett 2007.
15. Allen 2006, p. 373.
16. Senyonjo 2016, p. 86. For a discussion of Senyonjo's remarkable ministry, see Van Klinken 2020a.
17. Tutu 2004.
18. Allen 2006, p. 372.
19. Allen 2006, p. 372.
20. Allen 2006, p. 223.
21. Tutu 1997, p. x.
22. Tutu 1983, pp. 46–47.
23. See Clarke 1984, p. 7.
24. Tutu 1997, p. x.
25. Tutu 2012, p. 150.
26. See Motlhabi 2008.
27. Quoted in Motlhabi 2008, pp. 46–47.
28. Tutu 1997, p. ix.
29. Tutu 1997, p. ix.
30. Tutu 2012, p. 150.

31. Tutu 2012, p. 149.
32. Tutu 2012, p. 150.
33. Allen 2006, p. 391.
34. Battle 1997.
35. Allen 2006, p. 347.
36. Battle 1997, p. 5.
37. Battle 1997, p. 46.
38. Tutu 1999, p. 35.
39. Allen 2006, p. 396.
40. Mojola 2018, p. 66.
41. Kaoma 2018, p. 178.
42. Mawerenga 2018, pp. 173–74.
43. Also see Bongmba 2016.
44. Tutu 2015.
45. Tutu 2015, p. 388.
46. Thoreson 2008, p. 681.
47. Tutu 2012, p. 149.
48. Tutu 2012, pp. 149–50.
49. Thoreson 2008, p. 681.
50. E.g. see Matebeni 2014; McCarty III 2013.
51. Tutu 1999, p. 258.

2. GENDER, SEXUALITY AND A THEOLOGY OF FRUITFULNESS: MERCY ODUYOYE

1. Russell 2006, pp. 46–47.
2. Kanyoro 2006.
3. See Phiri and Nadar 2006.
4. Oduyoye, like many other African theologians, often writes about 'African culture' in the singular. That is not to ignore the diversity of cultures on the continent, but to reflect their belief in the commonalities across various African cultures.
5. Martey 1993.
6. Oduyoye 2001, p. 28.
7. Hadebe 2016, p. 2.
8. See Mutambara 2006.

9. Oduyoye 1995, p. 172.
10. Kanyoro 2002.
11. Oduyoye 2003, p. 44.
12. Oduyoye 2003, p. 51.
13. Oduyoye 2003, pp. 43–44.
14. Oduyoye 2019, p. 350.
15. For examples, see Van Klinken and Gunda 2012.
16. Oduyoye 2001, p. 79.
17. *Ibid.*
18. Oduyoye 2001, p. 78.
19. Oduyoye 2001, p. 116.
20. See Phiri and Nadar 2005.
21. Kanyoro and Njoroge 1996.
22. Oduyoye 2001, p. 83.
23. Oduyoye 2001, p. 84.
24. Germond and De Gruchy 1997.
25. Epprecht 2013, p. 67.
26. E.g. see Van Klinken 2017.
27. Kanyoro and Njoroge 1996.
28. Oduyoye 2019, p. 125.
29. Oduyoye 1993, p. 354. Oduyoye quotes Mbiti as grouping same-sex relationships with sexual perversions such as bestiality, and as stating that homosexuality is 'immoral, abnormal, unnatural, and a danger to society' (Mbiti, quoted in Oduyoye 1993, p. 355). To be fair on him, Mbiti made these statements in a 1973 publication, and his own thinking about the subject may well have changed later.
30. Oduyoye 1993, p. 361.
31. Oduyoye 1993, p. 355.
32. Oduyoye 1993, p. 347.
33. Oduyoye 1999, p. 105.
34. *Ibid.*
35. Oduyoye 1999, p. 113.
36. Oduyoye 1999, p. 118.
37. Kanyoro 2006.
38. Oduyoye 1999, p. 119.

39. Oduyoye 2001, p. 111.
40. Nadar 2012, p. 274.
41. Oduyoye 2001, p. 10.
42. Oduyoye 2001, p. 11.
43. Amoah and Oduyoye 1989.
44. Oduyoye 2001, p. 21.
45. Van Klinken 2019, p. 103.
46. See Van Klinken 2018.
47. Oduyoye 2001, p. 116.

3. REVOLUTIONARY IMAGINATION AND THE ECOLOGY OF HUMAN RIGHTS: JEAN-BLAISE KENMOGNE

1. Originally a German colony from 1884, after World War I Cameroon was partitioned between France and the United Kingdom, with the former controlling by far the largest geographical share of what, after independence, became one republic.
2. Ndjio 2013.
3. Corey-Boulet 2019, pp. 15–30.
4. Alternatives Cameroun 2010.
5. Quoted in Togue 2017, p. 253.
6. Awondo 2016, p. 107.
7. Awondo 2016, p. 110.
8. Lyonga 2016.
9. The official name being Cercle International pour la Promotion de la Création (CIPCRE).
10. CIPCRE n.d.
11. See Kenmogne 2015.
12. Quotations from this book in the present chapter have been translated by Adriaan van Klinken.
13. Kenmogne and Mana 2012, p. 34.
14. Kenmogne and Mana 2012, p. 36.
15. See Awondo et al. 2012, pp. 150–52.
16. Eboussi Boulaga 2007; Gueboguo 2012.
17. Mbembe 2010.
18. Kenmogne and Mana 2012, p. 31.

19. Kenmogne and Mana 2012, p. 32.
20. Kenmogne and Mana 2012, p. 35.
21. Kenmogne and Mana 2012, p. 64.
22. Gospel of John 8: 7 (New International Version).
23. Kenmogne and Mana 2012, p. 69.
24. On biblical hermeneutics and the debate on homosexuality in Africa, see the article by another Cameroonian scholar, Elias Bongmba 2015.
25. Kenmogne and Mana 2012, p. 67.
26. Kenmogne and Mana 2012, p. 73.
27. Kenmogne and Mana 2012, pp. 66, 69, 70.
28. Mbetbo 2013.
29. Kenmogne and Mana 2012, p. 76.
30. Matthew 25: 31–46. See Dube 2008.
31. Kenmogne and Mana 2012, p. 73.
32. Kenmogne and Mana 2012, p. 76. For the biblical parable, see Gospel of Luke, 10: 25–37.
33. Kenmogne and Mana 2012, p. 74.
34. Kenmogne and Mana 2012, p. 75.
35. Kenmogne and Mana 2012, p. 78.
36. Mbetbo 2013, p. 79.
37. Kenmogne and Mana 2012, p. 11.
38. Kenmogne and Mana 2012, p. 58. For an introduction in English to Kä Mana's thinking, see Kä Mana (2002); specifically for his concept of *imaginaire*, see Dedji 2001.
39. Only one of his many books has been translated into English; see Mana 2002.
40. Mana, quoted in Dedji 2001, p. 264.
41. Mana 2002, p. 3.
42. Mana 2002, p. 27.
43. Mana 2002, p. 21.
44. Mana 2004, p. 83.
45. Kenmogne and Mana 2011, p. 58.
46. Mana 2002, p. 71.
47. See Ndjio 2013.
48. Mana 2002, p. 19.

49. Kenmogne and Mana 2012, p. 24.
50. Kenmogne 2015.
51. Kenmogne 2014.

4. AFFIRMING HUMAN DIVERSITY AND EMBODIMENT IN THE FACE OF HIV: MUSA W. DUBE

1. See for example Browning 2011 and Chitando 2009.
2. Van Klinken and Gunda 2012, pp. 131–32.
3. Genesis 1: 26–27, 31.
4. Dube 2008, p. 40.
5. Dube 2007, pp. 129, 135, 138.
6. Dube 2003, p. 210.
7. *Ibid.*
8. Dube 2003, p. 214.
9. Dube 2010, p. 145.
10. Dube 2015.
11. Gospel of Mark 5: 21–43.
12. Dube 2009c.
13. Dube 2009c, p. 140.
14. Dube 2005, pp. 180–81 (emphasis added).
15. Dube 2008.
16. Dube 2001.
17. Dube 2003, p. 210.
18. See Epprecht 2008.
19. Dube 2003, p. 201.
20. Dube 2007.
21. Dube 2007, p. 20 (italics original).
22. Dube 2007, p. 9.
23. 1 Corinthians 12: 23–31.
24. Dube 2007, pp. 16, 72, 75–76. See also Van Klinken 2010.
25. 1 Corinthians 12: 26.
26. Dube 2006, p. 141.
27. Dube 2007, p. 56.
28. Dube 2008.
29. Dube 2003, p. 213.

30. Dube 2003, p. 214.
31. Dube 2009a and 2009b.
32. Njoroge 2008, p. 119.
33. See Gunda 2010.
34. Dube 2003, p. 212.

5. TOWARDS SEXUALLY COMPETENT CHURCHES: THE ECUMEN-
ICAL HIV AND AIDS INITIATIVES AND ADVOCACY

1. This chapter has been informed by the insider knowledge of one of
the co-authors, Ezra Chitando, who since 2005 has been part of the
work of EHAIA.
2. See WCC n.d.; Brash 1995.
3. Maxson 2016.
4. Kurian 2016; Njoroge 2016. The word 'ecumenical' refers to efforts by
Christians of different denominations and traditions to develop closer
relationships and better mutual understanding.
5. WCC 1997.
6. Parry 2008.
7. Kelly 2010.
8. Njoroge 2016.
9. Chitando and Chirongoma 2013.
10. Njoroge 2009, p. 3.
11. The Greek word *kairos* is used in the New Testament. It became particularly significant in church and theology circles in Africa due to the
publication of the 1985 *Kairos Document*, in which a group of mainly
black South African theologians critiqued apartheid and called the
church to take a prophetic stance against it.
12. African Union 2015.
13. E.g. Luke 4: 18–19.
14. Njoroge 2013.
15. Genesis 1: 27.
16. Ajibade 2016, p. 114.
17. Igo 2005; Chitando 2007; Igo 2009; Parry 2013; Chitando and Njoroge
2016.
18. Chitando and Nickles 2012.

19. Psalm 139: 14.

20. Dube 2003.

21. Chitando 2015.

22. Dube 2003; Chitando 2008.

23. Parry 2008, p. 28.

24. Njoroge 2008, p. 115.

25. Njoroge 2013.

26. Almedal 2010.

27. Mofokeng 1988, p. 36.

28. Ujamaa Centre 2014.

29. West 1999.

30. Gunda 2017, 2.

31. Acts 10: 15.

32. Mark 12: 31.

33. Wilson and Lawson 2016.

6. BUILDING A PROGRESSIVE PAN-AFRICAN CHRISTIAN MOVE-
   MENT: THE FELLOWSHIP OF AFFIRMING MINISTRIES

1. See de Lange and Gaum 2015.

2. See Macaulay 2010.

3. TFAM n.d 'About Us'.

4. City of Refuge, n.d.

5. Flunder 2015, p. 117.

6. TFAM n.d. 'About Us'.

7. *Ibid.*

8. *Ibid.*

9. Lewin 2018, pp. 116–17.

10. Flunder 2015, p. 120.

11. Lewin 2018.

12. Interview with Joseph Tolton, by Adriaan van Klinken, Nairobi, 24 February 2016.

13. These are currently listed on the website as countries where TFAM is active (TFAM Global, 'Where We Work').

14. TFAM Global, 'Our Method'.

15. Jjuuko 2017, p. 298.

16. TFAM, 'The Fellowship Global'.
17. See Van Klinken 2020b.
18. Quoted in Alison Amyx, 2015. 'Black Pastors Launch African Tour to Counteract Rick Warren's Anti-Gay Movement', Believe Out Loud. Available at: https://www.believeoutloud.com/voices/article/black-pastors-launch-african-tour-to-counteract-rick-warrens-anti-gay-movement/ (accessed 19 February 2020).
19. See Kaoma 2009, 2012; Van Klinken 2017.
20. Nyiawung 2010.
21. Interview with Joseph Tolton, by Adriaan Van Klinken, Nairobi, 24 February 2016. In Pentecostal language, 'anointing' refers to a person having received the Holy Spirit.
22. One of the authors, Adriaan van Klinken, watched Tolton preach in Kenya several times.
23. TFAM Global, 'Our Project'.
24. African LGBTI Manifesto 2010.
25. The Fellowship Global 2013.
26. TFAM Global, 'Interconnected Justice'.
27. The Fellowship Global 2013.
28. TFAM Global, 'Interconnected Justice'.
29. *Ibid.*
30. Heather Hahn, 9 September 2019. 'First church in Africa becomes reconciling', United Methodist News. Available at: https://www.umnews.org/en/news/first-church-in-africa-becomes-reconciling (accessed 20 February 2020).
31. Kennedy Mwita, 15 February 2019. 'Kenya and the Future of the UMC', United Methodist Affirmation. Available at: http://www.umaffirm.org/site/current-events/24-latest-news/174-kenya-and-the-future-of-the-umc (accessed 20 February 2020).
32. The Fellowship Global 2013.
33. This section is based on ethnographic research conducted by one of the authors of this book, Adriaan van Klinken, in the CAC since 2015. For a much more in-depth account, see chapter 4 in Van Klinken 2019.
34. CAC uses the term 'community' rather than 'church' in its name because of legal reasons. They are officially registered with the Kenyan authorities as a community-based organisation, not as a religious society.

35. Obinyan 2020.
36. The ruling was postponed till May, and turned out to be negative.
37. Lyrics by David Kai.
38. See Genesis 9: 13–7.
39. CAC Kenya, 2019.
40. Nathan 2012, p. 281.
41. See Lewin 2018, p. 149; Van Klinken 2019, pp. 172–73.

7. RECLAIMING THE QUEER BODY: NIGERIAN LGBT LIFE STORIES OF SEXUALITY AND FAITH

1. From Botswana, see MacAllister 2016; from Malawi, see Xaba and Biruk 2016; from Ethopia, see Lisanework 2019; from Kenya, see Mwachiro 2013 and The Nest 2015; from Somalia, see Jama 2015; from Nigeria, see Dibia and Makanjuola 2020, and Mohammed et al.
2. Nadar 2014.
3. Azuah 2016. The subtitle of this book refers to lesbian, gay, bisexual and transgender identities, and in the text the acronym lgbt (rather than lgbti) is used, which we will follow in this chapter.
4. Azuah 2016, p. 7.
5. A minority of the stories in the volume refer to Nigerian Muslim contexts and experiences, but the majority reflect a Christian background. For the purpose of this chapter, we focus on the stories that relate to Christianity.
6. Although there are different forms of Christian expression in Nigeria (as elsewhere), in this chapter we adopt the generic term 'Church' for all of them. When it comes to homosexuality, they tend to sing from the same hymn book and condemn it. We retain the capital 'C' to indicate the singular use.
7. On the theme of narrative queer theologies in Africa, see Van Klinken 2018.
8. Azuah 2016, p. 61.
9. See Oguntola-Laguda and Van Klinken 2016.
10. Obadare 2015, p. 64.
11. See Mbembe 2001.

12. Sylvester 2006.
13. Azuah 2016, p. 126.
14. Azuah 2016, p. 60.
15. Azuah 2016, pp. 63–64.
16. Azuah 2016, pp. 196–97.
17. Green-Simms and Azuah 2012.
18. Azuah 2016, p. 259.
19. Azuah 2016, p. 51.
20. Azuah 2016, p. 70. Also see Phiri 2016.
21. Azuah 2016, p. 89.
22. Azuah 2016, p. 248.
23. Azuah 2016, p. 47.
24. Azuah 2016, p. 208.
25. Azuah 2016, p. 43.
26. Azuah 2016, p. 30.
27. Azuah 2016, p. 134.
28. Azuah 2016, p. 88.
29. Azuah 2016, pp. 203–4.
30. Azuah 2016, pp. 85, 52, 135.
31. Azuah 2016, p. 36.
32. Azuah 2016, p. 138.
33. Azuah 2016, p. 50.
34. Azuah 2016, p. 61.
35. Azuah 2016, p. 206.
36. Azuah 2016, p. 234.
37. Azuah 2016, p. 160.
38. Azuah 2016, p. 232.
39. Azuah 2016, p. 65.
40. E.g. see Azuah 2016, pp. 35, 51, 59, etc.
41. Azuah 2016, p. 51.
42. Azuah 2016, pp. 117–18, 199.
43. Azuah 2016, p. 178.
44. Azuah 2016, pp. 79–82.
45. Azuah 2016, p. 72.
46. Azuah 2016, p. 38.

47. Azuah 2016, p. 190.
48. Azuah 2016, p. 197.
49. Azuah 2016, p. 185.
50. Azuah 2016, p. 193.
51. Azuah 2016, p. 203.
52. Grillo, Van Klinken and Ndzovu 2019, p. 83.
53. Azuah 2016, p. 214. His bio says that Rowland Jide is the first openly gay preacher in Nigeria and is the founder and pastor of House of Rainbow Fellowship (p. 268).
54. Azuah 2016, p. 220.
55. Oduyoye 2001, p. 88–89.
56. Azuah 2016, p. 229.
57. *Ibid.*
58. Azuah 2016, p. 70.
59. Azuah 2016, p. 232.
60. Azuah 2016, p. 104.
61. Azuah 2016, p. 70.
62. Azuah 2016, pp. 38, 219.
63. Azuah 2016, p. 139.
64. Aragón 2018.

8. THE ART OF WORDS: LGBTQ POETRY, CHRISTIANITY AND FLOURISHING IN AFRICA

1. Mwangi 2014.
2. See Spivak 1988. On queer arts of resistance, see Van Klinken 2019.
3. Khadhani and Zimunya 1981.
4. Animashaun et al. 2016. The subtitle of this volume uses the acronym LGBTQ which we will follow in this chapter (but in lower case). Two other recent collections are Azuah and Omas 2018, which includes poems by a range of Nigerian queer writers, and Oriogun 2020, which includes poems by one Nigerian author. For the purpose of this chapter, we opted to focus on the collection that has pan-African content as it allows us to bring in voices from some countries not featured in other chapters of this book.
5. The volume under discussion also includes some short prose texts, a few

of which are also part of our discussion in this chapter. Much of what we say here about poetry also applies to prose writing.

6. Mukhuba 2017.

7. Wassiliwizky et al. 2017, p. 1237.

8. Osike 2018, p. 50.

9. Animashaun et al. 2016, p. 129. All following quotations from this poem are from this page.

10. Haggard is an American evangelical pastor who in 2006 was forced to step down from his various positions after a male sex-worker alleged that Haggard had made use of his sexual services for three years—a period during which Haggard was actively campaigning against same-sex marriage.

11. Dube in his poem uses the term 'evangelical'. The categories of Evangelicalism and Pentecostalism are closely related and partly over-lapping.

12. See Chitando and Van Klinken 2016.

13. Lyonga 2016.

14. Van Klinken 2013.

15. Kalu 2008, p. 98.

16. Animashaun et al. 2016, p. 121. All following quotations from this text are from the same page.

17. On African eco-feminism, see Pasi 2016.

18. Olupona 2014, p. 23.

19. I Kings 19: 12. Bible quotations are from the New International Version.

20. Animashaun et al. 2016, p. 85. All following quotations from this poem are from this page.

21. Paraphrasing Romans 8: 31.

22. Animashaun et al. 2016, p. 9. All following quotations from this poem are from this page.

23. Animashaun et al. 2016, p. 16. All following quotations from this poem are from this page.

24. Annan 2016.

25. West 2011.

26. E.g. see I John 4: 7–8. Also see chapter 4 about Musa Dube in this book, where the same point is discussed.

9. INFINITE POSSIBILITIES IN A NIGERIAN LESBIAN LOVE STORY: *UNDER THE UDALA TREES*

1. Green-Simms 2016.
2. Adogame 2010, pp. 2–3.
3. Okparanta 2015, p. 325.
4. An Igbo name, meaning as much as 'Good journey in life'.
5. Meaning 'honest', and a name with a highly symbolic meaning, as it was carried by a legendary sixteenth-century Hausa warrior queen, and by the mother of the Prophet Muhammad.
6. Okparanta 2015, pp. 220–21.
7. Okparanta 2015, p. 320.
8. Given this name, one would expect it to be a Sabbath-worshipping church, as some Nigerian Pentecostal churches (used to) be, but the novel explicitly states that Ijeoma and her parents went there 'every Sunday' (Okparanta 2015, p. 11).
9. Okparanta 2015, p. 11.
10. Ojo 2006.
11. The novel does not explicitly label the sexuality of Ijeoma, or that of the other women, with words such as gay, lesbian, bisexual and queer. This reflects the historical setting of the 1970s, when such terminology was virtually absent in countries such as Nigeria.
12. Ogoti 2019.
13. Agukoronye 2001, p. 95.
14. Okparanta 2015, p. 309.
15. Isiugo-Abanihe 1994.
16. Okparanta 2015, pp. 44–46.
17. Okparanta 2015, p. 105.
18. Okparanta 2015, p. 125.
19. Korte 2010.
20. Wariboko 2014, p. 112.
21. Okparanta 2015, p. 12.
22. Okparanta 2015, p. 13.
23. *Ibid.*
24. Okparanta 2015, p. 42.
25. Okparanta 2015, pp. 71–72.

26. Wariboko 2014, p. 104.
27. Okparanta 2015, p. 86.
28. Wariboko 2014, p. 6.
29. Okparanta 2015, p. 72.
30. Okparanta 2015, p. 87.
31. Okparanta 2015, p. 88.
32. See Van Klinken 2013; Hackman 2018.
33. Okparanta 2015, p. 92.
34. Okparanta 2015, p. 196.
35. Hackman 2018, p. 91.
36. Okparanta 2015, p. 323.
37. Okparanta 2015, p. 68.
38. Okparanta 2015, p. 23.
39. Okparanta 2015, pp. 82–83.
40. Okparanta 2015, p. 83.
41. Okparanta 2015, p. 74.
42. Okparanta 2015, p. 80.
43. Okparanta 2015, p. 81.
44. Okparanta 2015, p. 82.
45. Okparanta 2015, p. 83.
46. Okparanta 2015, p. 159.
47. Okparanta 2015, p. 229.
48. Okparanta 2015, pp. 159, 231.
49. Okparanta 2015, p. 192.
50. Okparanta 2015, p. 201.
51. Okparanta 2015, p. 202.
52. Gunda 2010, p. 22.
53. Okparanta 2015, p. 83.
54. Frateur 2019, p. 78.
55. Okparanta 2015, pp. 321–22.

10. CHRISTIANITY AND VISUAL ACTIVISM IN KENYAN QUEER FILM: *RAFIKI* AND *SAME LOVE*

1. Macharia 2015, p. 140.
2. Simms-Green 2018, p. 653.

3. Azuah 2018, p. 12.
4. Azuah 2018, p. 13–14.
5. See Van Klinken 2019, pp. 59–60.
6. Maupeu 2010, p. 402.
7. See Kidula 2012; Ntarangwi 2016.
8. Osinubi 2019, p. 72.
9. Osinubi 2019, p. 70.
10. Ombagi 2018, p. 107.
11. Quoted in Stoyan Zaimov, 18 May 2015. '700 Kenyan Evangelical Pastors Urge Obama Not to "Preach" Gay Marriage Support During Visit', *The Christian Post*. Available at: https://www.christianpost.com/news/700-kenyan-evangelical-pastors-urge-obama-not-to-preach-gay-marriage-support-during-visit-archbishop-accuses-obama-of-ruining-american-society.html (accessed 24 March 2020).
12. See Van Klinken 2019, pp. 41–42.
13. See Van Klinken 2013; Lyonga 2016.
14. Parsitau 2015.
15. Gospel of Matthew 19: 26.
16. Du Bois 2007 [1920], p. 1.

CONCLUSION

1. Eze 2011, pp. 9–10.
2. Ndlovu-Gatsheni 2018.
3. Ekine and Abbas 2013, p. 3.
4. African LGBTI Manifesto 2010.
5. The Banjul Charter, also named the African Charter on Human and Peoples' Rights, is the official human rights instrument that promotes and protects human rights and freedoms on the African continent.
6. Atiemo 2013.
7. Nyanzi 2014, p. 67.
8. Homewood 2020, p. 126.
9. Mbembe 2017, p. 174.

BIBLIOGRAPHY

'African LGBTI Manifesto'. 18 April 2010, Nairobi. Available at: http://www.fahamu.org/mbbc/wp-content/uploads/2011/09/African-LGBTI-Manifesto-2010.pdf (accessed 19 February 2020).

Adogame, Afe. 2020. 'Editorial: Religion in African Literary Writing', *Studies in World Christianity* 16 (1), 1–5.

African Union. 2015. *Agenda 2063: The Africa We Want (Popular Version)*. Addis Ababa: African Union.

Agukoronye, Okechukwu C. 2001. 'Landscape Practices in Traditional Igbo Society, Nigeria', *Landscape Research* 26 (2), 85–98.

Ajibade, Ijeoma. 2016. 'The Image of God: Recognizing God within Key Populations', in Gillian Paterson and Callie Long (eds.), *Dignity, Freedom, and Grace: Christian Perspectives on HIV, AIDS, and Human Rights*. Geneva: World Council of Churches, 109–15.

Allen, John. 2006. *Rabble-Rouser for Peace. The Authorized Biography of Desmond Tutu*. New York: Free Press.

Almedal, Calle. 2010. 'Building HIV Competent Churches: Problem Areas for Churches to Discuss', in Erlinda N. Senturias and Liza B. Lamis (eds.), *Building HIV Competent Churches: Called to Prophesy, Reconcile and Heal*. Hong Kong: Christian Council of Asia, 142–47.

Atiemo, Abamfo Ofori. 2013. *Religion and the Inculturation of Human Rights in Ghana*. London: Bloomsbury.

Alternatives Cameroun, Centre for Human Rights at the University of Pretoria, Global Rights, and International Gay and Lesbian Human Rights Commission. 2010. *The Status of Lesbian, Gay, Bisexual and*

Transgender Rights in Cameroon: A Shadow Report. Available at: https://www2.ohchr.org/english/bodies/hrc/docs/ngos/LGBTI_Cameroon_HRC99.pdf (accessed 29 December 2019).

Amoah, Elizabeth, and Mercy Oduyoye. 1989. 'The Christ for African Women', in Virginia Fabella and Mercy Oduyoye (eds.), *With Passion and Compassion: Third World Women Doing Theology*. Maryknoll, NY: Orbis Books, 35–46.

Animashaun, Abayomi, et al. (eds.). 2016. *Walking the Tightrope: Poetry and Prose by LGBTQ Writers from Africa*. Maple Shade, NJ: Tincture.

Annan, Kofi. 2016. 'Religion, Pluralism and Democracy', Kofi Annan Foundation. Available at: https://www.kofiannanfoundation.org/supporting-democracy-and-elections-with-integrity/bali-democracy-forum/ (accessed 7 May 2020).

Aragón, Asunción. 2018. 'Breaking/Voicing the Silence: Diriye Osman's *Fairy Tales for Lost Children*', *African Literature Today* 36, 123–34.

Arnfred, Signe (ed.). 2005. *Re-thinking Sexualities in Africa*. Uppsala: Nordiska Afrikainstitutet.

Art Attack. 15 February 2016. *Same Love (Remix)*. YouTube. Available at: https://www.youtube.com/watch?v=8EataOQvPII.

Awondo, Patrick, et al. 2012. 'Homophobic Africa? Toward a More Nuanced View', *African Studies Review* 55 (3), 145–68.

Awondo, Patrick. 2010. 'The Politicisation of Sexuality and Rise of Homosexual Movements in Post-colonial Cameroon', *Review of African Political Economy* 37 (125), 315–28.

———. 2016. 'Religious Leadership and the Re-Politicisation of Gender and Sexuality in Cameroon', *Journal of Theology for Southern Africa* 155, 105–20.

Azuah, Unoma (ed.). 2016. *Blessed Body: The Secret Lives of Nigerian Lesbian, Gay, Bisexual and Transgender*. Jackson, TN: Cookingpot Publishing.

———. 2018. 'Visual Activism: Documentary Born This Way', Queer Theory in Film and Fiction, special issue of *African Literature Today* 36, 7–16.

Azuah, Unoma, and Michelle Omas (eds.). 2018. *Mounting the Moon: Queer Nigerian Poems*. Jackson, TN: Cookingpot Publishing.

Battle, Michael. 1997. *Reconciliation: The Ubuntu Theology of Desmond Tutu*. Cleveland, OH: The Pilgrim Press.

Bediako, Kwame. 1992. *Theology and Identity: The Impact of Culture upon Christian Thought in the Second Century and in Modern Africa*. Oxford: Regnum Books.

———. 1995. *Christianity in Africa: The Renewal of a Non-Western Religion*. Edinburgh: Edinburgh University Press.

Bongmba, Elias K. 2015. 'Hermeneutics and the Debate on Homosexuality in Africa', *Religion and Theology* 22 (1–2), 69–99.

———. 2016. 'Homosexuality, Ubuntu, and Otherness in the African Church', *Journal of Religion and Violence* 4 (1), 15–37.

Brash, Alan A. 1995. *Facing Our Differences: The Churches and Their Gay and Lesbian Members*. Geneva: World Council of Churches.

Brittain, Christopher Craig, and Andrew McKinnon. 2018. *The Anglican Communion at a Crossroads: The Crises of a Global Church*. University Park, PA: Pennsylvania State University Press.

Browning, Melissa D. 2011. '"Hanging Out a Red Ribbon": Listening to Musa Dube's Postcolonial Feminist Theology', *Journal of Race, Ethnicity and Religion* 2 (13), 1–27. Available at: http://raceandreligion.com/JRER/Volume_2_(2011)_files/Browning%202%2013.pdf (accessed 13 May 2020).

CAC Kenya. 19 February 2019. 'Faith Voices for Decriminalisation Inter-Faith Service'. Available at: https://cac-kenya.com/2019/02/19/faith-voices-for-decrim-inter-faith-service/ (accessed 20 February 2020).

Chianeque, Luciano Chanhelela. 2015. 'Churches Need to Do More to Tackle HIV and AIDS', World Council of Churches. Available at: https://www.oikoumene.org/en/press-centre/news/churches-need-to-do-more-to-tackle-hiv-and-aids (accessed 18 September 2020).

Chitando, Ezra. 2007. *Living with Hope: African Churches and HIV/AIDS*. Geneva: World Council of Churches.

——— (ed.). 2008. *Mainstreaming HIV and AIDS in Theological Education: Experiences and Explorations*. Geneva: World Council of Churches.

——— 2009. *Troubled but not Destroyed: African Theology in Dialogue with HIV and AIDS*. Geneva: World Council of Churches.

———— (ed.). 2015. *Engaging with the Past: Same-Sex Relationships in Pre-Colonial Zimbabwe*. Harare: EHAIA.

Chitando, Ezra and Peter Nickles (eds.). 2012. *What's Faith got to do with it? A Global Multifaith Discussions on HIV Responses*. Johannesburg: INERELA.

Chitando, Ezra, and Sophia Chirongoma (eds.). 2013. *Justice Not Silence: Churches Facing Sexual and Gender-Based Violence*. Stellenbosch: EFSA.

Chitando, Ezra, and Tapiwa P. Mapuranga. 2016. 'Unlikely Allies? Lesbian, Gay, Bisexual, Transgender and Intersex (LGBTI) Activists and Church Leaders in Africa', in Ezra Chitando and Adriaan van Klinken (eds.), *Christianity and Controversies over Homosexuality in Contemporary Africa*. London and New York: Routledge, 171–83.

Chitando, Ezra, and Nyambura Njoroge (eds.). 2016. *Abundant Life: The Churches and Sexuality*. Geneva: World Council of Churches.

Chitando, Ezra, and Adriaan van Klinken (eds.). 2016. *Christianity and Controversies over Homosexuality in Contemporary Africa*. London and New York: Routledge.

Chitando, Ezra, and Pauline Mateveke. 2017. 'Africanizing the Discourse on Homosexuality: Challenges and Prospects', *Critical African Studies* 9 (1), 124–40.

CIPCRE (Cercle International pour la Promotion de la Création). n.d. Available at: http://cipcre.org/ (accessed 29 December 2019).

City of Refuge. n.d. 'Rev. Dr. Yvette A. Flunder'. Available at: http://www.cityofrefugeucc.org/uploads/8/1/7/2/81728266/yflunderupdated_bio_2015.pdf (accessed 17 February 2020).

Clarke, R. G. 1984. 'Apartheid is a Heresy', *Reality* 16 (2), 7–9.

Comaroff, John, and Jean L. Comaroff. 2015. *Theory from the South: Or, How Euro-America is Evolving Toward Africa*. Abingdon and New York: Routledge.

Corey-Boulet, Robbie. 2019. *Love Falls on Us: A Story of American Ideas and African LGBT Lives*. London: Zed Books.

De Lange, Ecclesia, and Laurie Gaum. 2015. 'Embodying More of Christ's Body: A Movement Towards Inclusivity Regarding Sexual Orientation and Gender Identity Within the Church', in Ernst Conradie and Miranda Pillay (eds.), *Ecclesial Reform and Deform Movements in the South African Context*. Stellenbosch: Sun Press, 18–29.

Dedji, Valentin. 2001. 'The Ethical Redemption of African *Imaginaire*: Ka Mana's Theology of Reconstruction', *Journal of Religion in Africa* 31 (3), 254–74.

Dibia, Jude, and Olumide F. Makanjuola (eds.). 2020. *Queer Men's Narratives*. Abuja: Cassava Republic.

Dube, Musa W. 2001. 'Preaching to the Converted: Unsettling the Christian Church', *Ministerial Formation* 93, 38–50.

———. 2003. 'Service for/on Homosexuals', in Musa W. Dube (ed.), *Africa Praying: A Handbook on HIV/AIDS Sensitive Sermon Guidelines and Liturgy*. Geneva: World Council of Churches, 210–14.

———. 2005. 'Rahab is Hanging Out a Red Ribbon: One African Woman's Perspective on the Future of Feminist New Testament Scholarship', in Kathleen O'Brien Wicker et al. (eds.), *Feminist New Testament Studies: Global and Future Perspectives*. New York: Palgrave Macmillan, 177–202.

———. 2006. 'Adinkra! Four Hearts Joined Together: On Becoming Healer/Teachers of African Indigenous Religion/s in HIV & AIDS Prevention', in Isabel A. Phiri and Sarojini Nadar (eds.), *African Women, Religion, and Health: Essays in Honor of Mercy Amba Ewudziwa Oduyoye*. Maryknoll, NY: Orbis Books, 131–56.

———. 2007. *A Theology of Compassion in the HIV & AIDS Era*. Module 7, The HIV&AIDS Curriculum for TEE Programmes and Institutions in Africa. Geneva: World Council of Churches, Ecumenical HIV and AIDS Initiative in Africa.

———. 2008. *The HIV & AIDS Bible: Selected Essays*. Scranton, PA: Scranton Press.

———. 2009a. 'HIV and AIDS Research and Writing in the Circle of Concerned African Women Theologians, 2002–2006', in Nontando Hadebe and Ezra Chitando (eds.), *Compassionate Circles: African Women Theologians Facing HIV*. Geneva: World Council of Churches, 173–96.

———. 2009b. 'In the Circle of Life: African Women Theologians' Engagement with HIV and AIDS', in Nontando Hadebe and Ezra Chitando (eds.), *Compassionate Circles: African Women Theologians Facing HIV*. Geneva: World Council of Churches, 197–236.

———. 2009c. 'Talitha cum Hermeneutics of Liberation: Some African

Women's Ways of Reading the Bible', in Alejandro F. Botta and Pablo R. Andinach (eds.), *The Bible and the Hermeneutics of Liberation.* Atlanta: Society of Biblical Literature, 133–46.

———. 2010. 'Centering the Body', in Ezra Chitando and Peter Nickles (eds.), *What's Faith Got to Do with It? A Global Multifaith Discussion on HIV Responses.* Johanesburg: INERELA, 142–47.

———. 2015. '"And God Saw that it was Very Good": An Earth-friendly Theatrical Reading of Genesis 1 Introduction: Sitting in the Theatre of Creation', *Black Theology* 13 (3), 230–46.

Du Bois, W. E. B. 2007 (originally published 1920). *Darkwater: Voices from Within the Veil.* New York: Cosimo Books.

Eboussi Boulaga, Fabien (ed.). 2007. 'Dossier: L'homosexualité est bonne à penser', *Terroirs: revue africaine de sciences sociales et de culture,* nos. 1–2.

Ekine, Sokari, and Hakima Abbas. 2013. 'Introduction', in Hakima Abbas and Sokari Ekine (eds.), *Queer African Reader.* Dakar: Pambazuka Press, 1–5.

Englund, Harri (ed.). 2011. *Christianity and Public Culture in Africa.* Athens, OH: Ohio University Press.

Epprecht, Marc. 2008. *Heterosexual Africa? The History of an Idea from the Age of Exploration to the Age of AIDS.* Athens, OH: Ohio University Press.

———. 2013. *Sexuality and Social Justice in Africa: Rethinking Homophobia and Forging Resistance.* London: Zed Books.

Eze, Chielozona. 2011. *Postcolonial Imagination and Moral Representations in African Literature and Culture.* Lanham, MD: Lexington Books.

Flunder, Yvette. 2015. 'Healing Oppression Sickness'. In Kathleen T. Talvacchia et al. (eds.), *Queer Christianities: Lived Religion in Transgressive Forms.* New York: New York University Press, 115–24.

Frateur, Amber. 2019. '"Adam and Eve, Not Eve and Eve"? Towards a Space for the Christian Legitimacy of Female Same-Sex Love in Chinelo Okparanta's *Under the Udala Trees'.* MA thesis, University of Ghent. Available at: https://scriptiebank.be/scriptie/2019/adam-and-eve-not-eve-and-eve-towards-space-christian-legitimacy-female-same-sex-love (accessed 13 May 2020).

Gaudio, Rudolph P. 2009. *Allah Made Us: Sexual Outlaws in an Islamic African City.* Malden, MA: Blackwell.

Germond, Paul, and Steve de Gruchy (eds.). 1997. *Aliens in the Household of God: Homosexuality and Christian Faith in South Africa*. Cape Town: David Philip.

Green-Simms, Lindsey. 2016. 'The Emergent Queer: Homosexuality and Nigerian Fiction in the 21st Century', *Research in African Literatures* 47 (2), 139–61.

———. 2018. 'Queer African Cinema, Queer World Cinema', *College Literature* 45 (4), 652–58.

Green-Simms, Lindsey, and Unoma Azuah. 2012. 'The Video-Closet: Nollywood's Gay-Themed Movies', *Transition* 107, 32–49.

Greenough, Chris. 2020. *Queer Theologies: The Basics*. London and New York: Routledge.

Grillo, Laura, et al. 2019. *Religions in Contemporary Africa: An Introduction*. London and New York: Routledge.

Gueboguo, Charles. 2006. *La question homosexuelle en Afrique: Le cas du Cameroun*. Paris: L'Harmattan.

Gunda, Masiiwa R. 2010. *The Bible and Homosexuality in Zimbabwe: A Socio-historical Analysis of the Political, Cultural and Christian Arguments in the Homosexual Public Debate with Special Reference to the Use of the Bible*. Bamberg: University of Bamberg Press.

———. 2017. 'Is it in the Bible? Understanding the Critical Role of the Text of the Bible in African Christianity', in Masiiwa R. Gunda and Jim Naughton (eds.), *On Sexuality and Scripture: Essays, Bible Studies and Personal Reflections by the Chicago Group Consultation, the Ujamaa Centre, and their Friends*. Pietermaritzburg: Cluster Publication, 4–7.

Hackman, Melissa. 2018. *Desire Work: Ex-Gay and Pentecostal Masculinity in South Africa*. Durham, NC: Duke University Press.

Hadebe, Nontando. 2016, '"Moving in Circles"—a *Sankofa-Kairos* Theology of Inclusivity and Accountability Rooted in Trinitarian Theology as a Resource for Restoring the Liberating Legacy of The Circle of Concerned African Women Theologians', *Verbum et Ecclesia* 3 (2), 1–6. Available at: https://verbumetecclesia.org.za/index.php/ve/article/view/1573/2828 (accessed 13 May 2020).

Hassett, Miranda K. 2007. *Anglican Communion in Crisis: How Episcopal Dissidents and Their African Allies Are Reshaping Anglicanism*. Princeton, NJ: Princeton University Press.

Homewood, Nathanael J. 2020. 'Leaky Anuses, Loose Vaginas, and Large Penises: A Hierarchy of Sexualized Bodies in the Pentecostal Imaginary', in S.N. Nyeck (ed.), *Routledge Handbook of Queer African Studies*. London and New York: Routledge, 113–28.

Igo, Robert. 2005. *Listening with Love: Pastoral Counselling: A Christian Response to People Living with HIV*. Geneva: World Council of Churches.

———. 2009. *A Window into Hope: An Invitation to Faith in the Context of HIV and AIDS*. Geneva: World Council of Churches.

Ilo, Stan Chu. 2019. 'Amoris Laetitia and the Logic of Mercy and Integration in an Illuminative Church', in Stan Chu Ilo (ed.), *Love, Joy, and Sex: African Conversation on Pope Francis's Amoris Laetitia and the Gospel of Family in a Divided World*. Eugene, OR: Wipf and Stock, 201–36.

Isichei, Elizabeth. 1995. *A History of Christianity in Africa: From Antiquity to the Present*. Grand Rapids, MI: Eerdmans Publishing.

Isiugo-Abanihe, Uche C. 1994. 'The Socio-cultural Context of High Fertility Among Igbo Women', *International Sociology* 9 (2), 237–58.

Jama, Afdhere. 2015. *Being Queer and Somali: LGBT Somalis at Home and Abroad*. Place of publication not identified: Oracle Releasing.

Jjuuko, Adrian. 2017. 'The Protection and Promotion of LGBTI Rights in the African Regional Human Rights System: Opportunities and Challenges', in Sylvie Namwasa and Adrian Jjuuko (eds.), *Protecting the Human Rights of Sexual Minorities in Contemporary Africa*. Pretoria: Pretoria University Law Press, 260–300.

Kalu, Ogbu. 2008. *African Pentecostalism: An Introduction*. Oxford: Oxford University Press.

Kanyoro, Musimbi R. A. 2002. *Introducing Feminist Cultural Hermeneutics: An African Perspective*. Cleveland, OH: The Pilgrim Press.

———. 2006. 'Beads and Strands: Threading More Beads in the Story of the Circle', in Isabel Apawo Phiri and Sarojini Nadar (eds.), *African Women, Religion, and Health: Essays in Honor of Mercy Amba Ewudziwa Oduyoye*. Maryknoll, NY: Orbis Books, 19–42.

Kanyoro, Musimbi R. A., and Nyambura Njoroge (eds.). 1996. *Groaning in Faith: African Women in the Household of God*. Nairobi: Acton Publishers.

Kaoma, Kapya. 2009. *Globalizing the Culture Wars: U.S. Conservatives, African Churches and Homophobia*. Somerville, MA: Political Research Associates.

———. 2012. *Colonizing African Values: How the U.S. Christian Right Is Transforming Sexual Politics in Africa*. Somerville, MA: Political Research Associates.

———. 2018. *Christianity, Globalization, and Protective Homophobia: Democratic Contestation of Sexuality in Sub-Saharan Africa*. New York: Palgrave Macmillan.

Kaunda, Chammah J. (ed.). 2020. *Genders, Sexualities, and Spiritualities in African Pentecostalism*. New York: Palgrave Macmillan.

Kelly, Michael. 2010. *HIV and AIDS: A Social Justice Perspective*. Nairobi: Paulines Publications Africa.

Kenmogne, Jean-Blaise. 2014. *L'éthique des liens: Pour une approche holistique du développement et de la vie*. Yaoundé: Éditions CLÉ.

———. 2015. *Pour un humanisme écologique: Crise écologique contemporaine et enjeux d'humanité*. Yaoundé: Éditions CLÉ.

Kenmogne, Jean-Blaise, and Haman Mana. 2012. *Homosexualité, Église et Droits de l'Homme: Ouvrons le débat*. Yaoundé: Éditions CEROS.

Khadhani, Mudereri and Musaemura B. Zimunya (eds). 1981. *And Now the Poets Speak*. Gwelo: Mambo Press.

Kidula, Jean Ngoya. 2012. 'The Local and Global in Kenyan Rap and Hip Hop Culture', in Eric Charry (ed.), *Hip Hop Africa: New African Music in a Globalizing World*. Bloomington: Indiana University Press, 171–86.

Korte, Anne-Marie. 2010. 'Paradise Lost, Growth Gained: Eve's Story Revisited. Genesis 2–4 in a Feminist Theological Perspective', in Bob Becking and Susanne Hennecke (eds.), *Out of Paradise: Eve and Adam and their Interpreters*. Sheffield: Sheffield Phoenix Press, 140–56.

Kurian, Manoj. 2016. *Passion and Compassion: The Ecumenical Journey with HIV*. Geneva: World Council of Churches.

Lewin, Ellen. 2018. *Filled with the Spirit: Sexuality, Gender, and Radical Inclusivity in a Black Pentecostal Church Coalition*. Chicago and London: University of Chicago Press.

Lindhardt, Martin (ed.). 2014. *Pentecostalism in Africa: Presence and Impact of Pneumatic Christianity in Postcolonial Societies*. Leiden: Brill.

Lisanework, Zelly (ed.). 2019. *Tikur Engeda: Queer Stories from Ethiopia.* Addis Ababa: House of Guramayle.

Lyonga, Frida. 2016. 'The Homophobic Trinity: Pentecostal End-Time, Prosperity and Healing Gospels as Contributors to Homophobia in Cameroon', in Ezra Chitando and Adriaan van Klinken (eds.), *Christianity and Controversies over Homosexuality in Contemporary Africa.* London and New York: Routledge, 51–64.

Maathai, Wangari Muta. 2010. *Replenishing the Earth: Spiritual Values for Healing Ourselves and the World.* New York: Doubleday.

MacAllister, John (ed.). 2016. *Dipolelo Tsa Rona.* Gabarone: Setso Publishing.

Macaulay, Rowland Jide. 2010. '"Just as I am, without one plea": A Journey to Reconcile Sexuality and Spirituality', *Ethnicity and Inequalities in Health and Social Care* 3 (3), 6–13.

Macharia, Keguro. 2015. 'Archive and Method in Queer African Studies', *Agenda* 29 (1), 140–46.

Mana, Kä. 2002. *Christians and Churches of Africa Envisioning the Future: Salvation in Jesus Christ and the Building of a New African Society.* Yaoundé: Editions Clé.

————. 2004. 'Culture, société et sciences humaines dans la lute contre le VIH-SIDA en Afrique', in Kä Mana, Jean-Blaise Kenmogne and Hélène Yinda (eds.), *Religion, culture et VIH-SIDA en Afrique.* Yaoundé: Editions Sherpa, 66–83.

Martey, Emmanuel. 1993. *African Theology: Inculturation and Liberation.* Maryknoll, NY: Orbis Books.

Massoud, Mark F. 2003. 'The Evolution of Gay Rights in South Africa', *Peace Review* 15 (3), 301–7.

Matebeni, Zethu. 2014. *Reclaiming Afrikan: Queer Perspectives on Sexual and Gender Identities.* Athlone: Modjaji Books.

Matebeni, Zethu, and Jabu Pereira. 2014. 'Preface', in Zethu Matebeni (ed.), *Reclaiming Afrikan: Queer Perspectives on Sexual and Gender Identities.* Athlone: Modjaji Books, 7–9.

Maupeu, Hervé. 2010. 'Political Activism in Nairobi: Violence and Resilience of Kenyan Authoritarianism', in Hélène Charton-Bigot and Deyssi Rodriguez-Torres (eds.), *Nairobi Today: The Paradox of a Fragmented City.* Dar es Salaam: Mkuki na Nyota, 381–405.

Mawerenga, Jones Hamburu. 2018. *The Homosexuality Debate in Malawi*. Mzuzu: Mzuni Press.

Maxson, Natalie. 2016. *Journey for Justice: The Story of Women in the WCC* (revised edition). Geneva: World Council of Churches.

Maxwell, David. 2002. 'Introduction', in David Maxwell and Ingrid Lawrie (eds.), *Christianity and the African Imagination: Essays in Honour of Adrian Hastings*. Leiden: Brill, 1–24.

Mbembe, Achille. 2001. *On the Postcolony*. Berkeley, CA: University of California Press.

———. 2010. *Sortir de la grande nuit: Essai sur l'Afrique décolonisée*. Paris: La Découverte.

———. 2017. *Critique of Black Reason*. Durham, NC and London: Duke University Press.

Mbetbo, Joachim Ntetmen. 2013. 'Internalised Conflicts in the Practice of Religion Among Kwandengue Living with HIV in Douala, Cameroun', *Culture, Health and Sexuality* 15 (sup. 1), 76–87.

McCarty, James W. III. 2013. 'A Paradoxical Theology of Biology: Desmond Tutu's Social Ethics in Light of His Sermon at Southwark Cathedral', *Theology and Sexuality* 19 (1), 89–97.

Mofokeng, Takatso. 1988. 'Black Christians, the Bible and Liberation', *Journal of Black Theology* 2, 34–42.

Mohammed, Azeenarh, et al. (eds.) 2018. *She Called Me Woman: Nigeria's Queer Women Speak*. Abuja: Cassava Republic.

Mojola, Aloo Osotsi. 2018. 'The African Bantu Concept of Ubuntu in the Theology and Practice of Desmond Tutu and its Implications for African Biblical Hermeneutics', in Madipoane Masenya (Ngwan'a Mphahlele) and Kenneth N. Ngwa (eds.), *Navigating African Biblical Hermeneutics: Trends and Themes from our Pots and our Calabashes*. Newcastle: Cambridge Scholars, 57–69.

Moreau, Julie, and T.J. Tallie. 2020. 'Queer African Studies and Directions in Methodology', in S. N. Nyeck (ed.), *Routledge Handbook of Queer African Studies*. London and New York: Routledge, 49–61.

Motlhabi, Mokgethi. 2008. *African Theology/Black Theology in South Africa: Looking Back, Moving On*. Pretoria: UNISA Press.

Mukhuba, Theophilus T. 2017. 'An Analysis of Jack Mapanje's Poetry with

Particular Reference to his Use of Obscuring Devices', *International Journal of Applied Linguistics & English Literature* 6 (7), 30–4.

Muparamoto, Nelson. 2016. 'Enduring and Subverting Homophobia: Religious Experiences of Same-Sex Loving People in Zimbabwe', in Ezra Chitando and Adriaan van Klinken (eds.), *Christianity and Controversies Over Homosexuality in Contemporary Africa*. London and New York: Routledge, 153–56.

Mutambara, Maaraidzo. 2006. 'African Women Theologies Critique Inculturation', in Edward Antonio (ed.), *Inculturation and Postcolonial Discourse in African Theology*. Leuven: Peter Lang, 173–92.

Mwachiro, Kevin. 2014. *Invisible: Stories from Kenya's Queer Community*. Nairobi: Goethe-Institut.

Mwangi, Evan. 2014. 'Queer Agency in Kenya's Digital Media', *African Studies Review* 57 (2), 93–113.

Nadar, Sarojini. 2012. 'Feminist Theologies in Africa', in Elias Bongmba (ed.), *The Wiley-Blackwell Companion to African Religions*. Malden and Oxford: Wiley-Blackwell, 269–78.

———. 2014. '"Stories are Data with Soul"—Lessons from Black Feminist Epistemology', *Agenda* 28 (1), 18–28.

Nathan, Roland A. 2012. 'Blessed Be the Tie That Binds: African Diaspora Christian Movements and African Unity', in Mammo Muchie et al. (eds.), *The Africana World: From Fragmentation to Unity and Renaissance*. Pretoria: Africa Institute of South Africa, 275–86.

Ndjio, Basile. 2013. 'Sexuality and Nationalist Ideologies in Post-colonial Cameroon', in Saskia Wieringa and Horacio Sivori (eds.), *The Sexual History of the Global South: Sexual Politics in Africa, Asia and Latin America*. London: Zed Books, 120–43.

Ndlovu-Gatsheni, Sabelo J. 2018. *Epistemic Freedom in Africa: Deprovincialization and Decolonization*. London and New York: Routledge.

Ngũgĩ wa Thiong'o. 1986. *Decolonising the Mind: The Politics of Language in African Literature*. London: Heinemann.

———. 2009. *Re-membering Africa*. Nairobi: East African Educational Publishers.

Njoroge, Nyambura J. 2008. 'Beyond Suffering and Lament: Theology of Hope and Life', in Darren C. Marks (ed.), *Shaping a Global Theological Mind*. Aldershot: Ashgate, 113–20.

———. 2009. *Gender Justice, Ministry and Healing: A Christian Response to the HIV Epidemic*. Progressio Comment. London: Progressio.

———. 2013. 'Daughters of Africa Heed the Call for Justice, Peace, and Fullness of Life', *International Review of Mission* 102 (1), 30–43.

———. 2016. 'Ecumenical HIV Theology from Womb to Tomb', in Jacquineau Azetsop (ed.), *HIV & AIDS in Africa: Christian Reflection, Public Health, Social Transformation*. Maryknoll, NY: Orbis Books, 198–214.

Ntarangwi, Mwenda. 2016. *The Street is My Pulpit: Hip Hop and Christianity in Kenya*. Urbana: University of Illinois Press.

Nyanzi, Stella. 2014. 'Queering Queer Africa', in Zethu Matebeni (ed.), *Reclaiming Afrikan: Queer Perspectives on Sexual and Gender Identities*. Athlone: Modjaji Books, 65–68.

Nyiawung, Mbengu D. 2010. 'The Prophetic Witness of the Church as an Appropriate Mode of Public Discourse in African Societies', *HTS Theological Studies* 66 (1), 1–8.

Nyeck, S.N. (ed). 2020. *Routledge Handbook of Queer African Studies*. London and New York: Routledge.

Obadare, Ebenezer. 2015. 'Sex, Citizenship and the State in Nigeria: Islam, Christianity and the Emergent Struggle over Intimacy', *Review of African Political Economy* 42 (143), 62–76.

Obinyan, Aiwan. 2020. *Kenyan, Christian, Queer* (documentary film). London: AiAi Studios.

Oduyoye, Mercy A. 1986. *Hearing and Knowing: Theological Reflections on Christianity in Africa*. Maryknoll, NY: Orbis Books.

———. 1993. 'A Critique of Mbiti's View on Love and Marriage in Africa', in Jacob K. Olupona and Sulayman S. Nyang (eds.), *Religious Plurality in Africa: Essays in Honour of John S. Mbiti*. Berlin: Mouton de Gruyter, 341–64.

———. 1995. *Daughters of Anowa: African Women and Patriarchy*. Maryknoll, NY: Orbis Books.

———. 1999. 'A Coming Home to Myself: The Childless Woman in the West African Space', in Margaret A. Farley and Serene Jones (eds.), *Liberating Eschatology: Essays in Honor of Letty M. Russell*. Louisville, KY: Westminster John Knox Press, 105–22.

————. 2001. *Introducing African Women's Theology.* Cleveland, OH: The Pilgrims Press.

————. 2003. 'African Culture and the Gospel: Inculturation from an African Woman's Perspective', in Mercy A. Oduyoye and Hendrik Vroom (eds.), *One Gospel—Many Cultures: Case Studies and Reflections on Cross-Cultural Theology.* Amsterdam: Rodopi, 39–62.

————. 2019. *Re-membering Me: Memoirs of Mercy Amba Oduyoye.* Ibadan: Sefer.

Ogoti, Vincent R. 2019. 'Soundscape and narrative dynamics in Chinelo Okparanta's *Under the Udala Trees*', *Journal of the African Literature Association* 13 (3), 291–305.

Oguntola-Laguda, Danoye, and Adriaan van Klinken. 2016. 'Uniting a Divided Nation? Nigerian Muslim and Christian Responses to the Same-Sex Marriage (Prohibition) Act', in Adriaan van Klinken and Ezra Chitando (eds.), *Public Religion and the Politics of Homosexuality in Africa.* London and New York: Routledge, 34–48.

Ojo, Matthews A. 2006. *The End-Time Army: Charismatic Movements in Modern Nigeria.* Trenton, NJ: Africa World Press.

Okparanta, Chinelo. 2015. *Under the Udala Trees.* London: Granta Publications.

Olupona, Jacob. 2014. *African Religions: A Very Short Introduction.* New York: Oxford University Press.

Ombagi, Eddie. 2019. 'Nairobi is a Shot of Whisky: Queer (Ob)scenes in the City', *Journal of African Cultural Studies* 31 (1), 106–19.

Oriogun, Romeo. 2020. *Sacrament of Bodies.* Lincoln: University of Nebraska Press.

Orobator, Agbonkhianmeghe E. 2005. *From Crisis to Kairos: The Mission of the Church in the Time of HIV/AIDS, Refugees and Poverty.* Maryknoll, NY: Orbis Books.

Osike, Ifediora. 2018. 'Contemporary African Poetry: A Postcolonial Reading of Iquo Eke's *Symphony of Becoming* and Ifeanyi Nwaeboh's *Stampede of Voiceless Ants*', *Africology: The Journal of Pan African Studies* 11 (4), 49–60.

Osinubi, Taiwo Adetunji. 2019. 'Queer Subjects in Kenyan Cinema: Reflections on Rafiki', *Eastern African Literary and Cultural Studies* 5 (1), 70–77.

Parry, Sue. 2008. *Beacons of Hope: HIV Competent Churches—A Framework for Action*. Geneva: World Council of Churches.

———. 2013. *Practicing Hope: A Handbook for Building HIV and AIDS Competence in the Churches*. Geneva: World Council of Churches.

Parsitau, Damaris. 2015. 'Embodying Holiness: Gender, Sex and Bodies in a Neo-Pentecostal Church in Kenya', in Augustine Agwuele (ed.), *Body Talk and Cultural Identity in the African World*. London: Equinox, 181–201.

Pasi, Juliet. 2016. 'Writing Nature from the Feminine: An Ecofeminist Analysis of the Gardens in Tsitsi Dangarembga's *The Book of Not*', *Journal of Literary Studies* 32 (1), 17–31.

Phiri, Isabel Apawo, and Sarojini Nadar (eds.). 2005. *On Being Church: African Women's Voices and Visions*. Geneva: WCC Publications.

———. 2006. '"Treading Softly but Firmly": African Women, Religion, and Health', in Isabel Apawo Phiri and Sarojini Nadar (eds.), *African Women, Religion, and Health: Essays in Honor of Mercy Amba Ewudziwa Oduyoye*. Maryknoll, NY: Orbis Books, 1–18.

Phiri, Lilly. 2016. 'Born this Way: The Imago Dei in Men who Love Other Men in Lusaka, Zambia', in Ezra Chitando and Adriaan van Klinken (eds.), *Christianity and Controversies over Homosexuality in Contemporary Africa*. London and New York: Routledge, 157–70.

Russell, Letty M. 2006. 'Mercy Amba Ewudziwa Oduyoye: Wise Women Bearing Gifts', in Isabel Apawo Phiri and Sarojini Nadar (eds.), *African Women, Religion, and Health: Essays in Honor of Mercy Amba Ewudziwa Oduyoye*. Maryknoll, NY: Orbis Books, 43–58.

Senyonjo, Christopher. 2016. *In Defense of All God's Children: The Life and Ministry of Bishop Christopher Senyonjo*. New York: Morehouse Publishing.

Spivak, Gayatri C. 1988. 'Can the Subaltern Speak?' in C. Nelson and L. Grossberg (eds.), *Marxism and the Interpretation of Culture*. Basingstoke: Macmillan Education, 271–313.

Spronk, Rachel, and Thomas Hendriks. 2020. 'Mobilizing Religion, Queering Tradition', in Rachel Spronk and Thomas Hendriks (eds.), *Readings in Sexualities from Africa*. Bloomington, IN: Indiana University Press, 247–9.

Sylvester, Christine. 2006. 'Bare Life as a Development/Postcolonial Problematic', *The Geographical Journal* 172 (1), 66–77.

Tamale, Sylvia. 2011. 'Introduction', in Sylvia Tamale (ed.), *African Sexualities: A Reader*. Cape Town: Pambazuka Press, 1–8.

TFAM (The Fellowship of Affirming Ministries). n.d. 'About Us'. Available at: https://www.radicallyinclusive.org/about-us (accessed 17 February 2020).

———. n.d. 'The Fellowship Global'. Available at: https://www.radicallyinclusive.org/global (accessed 17 February 2020).

TFAM Global. n.d. 'Interconnected Justice'. Available at: http://tfamglobal.org/what-we-do/interconnected-justice/ (accessed 19 February 2020).

———. n.d. 'Our Method'. Available at: http://tfamglobal.org/who-we-are/our-method/ (accessed 19 February 2020).

———. n.d. 'Our Project'. Available at: http://tfamglobal.org/who-we-are/our-project/ (accessed 19 February 2020).

———. n.d. 'Where We Work'. Available at: http://tfamglobal.org/where-we-work/ (accessed 19 February 2020).

The Fellowship Global. 2013. 'Empowering Progressive Clergy in Africa'. Available at: http://thefellowshipglobal.org/wp-content/uploads/2014/05/Empowering-Progressive-Clergy-in-Africa.pdf (accessed 25 March 2016).

The Nest. 2015. *Stories of Our Lives*. Nairobi: The Nest Collective.

Thoreson, Ryan Richard. 2008. 'Somewhere over the Rainbow Nation: Gay, Lesbian and Bisexual Activism in South Africa', *Journal of Southern African Studies* 34 (3), 679–97.

Togue, Michel. 2017. 'The Status of Sexual Minority Rights in Cameroon', in Sylvie Namwase and Adrian Jjuuko (eds.), *Protecting the Human Rights of Sexual Minorities in Contemporary Africa*. Pretoria: Pretoria University Law Press, 245–59.

Tutu, Desmond. 1983. 'Apartheid and Christianity', in John W. de Gruchy and Charles Villa-Vicencio (eds.), *Apartheid is a Heresy*. Grand Rapids: Eerdmans, 39–47.

———. 1997. 'Foreword', in Paul Germond and Steve de Gruchy (eds.), *Aliens in the Household of God: Homosexuality and Christian Faith in South Africa*. Cape Town: David Philip, ix–x.

———. 1999. *No Future Without Forgiveness*. New York: Doubleday.

———. 2004. 'Sermon by Archbishop Desmond Tutu at Southwark Cathedral' (1 February 2004). Available at: https://www.anglicannews. org/news/2004/02/sermon-by-archbishop-desmond-tutu-at-southwark-cathedral.aspx (accessed 21 January 2020).

———. 2012. 'Afterword', in Michael G. Long, *Martin Luther King Jr., Homosexuality, and the Early Gay Rights Movement: Keeping the Dream Straight?* New York: Palgrave Macmillan, 149–50.

———. 2015. 'The First Word: To Be Human Is To Be Free', *Journal of Law and Religion* 30 (3), 386–90.

Ujamaa Centre. 2014. *Doing Contextual Bible Study: A Resource Manual* (revised edition). Available at: http://ujamaa.ukzn.ac.za/Libraries/manuals/Ujamaa_CBS_bible_study_Manual_part_1_2.sflb.ashx (accessed 13 May 2020).

Uko, Iniobong. 2018. 'Book Review: Unoma Azuah. *Blessed Body: The Secret Lives of Nigerian Lesbian, Gay, Bisexual & Transgender*', *African Literature Today* 36, 252–59.

Van Klinken, Adriaan. 2010. 'When the Body of Christ has AIDS: A Theological Metaphor for Global Solidarity in Light of HIV and AIDS', *International Journal of Public Theology* 4 (4), 446–65.

———. 2013. 'Gay Rights, the Devil and the End Times: Public Religion and the Enchantment of the Homosexuality Debate in Zambia', *Religion* 43 (4), 519–40.

———. 2015. 'Queer Love in a "Christian Nation": Zambian Gay Men Negotiating Sexual and Religious Identities', *Journal of the American Academy of Religion* 83 (4), 947–64.

———. 2017. 'Culture Wars, Race, and Sexuality: A Nascent Pan–African LGBT-Affirming Christian Movement and the Future of Christianity', *Journal of Africana Religions* 5 (2), 217–38.

———. 2018. 'Autobiographical Storytelling and African Narrative Queer Theology', *Exchange: Journal of Contemporary Christianities in Context* 47 (3), 211–29.

———. 2019. *Kenyan, Christian, Queer: Religion, LGBT Activism, and Arts of Resistance in Africa*. University Park, PI: Pennsylvania State University Press.

———. 2020a. 'Changing the Narrative of Sexuality in African Christianity:

Bishop Christopher Senyonjo's LGBT Advocacy', *Theology and Sexuality* 26 (1), 1–6.

———. 2020b. 'Queer Pan-Africanism in Contemporary Africa', in Reiland Rabaka (ed.), *The Routledge Handbook of Pan-Africanism*. London and New York, 343–54.

Van Klinken, Adriaan, and Masiiwa R. Gunda. 2012. 'Taking Up the Cudgels Against Gay Rights? Trends and Trajectories in African Christian Theologies on Homosexuality', *Journal of Homosexuality* 59 (1), 114–38.

Van Klinken, Adriaan, and Ezra Chitando (eds.). 2016. *Public Religion and the Politics of Homosexuality in Africa*. London and New York: Routledge.

Van Klinken, Adriaan, and Kwame E. Otu. 2017. 'Ancestors, Embodiment, and Sexual Desire? Wild Religion and the Body in the Story of a South African Lesbian Sangoma', *Body and Religion* 1 (1), 70–87.

Van Klinken, Adriaan, and Ebenezer Obadare. 2018. 'Christianity, Sexuality and Citizenship in Africa: Critical Intersections', *Citizenship Studies* 22 (6), 557–68.

Wainaina, Binyavanga. 2014. 'We Must Free Our Imaginations', parts 1–6, YouTube. Available at: https://www.youtube.com/watch?v=8uMwppw5AgU&t=2s.

———. 2015. 'Conversations with Baba', YouTube. Available at: https://www.youtube.com/watch?v=z5uAoBu9Epg.

Wariboko, Nimi. 2014. *Nigerian Pentecostalism*. Rochester, NY: University of Rochester Press.

Wassiliwizky, Eugen, et al. 2017. 'The Emotional Power of Poetry: Neural Circuitry, Psychophysiology and Compositional Principles', *Social Cognitive and Affective Neuroscience* 12 (8), 1229–40.

West, Gerald O. 1999. *The Academy of the Poor: Towards a Dialogical Reading of the Bible*. Sheffield: Sheffield Academic Press.

———. 2011. 'Sacred Texts—Particularly the Bible and the Qur'an—and HIV and AIDS: Charting the Textual Territory', in B. Haddad, (ed.), *Religion and HIV and AIDS: Charting the Terrain*. Pietermaritzburg: University of KwaZulu-Natal Press, 135–65.

———. 2016. *The Stolen Bible: From Tool of Imperialism to African Icon*. Leiden: Brill.

Wilson, Ayoko B. and Godson Lawson. 2016. 'Called to be Courageous: Churches and Sexual Minorities', in Ezra Chitando and Nyambura Njoroge (eds.), *Abundant Life: The Churches and Sexuality*. Geneva: World Council of Churches, 161–71.

World Council of Churches. 1997. *Facing AIDS: The Challenge, The Churches' Response*. Geneva: WCC Publications.

———. n.d. *Work on Issues of Human Sexuality—a Chronology*. http:// www.wcc-coe.org/wcc/who/sexuality.html (accessed 13 May 2020).

Xaba, Makhosazana, and Crystal Biruk (eds.). 2016. *Proudly Malawian: Life Stories from Lesbian and Gender-Nonconforming Individuals*. Johannesburg: GALA.

INDEX

Note: Page numbers followed by "*n*" refer to notes